Geometry Connections
Version 3.1

Managing Editor

Leslie Dietiker
Phillip and Sala Burton Academic High School
San Francisco, CA

Contributing Editors

Elizabeth Ellen Coyner
Christian Brothers High School
Sacramento, CA

Lara Lomac
Phillip and Sala Burton Academic
High School, San Francisco, CA

Leslie Nielsen
Isaaquah High School
Issaquah, WA

Barbara Shreve
San Lorenzo High School
San Lorenzo, CA

Lew Douglas
The College Preparatory School
Oakland, CA

Damian Molinari
Phillip and Sala Burton Academic
High School, San Francisco, CA

Karen O'Connell
San Lorenzo High School
San Lorenzo, CA

Michael Titelbaum
University of California
Berkeley, CA

David Gulick
Phillips Exeter Academy
Exeter, NH

Jason Murphy-Thomas
George Washington High School
San Francisco, CA

Ward Quincey
Gideon Hausner Jewish Day School
Palo Alto, CA

Illustrator

Kevin Coffey
San Francisco, CA

Technical Assistants

Erica Andrews
Elizabeth Burke
Carrie Cai
Daniel Cohen

Elizabeth Fong
Rebecca Harlow
Michael Leong
Thomas Leong

Marcos Rojas
Susan Ryan

Program Directors

Leslie Dietiker
Phillip and Sala Burton Academic High School
San Francisco, CA

Brian Hoey
Christian Brothers High School
Sacramento, CA

Judy Kysh, Ph.D.
Departments of Mathematics and Education
San Francisco State University

Tom Sallee, Ph.D.
Department of Mathematics
University of California, Davis

Contributing Editor of the Parent Guide:

Karen Wootten, Managing Editor
Odenton, MD

Technical Manager of Parent Guide and Extra Practice:

Rebecca Harlow
Stanford University
Stanford, CA

Editor of Extra Practice:

Bob Petersen, Managing Editor
Rosemont High School
Sacramento, CA

Assessment Contributors:

John Cooper, Managing Editor
Del Oro High School
Loomis, CA

Lara Lomac
Phillip and Sala Burton Academic High School,
San Francisco, CA

Barbara Shreve
San Lorenzo High School
San Lorenzo, CA

Leslie Dietiker
Phillip and Sala Burton Academic High School
San Francisco, CA

Damian Molinari
Phillip and Sala Burton Academic High School,
San Francisco, CA

2 3 4 5 6 7 8 9   10 09 08 07 06

Printed in the United States of America   Version 3.1

ISBN-10:   1-931287-58-9

ISBN-13: 978-1-931287-58-6

A Note to Students:

Welcome to Geometry! This courses
centers on the study of shapes. As you
study geometry, you will be investigating
new situations, discovering relationships,
and figuring out what strategies can be used
to solve problems. Learning to think this
way is useful in mathematical contexts and
other courses, as well as in situations
outside the classroom.

In meeting the challenges of geometry, you will not be working alone. During this course you will collaborate with other students as a member of a study team. Working in a team means speaking up and interacting with others. You will explain your ideas, listen to what others have to say, and ask questions if there is something you do not understand. In geometry, a single problem can often be solved more than one way. You will see problems in different ways than your teammates do. Each of you has something to contribute while you work on the lessons in this course.

Together, your team will complete problems and activities that will help you discover new mathematical ideas and methods. Your teacher will support you as you work, but will not take away your opportunity to think and investigate for yourself. The ideas in the course will be revisited several times and connected to other topics. If something is not clear to you the first time you work with it, don't worry—you will have more chances to build your understanding as the course continues.

Learning math this way has a significant advantage: as long as you actively participate, make sure everyone in your study team is involved, and ask good questions, you will find yourself understanding mathematics at a deeper level than ever before. By the end of this course, you will have an understanding of a variety of geometric principles and properties that govern the world around us. You will see how these principles and properties interweave so that you can use them together to solve new problems. With your teammates, you will meet mathematical challenges you would not have known how to approach before.

In addition to the support provided by your teacher and your study team, CPM has also created online resources to help you, including help with homework, a parent guide, and extra practice. You will find these resources and more at www.cpm.org.

We wish you well and are confident that you will enjoy learning geometry!

Sincerely,
The CPM Team

Geometry
Connections
Table of Contents

Student Edition

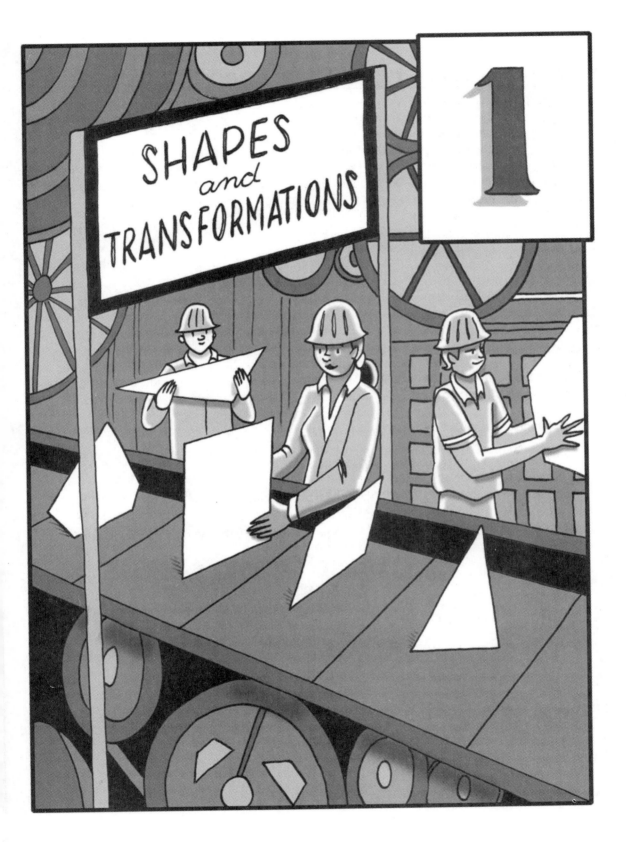

CHAPTER 1   Shapes and Transformations

Welcome to Geometry! *Geo* means Earth (*geography* is mapping the Earth, for example) and *metry* means measurement. Geometry applies the arithmetic, algebra and **reasoning** skills you have learned to the objects you see all around you. During this course, you will ask and answer questions such as "How can I describe this shape?", "How can I measure this shape?", "Is this shape symmetrical?", and "How can I convince others that what I think about this shape is true?"

This chapter begins with some activities that will introduce you to the big ideas of the course. Then you will apply motions to triangles and learn how to specify a particular motion. Finally, you will explore attributes of shapes that can be used to categorize and name them and find the probabilities of selecting shapes with certain properties from a "shape bucket."

Guiding Questions

Think about these questions throughout this chapter:

What is geometry?

How can I describe this shape?

How can I move it?

Is this shape symmetrical?

How can I communicate my ideas clearly?

In this chapter, you will:

➢ become familiar with basic geometric shapes and learn how to describe each one using its attributes, such as parallel sides or rotation symmetry.

➢ investigate three basic rigid transformations: reflection (flip), rotation (turn), and translation (slide).

➢ be introduced to probability and learn how to use probability to make predictions.

Chapter Outline

 Section 1.1 Investigations involving quilts, twisted strips of paper, rug designs, precise reasoning, and kaleidoscopes will introduce you to some basic building-blocks of geometry: shapes, motions, measurements, patterns, reasoning and symmetry.

 Section 1.2 You will learn about transformations as you study how to flip, turn, and slide shapes. Then you will learn how to use these motions to build new shapes and to describe symmetry.

 Section. 1.3 A "shape bucket" will introduce you to a variety of basic shapes that you will describe, classify and name according to their attributes. You will also learn about probability.

1.1.1 How can I design it?

Creating a Quilt Using Symmetry

Welcome to Geometry! But what is geometry? At the end of this chapter you will have a better understanding of what geometry is. To start, you will focus on several activities that will hopefully challenge you and introduce you to important concepts in geometry that you will study in this course. While all of the problems are solvable with your current math skills, some will be revisited later in the course so that you may apply new geometric tools to solve and extend them.

Today you will consider an example of how geometry is applied in the world around you. A very popular American tradition is to create quilts by sewing together remnants of cloth in intricate geometric designs. These quilts often integrate geometric shapes in repeated patterns that show symmetry. For centuries, quilts have been designed to tell stories, document special occasions, or decorate homes.

1-1.   DESIGNING A QUILT, Part One

How can you use symmetry to design a quilt? Today you will work with your team to design a patch that will be combined with other team patches to make a class quilt. Before you start, review the team roles, which are outlined on the next page.

a.   Each team member will receive four small squares. With a colored pencil or marker, shade in <u>half</u> of each square (one triangle) as shown at right. Each team member should use a different color.

b.   Next arrange your squares to make a larger 2-by-2 square (as shown at right) with a design that has **reflection symmetry**. A design has reflection symmetry if it can be folded in half so that both sides match perfectly. Make sure that you have arranged your pieces into a different symmetrical pattern than the rest of your team.

c.   Now, create a 4-by-4 square using the designs created by each team member as shown on the Lesson 1.1.1B Resource Page. Ask your teacher to verify that your designs are all symmetrical and unique. Then glue (or tape) all sixteen pieces carefully to the resource page and cut along the surrounding dashed square so that you have a blank border around your 4-by-4 square.

Problem continues on next page →

Problem continued from previous page.

    d.   Finally, discuss with your team what you all personally have in common. Come up with a team sentence that captures the most interesting facts. Write your names and this sentence in the border so they wrap around your 4-by-4 design.

To help you work together today, each member of your team has a specific job, assigned by your first name (or last name if team members have the same first name).

Team Roles

Resource Manager – If your name comes first alphabetically:

- Make sure the team has all of the necessary materials, such as colored pencils or markers and the Lesson 1.1.1A and 1.1.B Resource Pages.

- Ask the teacher when the **entire** team has a question. You might ask, *"No one has an idea? Should I ask the teacher?"*

- Make sure your team cleans up by delegating tasks. You could say, *"I will put away the _____ while you _____ ."*

Facilitator – If your name comes second alphabetically:

- Start the team's discussion by asking, *"What are some possible designs?"* or *"How can we make sure that all of our designs are symmetrical?"* or *"Are all of our designs different?"*

- Make sure that all of the team members get any necessary help. You don't have to answer all the questions yourself. A good facilitator regularly asks, *"Do you understand what you are supposed to do?"* and *"Who can answer _____'s question?"*

Recorder/Reporter – If your name comes third alphabetically:

- Coordinate the taping or gluing of the quilt pieces together onto the resource page in the orientation everyone agreed to.

- Take notes for the team. The notes should include phrases like, *"We found that we all had in common ..."* and explanations like, *"Each of our designs was found to be unique and symmetrical because ..."*

- Help the team agree on a team sentence: *"What do we all have in common?"* and *"How can I write that on our quilt?"*

Task Manager – If your name comes fourth alphabetically:

- Remind the team to stay on task and not to talk to students in other teams. You can suggest, *"Let's try coming up with different symmetrical patterns."*

- Keep track of time. Give your team reminders, such as *"I think we need to decide now so that we will have enough time to ..."*

1-2. DESIGNING A QUILT, Part Two

Your teacher will ask the Recorder/Reporters from each team to bring their finished quilt patches up to the board one at a time and tape them to the other patches. Be prepared to explain how you came up with your unique designs and interesting ideas about symmetry. Also be prepared to read your team sentence to the class. As you listen to the presentations, look for relationships between your designs and the other team designs.

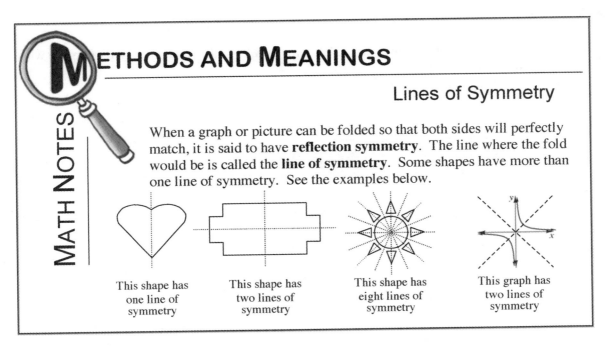

ETHODS AND MEANINGS

MATH NOTES

Lines of Symmetry

When a graph or picture can be folded so that both sides will perfectly match, it is said to have **reflection symmetry**. The line where the fold would be is called the **line of symmetry**. Some shapes have more than one line of symmetry. See the examples below.

This shape has one line of symmetry

This shape has two lines of symmetry

This shape has eight lines of symmetry

This graph has two lines of symmetry

Review & Preview

1-3. One focus of this Geometry course is to help you recognize and accurately identify a shape. For example, a **rectangle** is a four-sided shape with four right angles. Which of the shapes below can be called a rectangle? More than one answer is possible.

a.

b.

c.

d.

e.

f.

1-4.   Calculate the values of the expressions below. Show all steps in your process. The answers are provided for you to check your result. If you miss two or more of these and cannot find your errors, be sure to seek help from your team or teacher.
[Answers: a: 40, b: –6, c: 7, d: 59]

a. $2 \cdot (3(5+2)-1)$

b. $6-2(4+5)+6$

c. $3 \cdot 8 \div 2^2 +1$

d. $5-2 \cdot 3+6(3^2+1)$

1-5.   Match each table of data on the left with its rule on the right and **briefly explain** why it matches the data.

a.
x	1	0	–4	2	–2	–1
y	4	3	–1	5	1	2

(1) $y = x$

(2) $y = 3x - 1$

b.
x	–1	3	1	0	–2	2
y	–1	–9	–1	0	–4	–4

(3) $y = x + 3$

c.
x	3	–2	1	0	2	–3
y	12	7	4	3	7	12

(4) $y = x^2$

(5) $y = -x^2$

d.
x	–3	4	2	–2	0	–10
y	–10	11	5	–7	–1	–31

(6) $y = x^2 + 3$

1-6.   Simplify the expressions below as much as possible.

a. $2a + 4(7 + 5a)$

b. $4(3x + 2) - 5(7x + 5)$

c. $x(x + 5)$

d. $2x + x(x + 6)$

1-7.   **Examine** the graph at right. Then, in a sentence or two, suggest reasons why the graph rises at 11:00 AM and then drops at 1:15 PM.

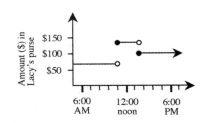

6

1.1.2 Can you predict the results?

Making Predictions and Investigating Results

Today you will **investigate** what happens when you change the attributes of a Möbius strip. As you **investigate**, you will record data in a table. You will then analyze this data and use your results to brainstorm further experiments. As you look back at your data, you may start to consider other related questions that can help you understand a pattern and learn more about what is happening. This Way of Thinking, called **investigating**, includes not only generating new questions, but also rethinking when the results are not what you expected.

1-8.   Working effectively with your study team will be an important part of the learning process throughout this course. Choose a member of your team to read aloud these Study Team Expectations:

STUDY TEAM EXPECTATIONS

Throughout this course you will regularly work with a team of students. This collaboration will allow you to develop new ways of thinking about mathematics, increase your ability to communicate with others about math, and help you strengthen your understanding by having you explain your thinking to someone else. As you work together,

- You are expected to share your ideas and contribute to the team's work.

- You are expected to ask your teammates questions and to offer help to your teammates. Questions can move your team's thinking forward and help others to understand ideas more clearly.

- Remember that a team that functions well works on the same problem together and discusses the problem while it works.

- Remember that one student on the team should not dominate the discussion and thinking process.

- Your team should regularly stop and verify that everyone on the team agrees with a suggestion or a solution.

- Everyone on your team should be consulted before calling on the teacher to answer a question.

1-9.   On a piece of paper provided by your teacher, make a "bracelet" by taping the two ends securely together. Putting tape on both sides of the bracelet will help to make sure the bracelet is secure. In the diagram of the rectangular strip shown at right, you would tape the ends together so that point A would attach to point C, and point B would attach to point D.

Now predict what you think would happen if you were to cut the bracelet down the middle, as shown in the diagram at right. Record your prediction in a table like the one shown below or on your Lesson 1.1.2 Resource Page.

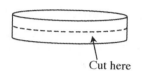

Cut here

	Experiment	Prediction	Result
1-9	Cut bracelet in half as shown in the diagram.		
1-10			
1-11			
1-12a			
1-12b			
1-12c			
1-12d			

Now cut your strip as described above and record your result in the first row of your table. Make sure to include a short description of your result.

1-10.   On a second strip of paper, label a point X in the center of the strip at least one inch away from one end.

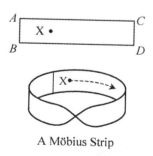

A Möbius Strip

Now turn this strip into a **Möbius strip** by attaching the ends together securely after making one twist. For the strip shown in the diagram at right, the paper would be twisted once so that point A would attach to point D. The result should look like the diagram at right.

Predict what would happen if you were to draw a line down the center of the strip from point X until you ran out of paper. Record your prediction, conduct the experiment, and record your result.

8

1-11. What do you think would happen if you were to cut your Möbius strip along the central line you drew in problem 1-10? Record your prediction in your table.

Cut just one of your team's Möbius strips. Record your result in your table. Consider the original strip of paper drawn in problem 1-9 to help you explain why cutting the Möbius strip had this result.

1-12. What else can you learn about Möbius strips? For each experiment below, first record your expectation. Then record your result in your table after conducting the experiment. Use a new Möbius strip for each experiment.

    a. What if the result from problem 1-11 is cut in half down the middle again?

    b. What would happen if the Möbius strip is cut one-third of the way from one of the sides of the strip? Be sure to cut a constant distance from the side of the strip.

    c. What if a strip is formed by 2 twists instead of one? What would happen if it were cut down the middle?

    d. If time allows, make up your own experiment. You might change how many twists you make, where you make your cuts, etc. Try to generalize your findings as you conduct your experiment. Be prepared to share your results with the class.

1-13. LEARNING REFLECTION

Think over how you and your study team worked today, and what you learned about Möbius strips. What questions did you or your teammates ask that helped move the team forward? What questions do you still have about Möbius strips? What would you like to know more about?

ETHODS AND MEANINGS

The Investigative Process

The **investigative process** is a way to study and learn new mathematical ideas. Mathematicians have used this process for many years to make sense of new concepts and to broaden their understanding of older ideas.

In general, this process begins with a **question** that helps you frame what you are looking for. For example, a question such as, *"What if the Möbius strip has 2 half-twists? What will happen when that strip is cut in half down the middle?"* can help start an investigation to find out what happens when the Möbius strip is slightly altered.

Once a question is asked, you can make an educated guess, called a **conjecture**. This is a mathematical statement that has not yet been proven.

Next, **exploration** begins. This part of the process may last awhile as you gather more information about the mathematical concept. For example, you may first have an idea about the diagonals of a rectangle, but as you draw and measure a rectangle on graph paper, you find out that your conjecture was incorrect. When this happens, you just experiment some more until you have a new conjecture to test.

When a conjecture seems to be true, the final step is to **prove** that the conjecture is always true. A proof is a convincing logical argument that uses definitions and previously proven conjectures in an organized sequence.

1-14. A major focus of this course is learning the **investigative process,** a process you used during the Möbius Strip activity in problems 1-9 through 1-12. One part of this process is asking mathematical questions.

Assume your teacher is thinking of a shape and wants you to figure out what shape it is. Write down three questions you could ask your teacher to determine more about his or her shape.

1-15. The shapes at right are examples of **equilateral triangles**. How can you describe an equilateral triangle? Make at least two statements that seem true for all equilateral triangles. Then trace these equilateral triangles on your paper and draw one more in a different orientation.

Examples of Equilateral Triangles

1-16. Match each table of data below with the most appropriate graph and **briefly explain** why it matches the data.

a. Boiling water cooling down.

Time (min)	0	5	10	15	20	25
Temp (°C)	100	89	80	72	65	59

b. Cost of a phone call.

Time (min)	1	2	2.5	3	4	5	5.3	6
Cost (cents)	55	75	75	95	115	135	135	155

c. Growth of a baby in the womb.

Age (months)	1	2	3	4	5	6	7	8	9
Length (inches)	0.75	1.5	3	6.4	9.6	12	13.6	15.2	16.8

Graph 1   Graph 2   Graph 3   Graph 4   Graph 5

1-17. Solve for the given variable. Show the steps leading to your solution. Check your solution.

a. $-11x = 77$

b. $5c + 1 = 7c - 8$

c. $\frac{x}{8} = 2$

d. $-12 = 3k + 9$

1-18. Calculate the values of the expressions below. Show all steps in your process.

a. $\frac{3(2+6)}{2}$

b. $\frac{1}{2}(14)(5)$

c. $7^2 - 5^2$

d. $17 - 6 \cdot 2 + 4 \div 2$

1.1.3 How can I predict the area?

Perimeter and Area of Enlarging Tile Patterns

One of the core ideas of geometry is the measurement of shapes. Often in this course it will be important to find the areas and perimeters of shapes. How these measurements change as a shape is enlarged or reduced in size is especially interesting. Today your team will apply algebraic skills as you **investigate** the areas and perimeters of similar shapes.

1-19.   CARPETMART

Your friend Alonzo has come to your team for help. His family owns a rug manufacturing company, which is famous for its unique and versatile designs. One of their most popular designs is shown at right. Each rug design has an "original" size as well as enlargements that are exactly the same shape.

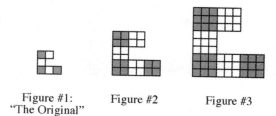

Figure #1:   Figure #2   Figure #3
"The Original"

Alonzo is excited because his family found out that the king of a far-away land is going to order an extremely large rug for one of his immense banquet halls. Unfortunately, the king is fickle and won't decide which rug he will order until the very last minute. The day before the banquet, the king will tell Alonzo which rug he wants and how big it will need to be. The king's palace is huge, so the rug will be VERY big!

Since the rugs are different sizes, and since each rug requires wool for the interior and fringe to wrap around the outside, Alonzo will need to quickly find the area and perimeter of each rug in order to obtain the correct quantities of wool and fringe.

Your Task: Your teacher will assign your team one of the rug designs to **investigate** (labeled (a) through (f) below). The "original" rug is shown in Figure 1, while Figures 2 and 3 are the next enlarged rugs of the series. With your team, create a table, graph, and rule for both the area and perimeter of your rug design. Then decide which representation will best help Alonzo find the area and perimeter for *any* figure number.

Problem continues on next page →

1-19.   *Problem continued from previous page.*

Be ready to share your analysis with the rest of the class. Your work must include the following:

- Diagrams for the rugs of the next two sizes (Figures 4 and 5) following the pattern shown in Figures 1, 2, and 3.

- A description of Figure 20. What will it look like? What are its area and perimeter?

- A table, graph, and rule representing the perimeter of your rug design.

- A table, graph, and rule representing the area of your rug design.

Rug Designs:

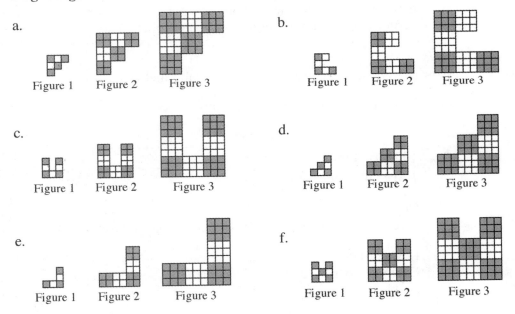

Further Guidance

1-20.   To start problem 1-20, first analyze the pattern your team has been assigned on graph paper, draw diagrams of Figures 4 and 5 for your rug design. Remember to shade Figures 4 and 5 the same way Figures 1 through 3 are shaded.

1-21.   Describe Figure 20 of your design. Give as much information as you can. What will it look like? How will the squares be arranged? How will it be shaded?

1-22. A table can help you learn more about how the perimeter changes as the rugs get bigger.

    a. Organize your perimeter data in a table like the one shown below.

Figure number	1	2	3	4	5	20
Perimeter (in units)						

    b. Graph the perimeter data for Figures 1 through 5. (You do not need to include Figure 20.) What shape is the graph?

    c. How does the perimeter grow? **Examine** your table and graph and describe how the perimeter changes as the rugs get bigger.

    d. Generalize the patterns you have found by writing an algebraic rule (equation) that will find the perimeter of any size rug in your design. That is, what is the perimeter of Figure n? Show how you got your answer.

1-23. Now analyze how the area changes with a table and graph.

    a. Make a new table, like the one below, to organize information about the area of each rug in your design.

Figure number	1	2	3	4	5	20
Area (in square units)						

    b. On a new set of axes, graph the area data for Figures 1 through 5. (You do not need to include Figure 20.) What shape is the graph?

    c. How does the area grow? Does it grow the same way as the perimeter? **Examine** your table and graph and describe how the area changes as the rugs get bigger.

    d. Write a rule that will find the area of Figure n. How did you find your rule? Be ready to share your **strategy** with the class.

Further Guidance section ends here.

1-24. The King has arrived! He demands a Rug #100, which is Figure 100 in your design. What will its perimeter be? Its area? **Justify** your answer.

14

METHODS AND MEANINGS

The Perimeter and Area of a Figure

The **perimeter** of a two-dimensional figure is the distance around its exterior (outside) on a flat surface. It is the total length of the boundary that encloses the interior (inside) region. See the example at right.

Perimeter = $5 + 8 + 4 + 6 = 23$ units

The **area** indicates the number of square units needed to fill up a region on a flat surface. For a rectangle, the area is computed by multiplying its length and width. The rectangle at right has a length of 5 units and a width of 3 units, so the area of the rectangle is 15 square units.

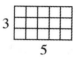

Area = $5 \cdot 3 = 15$ square units

1-25.   Read the Math Notes box for this lesson, which describes how to find the area and perimeter of a shape. Then **examine** the rectangle at right. If the perimeter of this shape is 120 cm, which equation below represents this fact? Once you have selected the appropriate equation, solve for x.

$2x + 5$

$6x - 1$

   a. $2x + 5 + 6x - 1 = 120$ 　　　　 b. $4(6x - 1) = 120$

   c. $2(6x - 1) + 2(2x + 5) = 120$ 　　 d. $(2x + 5)(6x - 1) = 120$

1-26.   Delilah drew 3 points on her paper. When she connects these points, must they form a triangle? Why or why not? Draw an example on your paper to support your **reasoning**.

1-27.   Copy the table below onto your paper. Complete it and write a rule relating x and y.

x	3	−1	0	2	−5	−2	1
y	0			−1			−2

1-28.   Rebecca placed a transparent grid of square units over each of the shapes she was measuring below. Using her grid, determine the area of each shape.

a.

b.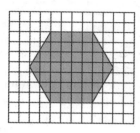

1-29.   Evaluate each expression below if $a = -2$ and $b = 3$.

a. $3a^2 - 5b + 8$

b. $\frac{2}{3}b - 5a$

c. $\frac{a+2b}{4} + 4a$

1.1.4 Are you convinced?

· ·

Logical Arguments

"I don't have my homework today because…" Is your teacher going to be convinced? Will it make a difference whether you say that the dog ate your homework or whether you bring in a note from the doctor? Imagine your friend says, "I know that shape is a square because it has four right angles." Did your friend tell you enough to convince you?

Many jobs depend on your ability to convince other people that your ideas are correct. For instance, a defense lawyer must be able to form logical arguments to persuade the jury or judge that his or her client is innocent. Today you are going to use a Way of Thinking called **reasoning and justifying** to focus on what makes a statement convincing.

TRIAL OF THE CENTURY

The musical group Apple Core has accused your math teacher, Mr. Bosky, of stealing its newest pop CD, "Rotten Gala." According to the police, someone stole the CD from the BigCD Store last Saturday at some time between 6:00 PM and 7:00 PM. Because your class is so well known for only reaching conclusions when sufficient evidence is presented, the judge has made you the jury! You are responsible for determining whether or not there is enough evidence to convict Mr. Bosky.

Carefully listen to the evidence that is presented. As each statement is read, decide:

- *Does the statement convince you? Why or why not?*

- *What could be changed or added to the statement to make it more convincing?*

Testimony

Mr. Bosky: *"But I don't like that CD! I wouldn't take it even if you paid me."*

Mr. Bosky: *"I don't have the CD. Search me."*

Mr. Bosky: *"I was at home having dinner Saturday."*

Casey: *"There were several of us having dinner with Mr. Bosky at his house. He made us a wonderful lasagna."*

Mrs. Thomas: *"All of us at dinner with Mr. Bosky left his house at 6:10 PM."*

Police Officer Yates: *"Driving as quickly as I could, it took me 30 minutes to go from Mr. Bosky's house to the BigCD store."*

Coach Teller: *"Mr. Bosky made a wonderful goal right at the beginning of our soccer game, which started at 7:00 PM. You can check the score in the local paper."*

Police Officer Yates: *"I also drove from the BigCD store to the field where the soccer game was. It would take him at least 40 minutes to get there."*

1-31.   THE FAMILY FORTUNE

You are at home when the phone rings. It is a good friend of yours who says, "Hey, your last name is Marston. Any chance you have a grandmother named Molly Marston who was REALLY wealthy? Check out today's paper." You glance at the front page:

Family Fortune Unclaimed

City officials are amazed that the county's largest family fortune may go unclaimed. Molly "Ol' Granny" Marston died earlier this week and it appears that she was survived by no living relatives. According to her last will and testament, "Upon my death, my entire fortune is to be divided among my children and grandchildren." Family members have until noon tomorrow to come forward with a written statement giving evidence that they are related to Ms. Marston or the money will be turned over to the city.

You're amazed – Molly is your grandmother, so your friend is right! However, you may not be able to collect your inheritance unless you can convince city officials that you are a relative. You rush into your attic where you keep a trunk full of family memorabilia.

a. You find several items that you think might be important in an old trunk in the attic. With your team, decide which of the items listed below will help prove that Ol' Molly was your grandmother.

Family Portrait — a photo showing three young children. On the back you see the date 1968.

Newspaper Clipping — an article from 1972 titled "Triplets Make Music History." The first sentence catches your eye: "Jake, Judy, and Jeremiah Marston, all eight years old, were the first triplets ever to perform a six-handed piano piece at Carnegie Hall."

Jake Marston's Birth Certificate — showing that Jake was born in 1964, and identifying his parents as Phillip and Molly Marston.

Your Learner's Permit — signed by your father, Jeremiah Marston.

Wilbert Marston's Passport — issued when Wilbert was fifteen.

b. Your team will now write a statement that will convince the city official (played by your faithful teacher!) that Ol' Molly was your grandmother. Be sure to support any claims that you make with appropriate evidence. Sometimes it pays to be convincing!

METHODS AND MEANINGS

Solving Linear Equations

In Algebra, you learned how to solve a linear equation. This course will help you apply your algebra skills to solve geometric problems. Review how to solve equations by reading the example below.

MATH NOTES

- **Simplify.** Combine like terms on each side of the equation whenever possible.

- **Keep equations balanced.** The equal sign in an equation tells you that the expressions on the left and right are balanced. Anything done to the equation must keep that balance.

$$3x - 2 + 4 = x - 6 \quad \text{Combine like terms}$$
$$3x + 2 = x - 6$$
$$-x = -x \quad \text{Subtract } x \text{ on both sides}$$
$$2x + 2 = -6$$
$$-2 = -2 \quad \text{Subtract 2 on both sides}$$
$$\frac{2x}{2} = \frac{-8}{2} \quad \text{Divide both sides by 2}$$
$$x = -4$$

- **Move your x-terms to one side of the equation.** Isolate all variables on one side of the equation and the constants on the other.

- **Undo operations.** Use the fact that addition is the opposite of subtraction and that multiplication is the opposite of division to solve for x. For example, in the equation $2x = -8$, since the 2 and the x are multiplied, then dividing both sides by 2 will get x alone.

Review & Preview

1-32. One goal of this course will be to review and enhance your algebra skills. Read the Math Notes box for this lesson. Then solve for x in each equation below, show all steps leading to your solution, and check your answer.

a. $34x - 18 = 10x - 9$

b. $4x - 5 = 4x + 10$

c. $3(x - 5) + 2(3x + 1) = 45$

d. $-2(x + 4) + 6 = -3$

1-33.   The day before Gerardo returned from a two-week trip, he wondered if he left his plants inside his apartment or outside on his deck. He knows these facts:

- If his plants are indoors, he must water them at least once a week or they will die.

- If he leaves his plants outdoors and it rains, then he does not have to water them. Otherwise, he must water them at least once a week or they will die.

- It has not rained in his town for 2 weeks.

When Gerardo returns, will his plants be dead? Explain your **reasoning**.

1-34.   For each of the equations below, solve for y in terms of x.

a. $2x - 3y = 12$ b. $5x + 2y = 7$

1-35.   Find the area of the rectangle at right. Be sure to include units in your answer.

8 mm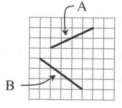

13 mm

1-36.   The **slope** of a line is a measure of its steepness and indicates whether it goes up or down from left to right. For example, the slope of the line segment A at right is $\frac{1}{2}$, while the slope of the line segment B is $-\frac{3}{4}$.

For each line segment below, find the slope. You may want to copy each line segment on graph paper in order to draw slope triangles.

a.   b.

c.   d.

1.1.5 What shapes can you find?

Building a Kaleidoscope

Today you will learn about angles and shapes as you study how a kaleidoscope works.

1-37.   BUILDING A KALEIDOSCOPE

How does a kaleidoscope create the complicated, colorful images you see when you look inside? A hinged mirror and a piece of colored paper can demonstrate how a simple kaleidoscope creates its beautiful repeating designs.

Your Task: Place a hinged mirror on a piece of colored, unlined paper so that its sides extend beyond the edge of the paper as shown at right. Explore what shapes you see when you look directly at the mirror, and how those shapes change when you change the angle of the mirror. Discuss the questions below with your team. Be ready to share your responses with the rest of the class.

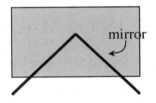

Discussion Points

What is this problem about? What is it asking you to do?

What happens when you change the angle (opening)
formed by the sides of the mirror?

How can you describe the shapes you see in the mirror?

1-38.   To complete your exploration, answer these questions together as a team.

a.   What happens to the shape you see as the angle formed by the mirror gets bigger (wider)? What happens as the angle gets smaller?

b.   What is the smallest number of sides the shape you see in the mirror can have? What is the largest?

c.   With your team, find a way to form a **regular hexagon** (a shape with six equal sides and equal angles).

d.   How might you describe to another team how you set the mirrors to form a hexagon? What types of information would be useful to have?

1-39.   A good way to describe an angle is by measuring how *wide* or *spread apart* the angle is. For this course, you should think of the measurement of an angle as representing the amount of rotation that occurs when you separate the two sides of the mirror from a closed position. The largest angle you can represent with a hinged mirror is 360°. This is formed when you open a mirror all the way so that the backs of the mirror touch. This is a called a **circular angle** and is represented by the diagram at right.

a.   Other angles may be familiar to you. For example, an angle that forms a perfect "L" or a quarter turn is a 90° angle, called a **right angle** (shown at right). You can see that four of these angles would form a circular angle.

What if the two mirrors are opened to form a straight line? What measure would that angle have? Draw this angle and label its degrees. How is this angle related to a circular angle?

b.   Based on the examples above, estimate the measures of these angles shown below. Then confirm your answer using a **protractor**, a tool that measures angles.

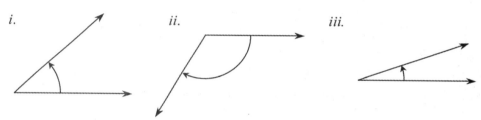

i.   *ii.*   *iii.*

1-40.   Now use your understanding of angle measurement to create some specific shapes using your hinged mirror. Be sure that both mirrors have the same length on the paper, as shown in the diagram at right.

These distances should be equal.

a.   Antonio says he can form an **equilateral triangle** (a triangle with three equal sides and three equal angles) using his hinged mirror. How did he do this? Once you can see the triangle in your mirror, place the protractor on top of the mirror. What is the measure of the angle formed by the sides of the mirror?

Problem continues on next page →

1-40.   *Problem continued from previous page.*

   b.   Use your protractor to set your mirror so that the angle formed is 90°. Be sure that the sides of the mirror intersect the edge of the paper at equal lengths. What is this shape called? Draw and label a picture of the shape on your paper.

   c.   Carmen's mirror shows the image at right, called a **regular pentagon**. She noticed that the five triangles in this design all meet at the hinge of her mirrors. She also noticed that the triangles must all the same size and shape, because they are reflections of the triangle formed by the mirrors and the paper.

   What must the sum of these five angles at the hinge be? And what is the angle formed by Carmen's mirrors? Test your conclusion with your mirror.

   d.   Discuss with your team and predict how many sides a shape would have if the angle that the mirror forms measures 40°. Explain how you made your prediction. Then check your prediction using the mirror and a protractor. Describe the shape you see with as much detail as possible.

1-41.   Reflect on what you learned during today's activity.

   a.   Based on this activity, what are some things that you think you will be studying in Geometry?

   b.   This activity was based on the question, *"What shapes can be created using reflections?"* What ideas from this activity would you want to learn more about? Write a question that could prompt a different, but related, future **investigation**.

METHODS AND MEANINGS

Types of Angles

When trying to describe shapes, it is convenient to classify types of angles. This course will use the following terms to refer to angles:

ACUTE: Any angle with measure **between** (but not including) 0° and 90°.

Less than 90°.

RIGHT: Any angle that measures 90°.

90°

OBTUSE: Any angle with measure **between** (but not including) 90° and 180°.

More than 90° and less than 180°.

STRAIGHT: Straight angles have a measure of 180° and are formed when the sides of the angle form a straight line.

180°

360°

CIRCULAR: Any angle that measures 360°.

1-42. Estimate the size of each angle below to the nearest 10°. A right angle is shown for reference so you should not need a protractor.

a.

b.

c.

1-43.   Using graph paper, draw a pair of xy-axes and scale them for $-6 \le x \le 6$ (x-values between and including -6 and 6) and $-10 \le y \le 10$ (y-values between and including -10 and 10). Complete the table below, substituting the x-values (inputs) to find the corresponding y-values (outputs) for the rule $y = x + 2$. Plot and connect the resulting points.

x (input)	-4	-3	-2	-1	0	1	2	3	4
y (output)									

1-44.   Angela had a rectangular piece of paper and then cut a rectangle out of a corner as shown at right. Find the area and perimeter of the resulting shape. Assume all measurements are in centimeters.

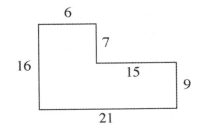

1-45.   For each equation below, solve for the given variable. If necessary, refer to the Math Notes box in Lesson 1.1.4 for guidance. Show the steps leading to your solution and check your answer.

a. $75 = 14y + 5$

b. $-7r + 13 = -71$

c. $3a + 11 = 7a - 13$

d. $2m + m - 8 = 7$

1-46.   On graph paper, draw four different rectangles that each have an area of 24 square units. Then find the perimeter of each one.

1.2.1 How do you see it?

Spatial Visualization and Reflections

Were you surprised when you looked into the hinged mirror during the Kaleidoscope Investigation of Lesson 1.1.5? Reflection can create many beautiful and interesting shapes and can help you learn more about the characteristics of other shapes. However, one reason you may have been surprised is because it is sometimes difficult to predict what a reflection will be. This is where spatial visualization plays an important role. **Visualizing**, the act of "picturing" something in your mind, is often helpful when working with shapes. In order to be able to **investigate** and describe a geometric concept, it is first useful to **visualize** a shape or action.

Today you will be **visualizing** in a variety of ways and will develop the ability to find reflections. As you work today, keep the following focus questions in mind:

How do I see it?

How can I verify my answer?

How can I describe it?

1-47.　　BUILDING BOXES

Which of the nets (diagrams) below would form a box with a lid if folded along the interior lines? Be prepared to defend your answer.

a.　　　　　　　b.　　　　　　　c.　　　　　　　d.

1-48.　　Have you ever noticed what happens when you look in a mirror? Have you ever tried to read words while looking in a mirror? What happens? Discuss this with your team. Then re-write the following words as they would look if you held this book up to a mirror. Do you notice anything interesting?

a.　　GEO　　　　　　　b.　　STAR　　　　　　　c.　　WOW

1-49.   When Kenji spun the flag shown at right very quickly about its
         pole, he noticed a three-dimensional shape emerge.

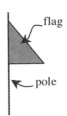

         a.   What shape did he see? Draw a picture of the three-
               dimensional shape on your paper and be prepared to
               defend your answer.

         b.   What would the flag need to look like so that a **sphere** (the
               shape of a basketball) is formed when the flag is rotated
               about its pole? Draw an example.

1-50.   REFLECTIONS

         The shapes created in the Kaleidoscope
         Investigation in Lesson 1.1.5 were the result
         of reflecting a triangle several times in a
         hinged mirror. However, other shapes can
         also be created by a reflection. For example,
         the diagram at right shows the result of
         reflecting a snowman across a line.

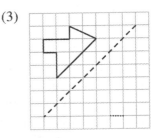

         original   image

         Line of
         reflection

         a.   Why do you think the image is called a reflection?
               How is the image different from the original?

         b.   On the Lesson 1.2.1 Resource Page provided by your teacher, use your
               visualization skills to imagine the reflection of each shape across the given
               line of refection. Then draw the reflection. Check your work by folding the
               paper along the line of reflection.

(1)   (2)   (3)

(4)   (5)   (6)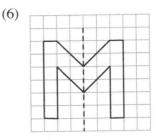

1-51. Sometimes, a motion appears to be a reflection when it really isn't. How can you tell if a motion is a reflection? Consider each pair of objects below. Which diagrams represent reflections across the given lines of reflection? Study each situation carefully and be ready to explain your thinking.

1-52. CONNECTIONS WITH ALGEBRA

What other ways can you use reflections? Consider how to reflect a graph as you answer the questions below.

a. On your Lesson 1.2.1 Resource Page, graph the parabola $y = x^2 + 3$ and the line $y = x$ for $x = -3, -2, -1, 0, 1, 2, 3$ on the same set of axes.

b. Now reflect the parabola over the line $y = x$. What do you observe? What happens to the x- and y-values of the original parabola?

1-53. LEARNING LOG

Throughout this course, you will be asked to reflect on your understanding of mathematical concepts in a Learning Log. Your Learning Log will contain explanations and examples to help you remember what you have learned throughout the course. It is important to write each entry of the Learning Log in your own words so that later you can use your Learning Log as a resource to refresh your memory. Your teacher will tell you where to write your Learning Log entries and how to structure or label them. Remember to label each entry with a title and a date so that it can be referred to later.

In this first Learning Log entry, describe what you learned today. For example, is it possible to reflect any shape? Is it possible to have a shape that, when reflected, doesn't change? How does reflection work? If it helps you to explain, sketch and label pictures to illustrate what you write. Title this entry "Reflections" and include today's date.

METHODS AND MEANINGS

Graphing an Equation

In Algebra, you learned how to graph an equation. During this course, you will apply your algebra skills to solve geometric problems. Review how to graph an equation by reading the example below.

- **Create a table of *x*-values.** Choose *x*-values that will show you any important regions of the graph of the equation. If you do not know ahead of time what the graph will look like, use the values $-4 \le x \le 4$ as shown at right.

$y = -x - 2$

x	−4	−3	−2	−1	0	1	2	3	4
y	2	1	0	−1	−2	−3	−4	−5	−6

- **Use the equation to find *y*-values.** Substitute each value of *x* into your equation and find the corresponding *y*-value. For example, for $y = -x - 2$, when $x = -3$, $y = -(-3) - 2 = 1$.

- **Graph the points using the coordinates from your table onto a set of $x \rightarrow y$ axes.** Connect the points and, if appropriate, use arrows to indicate that the graph of the equation continues in each direction.

- **Complete the graph.** Be sure your axes are scaled and labeled. Also label your graph with its equation as shown in the example above.

Review & Preview

1-54.   Review how to graph by reading the Math Notes box for this lesson. Then graph each line below on the same set of axes.

a. $y = 3x - 3$ b. $y = -\frac{2}{3}x + 3$ c. $y = -4x + 5$

1-55.   Estimate the size of each angle below to the nearest 10°. A
right angle is shown at right for reference so you do not need a
protractor.

a.   b.   c.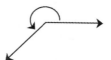

1-56.   The distance along a straight road is measured as shown in the diagram below. If the
distance between towns A and C is 67 miles, find the distance between towns A
and B.

1-57.   For each equation below, solve for x. Show all work. The answers are provided so
that you can check them. If you are having trouble with any solutions and cannot
find your errors, you may need to see your teacher for extra help (you can ask your
team as well). [**Solutions: a: 3.75, b: 3, c: 0, d: 3, e: ≈ 372.25, f: –3.4**]

a. $5x - 2x + x = 15$ b. $3x - 2 - x = 7 - x$

c. $3(x - 1) = 2x - 3 + 3x$ d. $3(2 - x) = 5(2x - 7) + 2$

e. $\frac{26}{57} = \frac{849}{5x}$ f. $\frac{4x+1}{3} = \frac{x-5}{2}$

1-58.   The three-dimensional shape at right is called a **cylinder**.
Its bottom and top bases are both circles, and its side is
perpendicular to the bases. What would the shape of a flag
need to be in order to generate a cylinder when it rotates
about its pole? (You may want to refer to problem 1-49 to
review how flags work.)

1.2.2 What if it is reflected more than once?

Rigid Transformations: Rotations and Translations

In Lesson 1.2.1, you learned how to change a shape by reflecting it across a line, like the ice cream cones shown at right. Today you will learn more about reflections and learn about two new types of transformations: rotations and translations.

original ┊ image

1-59. As Amanda was finding reflections, she wondered, "What if I reflect a shape twice over parallel lines?" **Investigate** her question as you answer the questions below.

   a. On the Lesson 1.2.2 Resource Page provided by your teacher, find △*ABC* and lines *n* and *p* (shown below). What happens when △*ABC* is reflected across line *n* to form △*A'B'C'* and then △*A'B'C'* is reflected across line *p* to form △*A"B"C"*? First **visualize** the reflections and then test your idea of the result by **drawing** both reflections.

   b. **Examine** your result from part (a). Compare the original triangle △*ABC* with the final result, △*A"B"C"*. What single motion would change △*ABC* to △*A"B"C"*?

   c. Amanda analyzed her results from part (a). "It looks like I could have just slid △*ABC* over!" Sliding a shape from its original position to a new position is called **translating**. For example, the ice cream cone at right has been **translated**. Notice that the image of the ice cream cone has the same *orientation* as the original (that is, it is not turned or flipped). What words can you use to describe a translation?

   d. The words **transformation** and **translation** sound alike and can easily be confused. Discuss in your team what these words mean and how they are related to each other.

1-60.   After answering Amanda's question in problem 1-59, her teammate asks, "What if the lines of reflection are not parallel? Is the result still a translation?" Find △*EFG* and lines *v* and *w* on the Lesson 1.2.2 Resource Page.

a.   First **visualize** the result when △*EFG* is reflected over *v* to form △*E′F′G′*, and then △*E′F′G′* is reflected over *w* to form △*E″F″G″*. Then **draw** the resulting reflections on the resource page. Is the final image a translation of the original triangle? If not, describe the result.

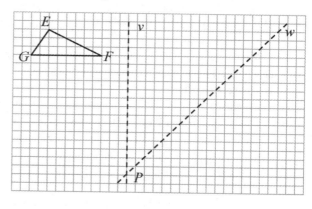

b.   Amanda noticed that when the reflecting lines are not parallel, the original shape is **rotated**, or turned, to get the new image. For example, the diagram at right shows the result when an ice cream cone is rotated about a point.

original   image

center of rotation

In part (a), the center of rotation is at point *P*, the point of intersection of the lines of reflection. Use a piece of tracing paper to test that △*E″F″G″* can be obtained by rotating △*EFG* about point *P*. To do this, first trace △*EFG* and point *P* on the tracing paper. While the tracing paper and resource page are aligned, apply pressure on *P* so that the tracing paper can rotate about this point. Then turn your tracing paper until △*EFG* rests atop △*E″F″G″*.

c.   The rotation of △*EFG* in part (a) is an example of a 90° clockwise rotation. The term "clockwise" refers to a rotation that follows the direction of the hands of a clock, namely ↻. A rotation in the opposite direction (↺) is called "counter-clockwise."

On your resource page, rotate the "block L" 90° counter-clockwise (↺) about point *Q*.

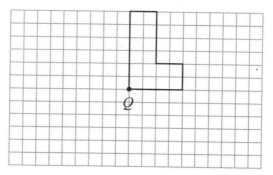

1-61.   NOTATION FOR TRANSFORMATIONS

In the diagram at right, the original square *ABCD* on the left was *translated* to the image square on the right. (We label a shape by labeling each corner.) The image location is different from the original, so we use different letters to label its **vertices** (corners).

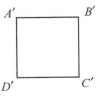

To keep track of how the vertices correspond, we call the image *A′B′C′D′*. The ′ symbol is read as "prime," so the shape on the right is called, "*A* prime *B* prime *C* prime *D* prime." *A′* is the image of *A*, *B′* is the image of *B*, etc. This notation tells you which vertices correspond.

a.   The diagram at right shows a different transformation of *ABCD*. Look carefully at the correspondence between the vertices. Can you rotate or reflect the original square to make the letters correspond as shown? If you can reflect, where would the line of reflection be? If you can rotate, where would the point of rotation be?

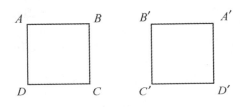

b.   The diagram at right shows a rotation. Copy the diagram (both squares and the point) and label the corners of the image square on the right. If you have trouble, ask your teacher for tracing paper. Describe the rotation.

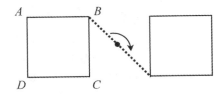

1-62.   CONNECTIONS WITH ALGEBRA

Examine how translations and rotations can affect graphs. On graph paper, graph the equation $y = \frac{1}{2}x - 3$.

a.   Draw the result if $y = \frac{1}{2}x - 3$ is translated up 4 units. You may want to use tracing paper. Write the equation of the result. What is the relationship of $y = \frac{1}{2}x - 3$ and its image?

b.   Now use tracing paper to rotate $y = \frac{1}{2}x - 3$ 90° clockwise (↻) about the point $(0, 0)$. Write the equation of the result. What is the relationship of $y = \frac{1}{2}x - 3$ and this new image?

METHODS AND MEANINGS

Rigid Transformations

A transformation that preserves the size, shape, and orientation of a figure while *sliding* it to a new location is called a **translation.**

A transformation that preserves the size and shape of a figure across a line to form a mirror image is called a **reflection**. The mirror line is a **line of reflection**. One way to find a reflection is to *flip* a figure over the line of reflection.

A transformation that preserves the size and shape while *turning* an entire figure about a fixed point is called a **rotation**. Figures can be rotated either clockwise (↻) or counterclockwise (↺).

When labeling a transformation, the new figure (image) is often labeled with **prime notation**. For example, if $\triangle ABC$ is reflected across the vertical dashed line, its image can be labeled $\triangle A'B'C'$ to show exactly how the new points correspond to the points in the original shape. We also say that $\triangle ABC$ is **mapped** to $\triangle A'B'C'$.

1-63.   The diagram at right shows a flat surface containing a line and a circle with no points in common. Can you **visualize** moving the line and/or circle so that they intersect at exactly one point? Two points? Three points? Explain each answer and illustrate each with an example when possible.

1-64.   Decide which transformation was used on each pair of shapes below. Some may
have undergone more than one transformation.

a.   b.   c.

d.   e.   f.

1-65.   The **perimeter** (the sum of the side lengths) of the
triangle at right is 52 units. Write and solve an
equation based on the information in the diagram.
Use your solution for x to find the measures of each
side of the triangle. Be sure to confirm that your
answer is correct.

1-66.   Bertie placed a transparent grid made up of unit squares over each of the shapes she
was measuring below. Using her grid, approximate the area of each region.

a.   b.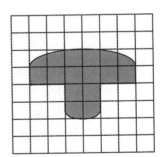

1-67.   For each equation below, find y if $x = -3$.

a. $y = -\frac{1}{3}x - 5$ b. $y = 2x^2 - 3x - 2$ c. $2x - 5y = 4$

1.2.3 How can I move it?

···

Using Transformations

In Lesson 1.1.1, your class made a quilt using designs based on a geometric shape. Similarly, throughout American history, quilters have created quilts that use

Sue Sales, *Hearts.*

transformations to create intricate geometric designs. For example, the quilt at right is an example of a design based on rotation and reflection, while the quilt at left contains translation, rotation, and reflection.

Today, you will work with your team to discover ways to find the image of a shape after it is rotated, translated, or reflected.

Sue Sales, *Balance From Within.*

1-68. Here are some situations that occur in everyday life. Each one involves one or more of the basic transformations: reflection, rotation or translation. State the transformation(s) involved in each case.

a. You look in a mirror as you comb your hair.

b. While repairing your bicycle, you turn it upside down and spin the front tire to make sure it isn't rubbing against the frame.

c. You move a small statue from one end of a shelf to the other.

d. You flip your scrumptious buckwheat pancakes as you cook them on the griddle.

e. The bus tire spins as the bus moves down the road.

f. You examine the footprints made in the sand as you walked on the beach.

1-69.   ROTATIONS ON A GRID

Consider what you know about rotation, a motion that turns a shape about a point. Does it make any difference if a rotation is clockwise (↻) versus counterclockwise (↺)? If so, when does it matter? Are there any circumstances when it does not matter? And are there any situations when the rotated image lies exactly on the original shape?

Investigate these questions as you rotate the shapes below about the given point on the Lesson 1.2.3 Resource Page. Use tracing paper if needed. Be prepared to share your answers to the questions posed above.

a.   180° ↻   b.   180° ↺   c.   90° ↻   d.   90° ↺

e.   270° ↻   f.   360° ↻   g.   180°   h.   90°

1-70.   TRANSLATIONS ON A GRID

The formal name for a slide is a translation. (Remember that translation and transformation are different words.) △A′B′C′ at right is the result of translating △ABC.

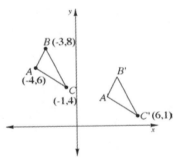

a.   Describe the translation. That is, how many units to the right and how many units down does the translation move the triangle?

b.   On graph paper, plot △EFG if E(4, 5), F(1, 7), and G(2, 0). Find the coordinates of △E′F′G′ if △E′F′G′ is translated the same way as △ABC was in part (a).

c.   △X′Y′Z′ is the result of performing the same translation on △XYZ. If X′(2, −3), Y′(4, −5), and Z′(0, 1), name the coordinates of X, Y, and Z.

1-71.   Using tracing paper, reflect △ABC across line l at right to form △A′B′C′. One way to do this is to trace the triangle and the line of reflection. Fold the tracing paper along the line of reflection and trace the triangle on the other side of the line of reflection. Then unfold the tracing paper and observe the original triangle and its reflection. Label the reflection △A′B′C′.

Problem continues on next page →

1-71. *Problem continued from previous page.*

Use your ruler to draw three dashed lines, each one joining one vertex of the original triangle with its image in the reflected triangle. Describe any geometric relationships you notice between each dashed line and the line of reflection.

1-72. How is the result from problem 1-71 useful? Consider reflecting a **line segment** (the portion of a line between two points) across a line that passes through one of its endpoints. For example, what would be the result when $\overline{AB}$ is reflected across $\overrightarrow{BC}$?

a. Copy $\overline{AB}$ and $\overrightarrow{BC}$ and draw $\overline{A'B}$, the reflection of $\overline{AB}$. When points A and A' are connected, what shape is formed?

b. Use what you know about reflection to make as many statements as you can about the shape from part (a). For example, are there any sides that must be the same length? Are there any angles that must be equal? Is there anything else special about this shape?

c. When two sides of a triangle have the same length, that triangle is called **isosceles**. In your Learning Log, describe all the facts you know about isosceles triangles. Be sure to include a diagram. Label this entry "Isosceles Triangles" and include today's date.

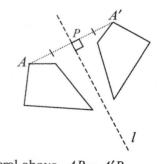

METHODS AND MEANINGS

More on Reflections

When a figure is reflected across a line of reflection, such as the quadrilateral at right, it appears that the figure is "flipped" over the line.

However, there are other interesting relationships between the original figure and its image.

For instance, the line segment connecting each image point with its corresponding point on the original figure is perpendicular to (meaning that it forms a right angle with) the line of reflection.

In addition, the line of reflection bisects (cuts in half) the line segment connecting each image point with its corresponding point on the original figure. For example, for reflection of the quadrilateral above, $AP = A'P$.

1-73. Plot the following points on another sheet of graph paper and connect them in the order given. Then connect points A and D.

$$A(5, 3), B(5, -6), C(-4, -6), \text{ and } D(-4, 3)$$

    a. What is the resulting figure?

    b. Find the area of shape $ABCD$.

    c. If $ABCD$ is rotated 90° clockwise (↻) about the origin to form $A'B'C'D'$, what are the coordinates of the vertices of $A'B'C'D'$?

1-74. Solve for the variable in each equation below. Show the steps leading to your answer.

    a. $8x - 22 = -60$
              b. $\frac{1}{2}x - 37 = -84$

    c. $\frac{3x}{4} = \frac{6}{7}$
                d. $9a + 15 = 10a - 7$

1-75. Graph the rule $y = -\frac{3}{2}x + 6$ on graph paper. Label the points where the line intersects the x- and y-axes.

1-76. On graph paper, graph the line through the point $(0, -2)$ with slope $\frac{4}{3}$.

    a. Write the equation of the line.

    b. Translate the graph of the line up 4 and to the right 3 units. What is the result? Write the equation for the resulting line.

    c. Now translate the original graph down 5 units. What is the result? Write the equation for the resulting line.

1-77. Evaluate the expression $\frac{1}{4}k^5 - 3k^3 + k^2 - k$ for $k = 2$.

1.2.4 What shapes can I create with triangles?

Using Transformations to Create Shapes

In Lesson 1.2.3, you practiced reflecting, rotating and translating figures. Since these are rigid transformations, the image always had the same size and shape as the original. In this lesson, you will combine the image with the original to make new, larger shapes from four basic "building-block" shapes.

As you create new shapes, consider what information the transformation gives you about the resulting new shape. By the end of this lesson, you will have generated most of the shapes that will be the focus of this course.

1-78. THE SHAPE FACTORY

The Shape Factory, an innovative new company, has decided to branch out to include new shapes. As Product Developers, your team is responsible for finding exciting new shapes to offer your customers. The current company catalog is shown at right.

Since your boss is concerned about production costs, you want to avoid buying new machines and instead want to reprogram your current machines.

The factory machines not only make all the shapes shown in the catalog, but they also are able to rotate or reflect a shape. For example, if the half-equilateral triangle is rotated 180° about the **midpoint** (the point in the middle) of its longest side, as shown at right, the result is a rectangle.

Your Task: Your boss has given your team until the end of this lesson to find as many new shapes as you can. Your team's reputation, which has suffered recently from a series of blunders, could really benefit by an impressive new line of shapes formed by a triangle and its transformations. For each triangle in the catalog, determine which new shapes are created when it is rotated or reflected so that the image shares a side with the original triangle. Be sure to make as many new shapes as possible. Use tracing paper or any other reflection tool to help.

40

1-79.   Since there are so many possibilities to test, it is useful to start by considering the shapes that can be generated just from one triangle. For example:

   a.   Test what happens when the half-square is reflected across each side. For each result (original plus image), draw a diagram and describe the shape that you get. If you know a name for the result, state it.

   b.   The point in the middle of each side is called its middle point, or **midpoint** for short. Try rotating the half-square 180° about the midpoint of each side to make a new shape. For each result, draw a diagram. If you know its name, write it near your new shape.

   c.   Repeat parts (a) and (b) with each of the other triangles offered by the Shape Factory.

*Further Guidance
section ends here.*

1-80.   EXTENSIONS

What other shapes can be created by reflection and rotation? Explore this as you answer the questions below. You can **investigate** these questions in any order. Remember that the resulting shape includes the original shape and all of its images. Remember to record and name each result.

   •   What if you reflect an equilateral triangle twice, once across one side and another time across a different side?

   •   What if an equilateral triangle is repeatedly rotated about one vertex so that each resulting triangle shares one side with another until new triangles are no longer possible? Describe the resulting shape.

   •   What if you rotate a trapezoid 180° around the midpoint of one if its non-parallel sides?

1-81.   BUILDING A CATALOG

Your boss now needs you to create a catalog page that includes your shapes. Each entry should include a diagram, a name, and a description of the shape. List any special features of the shape, such as if any sides are the same length or if any angles must be equal. Use color and arrows to highlight these attributes in the diagram.

METHODS AND MEANINGS

Polygons

A **polygon** is defined as a two-dimensional closed figure made up of straight line segments connected end-to-end. These segments may not cross (intersect) at any other points.

At right are some examples of polygons.

Shape A at right is an example of a **regular polygon** because its sides are all the same length and its angles have equal measure.

MATH NOTES

Review & Preview

1-82. According to the graph at right, how much money would it cost to speak to an attorney for 2 hours and 25 minutes?

1-83. Lourdes has created the following challenge for you: She has given you three of the four points necessary to determine a rectangle on a graph. She wants you to find the points that "complete" each of the rectangles below.

a. (−1, 3), (−1, 2), (9, 2)

b. (3, 7), (5, 7), (5, −3)

c. (−5, −5), (1, 4), (4, 2)

d. (−52, 73), (96, 73), (96, 1483)

1-84. Find the area of the rectangles formed in parts (a), (b), and (d) of problem 1-83.

1-85.   Copy the diagrams below on graph paper. Then find the result when each indicated transformation is performed.

   a.   Reflect Figure A across line *l*.

   b.   Rotate Figure B 90° clockwise (↻) about point P.

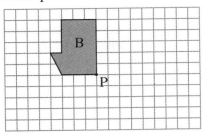

   c.   Reflect Figure C across line *m*.

   d.   Rotate Figure D 180° about point Q.

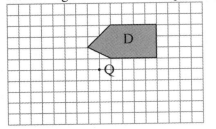

1-86.   At right is a diagram of a **regular hexagon** with center *C*. A polygon is regular if all sides are equal and all angles are equal. Copy this shape on your paper, then answer the questions below.

   a.   Draw the result of rotating the hexagon about its center 180°. Explain what happened. When this happens, the shape has **rotation symmetry**.

   b.   What is the result when the original hexagon is reflected across line *n*, as shown at right? A shape with this quality is said to have **reflection symmetry** and line *n* is a **line of symmetry** of the hexagon (not of the reflection).

   c.   Does a regular hexagon have any other lines of symmetry? That is, are there any other lines you could fold across so that both halves of the hexagon will match up? Find as many as you can.

1.2.5 What shapes have symmetry?

Symmetry

You have encountered symmetry several times in this chapter. For instance, the quilt your class created in Lesson 1.1.1 contained symmetry. The shapes you saw in the hinged mirrors during the kaleidoscope investigation were also symmetric. But so far, you have not developed a test for determining whether a polygon is symmetric. And since symmetry is related to transformations, how can we use transformations to describe this relationship? This lesson is designed to deepen your understanding of symmetry.

By the end of this lesson, you should be able to answer these target questions:

What is symmetry?

How can I determine whether or not a polygon has symmetry?

What types of symmetry can a shape have?

1-87.   REFLECTION SYMMETRY

In problem 1-1, you created a quilt panel that had **reflection symmetry** because if the design were reflected across the line of symmetry, the image would be exactly the same as the original design. See an example of a quilt design that has reflection symmetry at right.

Obtain the Lesson 1.2.5 Resource Page. On it, **examine** the many shapes that will be our focus of study in this course. Which of these shapes have reflection symmetry? Consider this as you answer the questions below.

a.   For each shape on the resource page, draw all the possible lines of symmetry. If you are not sure if a shape has reflection symmetry, trace the shape onto tracing paper and try folding the paper so that both sides of the fold match.

b.   Which types of triangles have reflection symmetry?

c.   Which types of quadrilaterals (shapes with four sides) have reflection symmetry?

d.   Which shapes on your resource page have more than three lines of symmetry?

1-88.   ROTATION SYMMETRY

In problem 1-87, you learned that many shapes have reflection symmetry. These
shapes remain unaffected when they are reflected across a line of symmetry.
However, some shapes remain unchanged when rotated about a point.

a.   **Examine** the shape at right. Can this shape be
        rotated so that its image has the same position
        and orientation as the original shape? Trace
        this shape on tracing paper and test your
        conclusion. If it is possible, where is the point
        of rotation?

b.   Jessica claims that she can rotate <u>all</u>
        shapes in such a way that they will not
        change. How does she do it?

c.   Since all shapes can be rotated 360°
        without change, that is not a very
        special quality. However, the shape in
        part (a) above was special because it
        could be rotated less than 360° and
        still remain unchanged. A shape with
        this quality is said to have **rotation
        symmetry**.

But what shapes have rotation symmetry? **Examine** the shapes on your Lesson
1.2.5 Resource Page and identify those that have rotation symmetry.

d.   Which shapes on the resource page have 90° rotation symmetry? That is,
        which can be rotated about a point 90° and remain unchanged?

1-89.   TRANSLATION SYMMETRY

In problems 1-87 and 1-88, you identified shapes that have reflection and rotation
symmetry. What about translation symmetry? Is there an object that can be
translated so that its end result is exactly the same as the original object? If so, draw
an example and explain why it has **translation symmetry**.

1-90.   CONNECTIONS WITH ALGEBRA

During this lesson, you have focused on the types of symmetry that can exist in geometric objects. But what about shapes that are created on graphs? What types of graphs have symmetry?

a.   **Examine** the graphs below. Decide which have reflection symmetry, rotation symmetry, translation symmetry, or a combination of these.

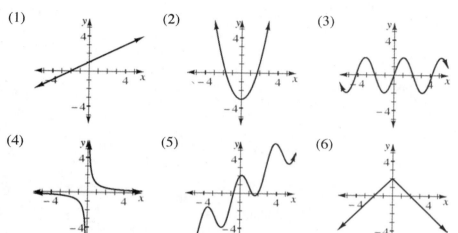

b.   If the y-axis is a line of symmetry of a graph, then its rule is referred to as **even**. Which of the graphs in part (a) have an even rule?

c.   If the graph has rotation symmetry about the origin (0, 0), its rule is called **odd**. Which of the graphs in part (a) have an odd rule?

1-91.   Reflect on what you have learned during this lesson. In your Learning Log, answer the questions posed at the beginning of this lesson, reprinted below. When helpful, give examples and draw a diagram.

What is symmetry?

How can I determine whether or not a polygon has symmetry?

What types of symmetry can a shape have?

METHODS AND MEANINGS

Slope of a Line and Parallel and Perpendicular Slopes

During this course, you will use your algebra tools to learn more about shapes. One of your algebraic tools that can be used to learn about the relationship of lines is slope. Review what you know about slope below.

The **slope** of a line is the ratio of the change in y (Δy) to the change in x (Δx) between any two points on the line. It indicates both how steep the line is and its direction, upward or downward, left to right.

$$\text{slope} = \frac{\text{vertical change}}{\text{horizontal change}} = \frac{\Delta y}{\Delta x}$$

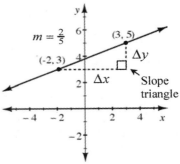

Lines that point upward from left to right have positive slope, while lines that point downward from left to right have negative slope. A horizontal line has zero slope, while a vertical line has undefined slope. The slope of a line is denoted by the letter m when using the $y = mx + b$ equation of a line.

One way to calculate the slope of a line is to pick two points on the line, draw a slope triangle (as shown in the example above), determine Δy and Δx, and then write the slope ratio. Be sure to verify that your slope correctly resulted in a negative or positive value based on its direction.

Parallel lines lie in the same plane (a flat surface) and never intersect. They have the same steepness, and therefore they grow at the same rate. Lines l and n at right are examples of parallel lines.

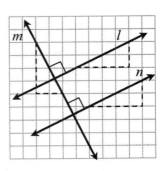

On the other hand, **perpendicular lines** are lines that intersect at a right angle. For example, lines m and n at right are perpendicular, as are lines m and l. Note that the small square drawn at the point of intersection indicates a right angle.

The **slopes of parallel lines** are the same. In general, the slope of a line parallel to a line with slope m is m.

The **slopes of perpendicular lines** are opposite reciprocals. For example, if one line has slope $\frac{4}{5}$, then any line perpendicular to it has slope $-\frac{5}{4}$. If a line has slope -3, then any line perpendicular to it has slope $\frac{1}{3}$. In general, the slope of a line perpendicular to a line with slope m is $-\frac{1}{m}$.

1-92.   On graph paper, graph each of the lines below on the same set of axes. What is the relationship between lines (a) and (b)? What about between (b) and (c)?

a. $y = \frac{1}{3}x + 4$ b. $y = -3x + 4$ c. $y = -3x - 2$

1-93.   The length of a side of a square is $5x + 2$ units. If the perimeter is 48 units, complete the following.

a.   Write an equation to represent this information.

b.   Solve for x.

c.   What is the area of the square?

1-94.   When the shapes below are reflected across the given line of reflection, the original shape and the image (reflection) create a new shape. For each reflection below, name the new shape that is created.

a.   b.   c.

d.   Use this method to create your own shape that has reflection symmetry. Add additional lines of symmetry. Note that the dashed lines of reflection in the figures above become lines of symmetry in the new shape.

1-95.   If a triangle has two equal sides, it is called **isosceles** (pronounced eye-SOS-a-lees). "Iso" means "same" and "sceles" is related to "scale." Decide whether each triangle formed by the points below is isosceles. Explain how you decided.

a.   (6, 0), (0, 6), (6, 6)   b.   (–3, 7), (–5, 2), (–1, 2)

c.   (4, 1), (2, 3), (9, 2)   d.   (1, 1), (5, –3), (1, –7)

1-96. Copy the diagrams below on graph paper. Then find each result when each indicated transformation is performed.

a. Reflect A across line *l*.

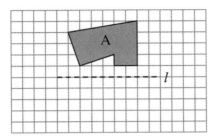

b. Rotate B 90° counterclockwise (↺) about point P.

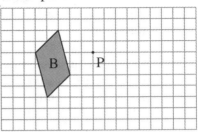

c. Rotate C 180° about point Q.

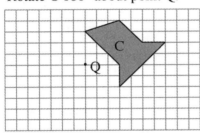

d. Reflect D across line *m*.

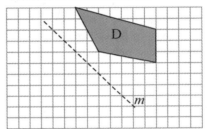

1.3.1 How can I classify this shape?

Attributes and Characteristics of Shapes

In Lesson 1.2.4, you generated a list of shapes formed by triangles and in Lesson 1.2.5, you studied the different types of symmetries that a shape can have. In Section 1.3, you will continue working with shapes to learn more about their attributes and characteristics. For example, which shapes have sides that are parallel? And which of our basic shapes are equilateral?

By the end of this lesson you should have a greater understanding about the attributes that make shapes alike and different. Throughout the rest of this course you will study these qualities that set shapes apart as well as learn how shapes are related.

1-97.   INTRODUCTION TO THE SHAPE BUCKET

Obtain a Shape Bucket and a Lesson 1.3.1B Resource Page from your teacher. The
Shape Bucket contains most of the basic geometric shapes you will study in this
course. Count the items and verify that you have all 16 shapes. Take the shapes out
and notice the differences between them. Are any alike? Are any strangely
different?

Once you have examined the shapes in your bucket, work as a team to build the
composite figures below (also shown on the resource page). Composite figures are
made by combining two or more shapes to make a new figure. On the Lesson 1.3.1B
Resource Page, show the shapes you used to build the composite shapes by filling in
their outlines within each composite shape.

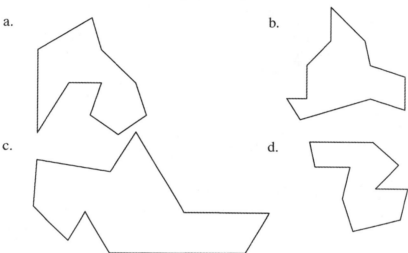

a.

b.

c.

d.

1-98.   VENN DIAGRAMS

Obtain a Venn diagram from your teacher.

a.   The **left** circle of
the Venn
diagram, Circle
#1, will represent
the attribute "has
at least one pair
of parallel sides"

**#1: Has at
least one pair
of parallel
sides**

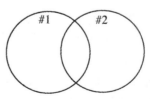

**#2: Has at
least two sides
of equal
length**

and the **right** side, Circle #2, will represent the attribute "has at least two sides
of equal length" as shown above. Sort through the shapes in the Shape Bucket
and decide as a team where each shape belongs. Be sure to record your
solution on paper. As you discuss this problem with your teammates, **justify**
your statements with reasons such as, "I think this shape goes here **because**..."

Problem continues on next page →

Geometry Connections

1-98.   *Problem continued from previous page.*

   b.   Next, reclassify the shapes for the new Venn diagram shown below. Describe
        each region in a sentence.

   **#1: Has only   #2: Has a
     three sides   right angle**

   c.   Finally, reclassify the shapes for the new Venn diagram shown below.
        Describe each region in a sentence.

   **#1: Has   #2: Has 180°
    reflection   rotation
    symmetry   symmetry**

METHODS AND **M**EANINGS

Venn Diagrams

MATH NOTES

A Venn diagram is a tool used to classify objects. It is usually
composed of two or more circles that represent different conditions.
An item is placed or represented in the Venn diagram in the
appropriate position based on the conditions it meets. See the
example below:

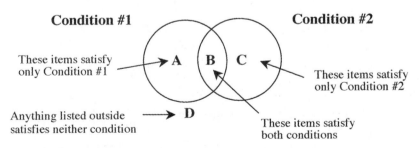

Condition #1   **Condition #2**

These items satisfy   **A   B   C**
only Condition #1   These items satisfy
                                                     only Condition #2

Anything listed outside   → **D**
satisfies neither condition   These items satisfy
                                            both conditions

1-99. Copy the Venn diagram below on your paper. Then show where each person described should be represented in the diagram. If a portion of the Venn diagram remains empty, describe the qualities a person would need to belong there.

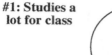 **#1: Studies a lot for class**   **#2: Has long hair**

a. Carol: *"I rarely study and enjoy braiding my long hair."*

b. Bob: *"I never do homework and have a crew cut."*

c. Pedro: *"I love joining after school study teams to prepare for tests and I like being bald!"*

1-100. Solve the equations below for *x*, if possible. Be sure to check your solution.

a. $\frac{3x-1}{4} = -\frac{5}{11}$

b. $(5-x)(2x+3) = 0$

c. $6 - 5(2x - 3) = 4x + 7$

d. $\frac{3x}{4} + 2 = 4x - 1$

1-101. **Examine** the figure graphed on the axes at right.

a. What happens when you rotate this figure about the origin 90°? 45°? 180°?

b. What other angle could the figure at right be rotated so that the shape does not appear to change?

c. What shape will stay the same no matter how many degrees it is rotated?

1-102. Copy △*ABC* at right on graph paper.

a. Rotate △*ABC* 90° counter-clockwise (↺) about the origin to create △*A'B'C'*. Name the coordinates of *C'*.

b. Reflect △*ABC* across the vertical line *x* = 1 to create △*A"B"C"*.

c. Translate △*ABC* so that *A'''* is at (4, –5). Name the coordinates of *B'''*.

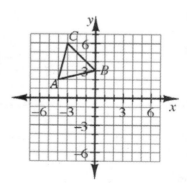

1-103.   Copy the table below, complete it, and write a rule relating *x* and *y*.

x	−3	−2	−1	0	1	2	3	4
y	−7			2	5			14

1.3.2 How can I describe it?

More Characteristics of Shapes

In Lesson 1.3.1, you used shapes to build new, unique, composite shapes. You also started to analyze the attributes (qualities) of shapes. Today you will continue to look at their attributes as you learn new vocabulary.

1-104.   Using your Venn diagram Resource Page from Lesson 1.3.1, categorize the shapes from the Shape Bucket in the Venn diagram as shown below. Record your results on paper.

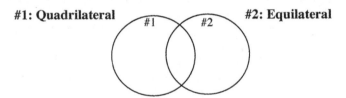

#1: Quadrilateral   #1   #2   **#2: Equilateral**

1-105.   DESCRIBING A SHAPE

How can you describe a square? With your class, find a way to describe a square using its attributes (special qualities) so that anyone could draw a square based on your description. Be as complete as possible. You may not use the word "square" in the description.

Square

1-106.   Each shape in the bucket is unique; that is, it differs from the others. You will be assigned a few shapes to describe **as completely as possible** for the class. But what is a complete description? As you work with your team to create a complete description, consider the questions below.

- What do you notice about your shape?

- What makes it different from other shapes?

- If you wanted to describe your shape to a friend on the telephone who cannot see it, what would you need to include in the description?

1-107.   GEOMETRY TOOLKIT

Obtain the Lesson 1.3.2A Resource Page entitled "Shapes Toolkit" from your teacher.

a.   Label each shape that you have learned about so far with its geometrical name.

b.   In the space provided, describe the shape based on the descriptions generated from problem 1-106. Leave space so that later observations can be added for each shape. Note that the description for **rectangle** has been provided as an example.

c.   On the diagram for each shape, mark sides that must have equal length or that must be parallel. Also mark any angles that measure 90°. See the descriptions below.

•   To show that two sides have the same length, use "tick marks" on the sides. However, to show that one pair of equal sides may not be the same length as the other pair of equal sides, you should use one tick mark on two of the opposite, equal sides and two tick marks on the other two opposite, equal sides, as shown below.

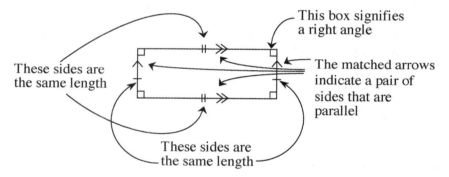

•   To show that the rectangle has two pairs of parallel sides, use one ">" mark on one pair of parallel sides and two ">>" marks on the other two parallel sides, as shown above.

•   Also mark any right angles by placing a small square at the right angle vertex (the corner). See the example above.

d.   The Shapes Toolkit Resource Page is the first page of a special information organizer, called your Geometry Toolkit, which you will be using for this course. It is a reference tool that you can use when you need to remember the name or description of a shape. Find a safe place in your Geometry binder to keep your Toolkit.

1-108.   **Examine** the Venn diagram below.

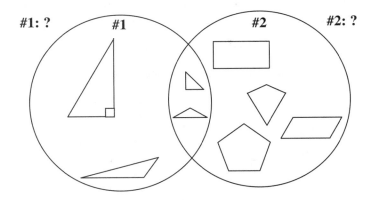

#1: ?   #1   #2   #2: ?

a.   What attribute does each circle represent? How can you tell?

b.   Where would the equilateral hexagon from your Shape Bucket go in this Venn? What about the trapezoid? Justify your **reasoning**.

c.   Create another shape that would belong outside both circles. Does your shape have a name that you have studied so far? If not, give it a new name.

1-109.   Elizabeth has a Venn diagram that she started at right. It turns out that the **only** shape in the Shape Bucket that could go in the intersection (where the two circles overlap) is a square! What are the possible attributes that her circles could represent? Discuss this with your team and be ready to share your ideas with the class.

1-110.   If no sides of a triangle have the same length, the triangle is called **scalene** (pronounced SCALE-een). However, if the triangle has two sides that are the same length, the triangle is called **isosceles** (pronounced eye-SOS-a-lees). Use the markings in each diagram below to decide if △ABC is isosceles or scalene. Assume the diagrams are not drawn to scale.

a.

b.

c.   ABDC is a square

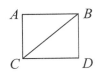

1-111.   In Lesson 1.3.3, you will start to learn how to make predictions in mathematics using probability. Decide if the following events must happen, cannot happen, or possibly will happen.

   a.   You will drink water some time today.

   b.   An earthquake will strike in your region tomorrow.

   c.   You will read a book.

   d.   If a shape is a trapezoid, it will have a pair of parallel sides.

   e.   You will shave your head this month.

1-112.   Without referring to your Shapes Toolkit, see if you can recall the names of each of the shapes below. Then check your answers with definitions from your Shapes Toolkit. How did you do?

   a.   b.   c.

   d.   e.   f.

1-113.   Copy the Venn diagram at right onto your paper. Then carefully place each capitalized letter of the alphabet below into your Venn diagram based on its type of symmetry.

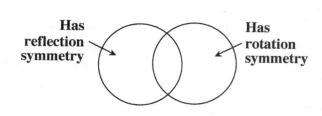

   A, B, C, D, E, F, G, H, I, J, K, L, M, N, O, P, Q, R, S, T, U, V, W, X, Y, Z

1-114.   **Multiple Choice:** Which equation below correctly represents the relationship of the sides given in the diagram at right?

   a. $3x - 2 + 2x + 17 = 360°$ b. $3x - 2 + 2x + 17 = 180°$

   c. $3x - 2 + 2x + 17 = 90°$ d. $3x - 2 = 2x + 17$

1.3.3 What are the chances?

Introduction to Probability

You have learned a great deal about the shapes in the Shape Bucket and with that knowledge can draw conclusions and make predictions. For example, if you are told that a shape is not a triangle, you could predict that it might be a quadrilateral.

One mathematical tool that can be used to predict how likely it is that something will happen is **probability**, the formal word for chance. There are many examples of the uses of probability in our lives. One such example is the weather. If a forecast predicts that there is a 95% likelihood of rain, you would probably bring a raincoat and umbrella with you for that day. If you buy a lottery ticket, the small print on the back of your ticket usually tells you the probability of randomly selecting winning numbers, which, unfortunately, is very low.

Your task today is to learn the principles of probability so that you can make predictions.

1-115.   WHAT'S THE CHANCE OF THAT HAPPENING?

In your teams, discuss the following list of events and consider the likelihood of each event occurring:

1. Your school's basketball team having a winning season this year

2. The sky being cloudy tomorrow

3. Your math teacher assigning homework tonight

4. The sun setting this evening

5. Meeting a famous person on the way home

6. Snow falling in Arizona in July

a.   Copy the probability line shown below on your paper. Where should these events lie? Place each event listed above at the appropriate location on the probability line. Do any events have no chance of happening? These should be placed on the left end of the number line. If you are sure the event will happen, place it on the right end.

|————————————————————————————————————|

NO CHANCE   MIGHT HAPPEN   CERTAIN TO
OF HAPPENING   HAPPEN

Problem continues on next page →

1-115.   *Problem continued from previous page.*

    b.   With your team, make up three new situations and place them on the probability line. One event should be certain to happen, one event should have no chance of happening, and one should possibly occur.

    c.   **Probability** can be written as a ratio, as a decimal, or as a percent. When using ratios or decimals, probability is expressed using numbers from 0 to 1. An event that has no chance of happening is said to have a probability of 0. An event that is certain to happen is said to have a probability of 1. Events that "might happen" will have values somewhere between 0 and 1. See the Math Notes box at the end of this lesson for more information about probability.

        Which events from part (a) have a probability of 0? A probability of 1? Which event has closest to a 25% chance? 50% chance?

1-116.   Probability is used to make predictions. For example, if you were to reach into the Shape Bucket and randomly pull out a shape, you could use probability to predict the chances of the shape having a right angle. Since there are 16 total shapes and 4 that have right angles, the probability is:

$$P\left(\text{right angle}\right) = \frac{4 \text{ shapes with right angles}}{16 \text{ total shapes}} = \frac{4}{16} = \frac{1}{4} = 0.25 = 25\%$$

The example above shows all forms of writing probability: $\frac{4}{16}$ (read "4 out of 16") is the probability as a ratio, 0.25 is its decimal form, and 25% is its equivalent percent.

Find the probabilities of randomly selecting the following shapes from a Shape Bucket that contains all 16 basic shapes.

    a.   P(quadrilateral)   b.   P(shape with an obtuse angle)

    c.   P(equilateral triangle)   d.   P(shape with parallel sides)

1-117.   What else can you predict about the shape randomly pulled from the Shape Bucket?

    a.   In your teams, describe at least two new probability conditions for the shapes in the bucket (like those in problem 1-116). One of the events should have a probability of 0 or a probability of 1. Write each P(condition) on a separate blank piece of paper and give it to your teacher.

    b.   Your teacher will select conditions generated by the class in part (a). For each condition, work with your team to determine the probability.

1-118.   Laura's team has a shape bucket that is missing several pieces. While talking to her teammates, Laura claims, "The probability of choosing a shape with four right angles is ¼ ."

Barbara adds, "Well…there are 2 shapes that have four right angles."

Montry responds, "I think you are both right."

What does Montry mean? Explain how Laura and Barbara could both be correct.

1-119.   What else can probability be used to predict? Analyze each of the situations below:

a.   What is the probability of randomly drawing a face card (king, queen or jack) from a deck of 52 cards, when you draw one card?

b.   Eduardo has in his pocket $1 in pennies, $1 in nickels, and $1 in dimes. If he randomly pulls out just one coin, what is the probability that he will pull out a dime?

c.   P(rolling an 8) with one regular die if you roll the die just once.

d.   P(dart hitting a shaded region) if the dart is randomly thrown and hits the target at right.

target

1-120.   In your Learning Log, write an entry describing what you learned today about probability. Be sure to show an example. Title this entry "Probability" and include today's date.

METHODS AND MEANINGS

Ratio and Probability

A comparison of two quantities is called a **ratio**. A ratio can be written as:

$$a : b \quad or \quad \frac{a}{b} \quad or \quad "a\ to\ b"$$

Each ratio has a numeric value that can be expressed as a fraction or decimal. For example, a normal deck of 52 playing cards has 13 cards with hearts. To compare the number of cards with hearts to the total number of playing cards, you could write:

$$\frac{Number\ of\ Hearts}{Total\ Number\ of\ Cards} = \frac{13}{52} = \frac{1}{4} = 0.25 \ .$$

Probability is a measure of the likelihood that an event will occur at random. It is expressed using numbers with values that range from 0 to 1, or from 0% to 100%. For example, an event that has no chance of happening is said to have a probability of 0 or 0%. An event that is certain to happen is said to have a probability of 1 or 100%. Events that "might happen" have values somewhere between 0 and 1 or between 0% and 100%.

The probability of an event happening is written as the ratio of the number of ways that the desired outcome can occur to the total number of possible outcomes (assuming that each possible outcome is equally likely).

$$P\left(event\right) = \frac{Number\ of\ Desired\ Outcomes}{Total\ Possible\ Outcomes}$$

For example, on a standard die, P(5) means the probability of rolling a 5. To calculate the probability, first determine how many possible outcomes exist. Since a die has six different numbered sides, the number of possible outcomes is 6. Of the six sides, only one of the sides has a 5 on it. Since the die has an equal chance of landing on any of its six sides, the probability is written:

$$P(5) = \frac{1\ side\ with\ the\ number\ five}{6\ total\ sides} = \frac{1}{6}\ or\ 0.1\overline{6}\ or\ approximately\ 16.7\%$$

Review & Preview

1-121.   **Examine** the shapes listed on your Shapes Toolkit. Name a shape that meets the following conditions: It has a pair of congruent sides, it has one right angle, and it has three vertices.

1-122.   Augustin is in line to choose a new locker at school. The locker coordinator has each student reach into a bin and pull out a locker number. There is one locker at the school that all the kids dread! This locker, # 831, is supposed to be haunted, and anyone who has used it has had strange things happen to him or her! When it is Augustin's turn to reach into the bin and select a locker number, he is very nervous. He knows that there are 535 lockers left and locker # 831 is one of them. What is the probability that Augustin reaches in and pulls out the dreaded locker # 831? Should he be worried? Explain.

1-123.   The four triangles at right are placed in a bag. If you reach into the bag without looking and pull out one triangle at random, what is the probability that:

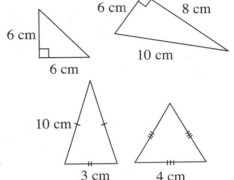

a.   the triangle is scalene?

b.   the triangle is isosceles?

c.   at least one side of the triangle is 6 cm?

1-124.   Rosalinda examined the angles at right and wrote the equation below.

$$(2x+1°)+(x-10°)=90°$$

a.   Does her equation make sense? If so, explain why her equation must be true. If it is not correct, determine what is incorrect and write the equation.

b.   If you have not already done so, solve her equation, clearly showing all your steps. What are the measures of the two angles?

c.   Verify that your answer is correct.

1-125.   Copy the table below on your paper and complete it for the rule $y = x^2 + 2x - 3$. Then graph and connect the points on graph paper. Name the x-intercepts.

x	−4	−3	−2	−1	0	1	2
y							

Chapter 1 Closure   What have I learned?

Reflection and Synthesis

The activities below offer you a chance to reflect on what you have learned in this chapter. As you work, look for concepts that you feel very comfortable with, ideas that you would like to learn more about, and topics you need more help with. Look for connections between ideas as well as connections with material you learned previously.

①   TEAM BRAINSTORM

With your team, brainstorm a list for each of the following two subjects. Be as detailed as you can. How long can you make your list? Challenge yourselves. Be prepared to share your team's ideas with the class.

Topics: What have you studied in this chapter? What ideas and words were important in what you learned? Remember to be as detailed as you can.

Connections: How are the topics, ideas, and words that you learned in previous courses connected to the new ideas in this chapter? Again, make your list as long as you can.

②   MAKING CONNECTIONS

The following is a list of the vocabulary used in this chapter. Make sure that you are familiar with all of these words and know what they mean. Refer to the glossary or index for any words that you do not yet understand.

angle	area	conjecture
equilateral	graph	image
line segment	measurement	parallel
perimeter	perpendicular	polygon
probability	protractor	random
ratio	reflection	regular hexagon
right angle	rotation	slope
solve	straight angle	symmetry
transformation	translation	triangle
Venn diagram	vertex (vertices)	

Problem continues on next page →

Geometry Connections

②   *Problem continued from previous page.*

Make a concept map showing all of the connections you can find among the key words and ideas listed above. To show a connection between two words, draw a line between them and explain the connection, as shown in the example below. A word can be connected to any other word as long as there is a justified connection. For each key word or idea, provide a sketch of an example.

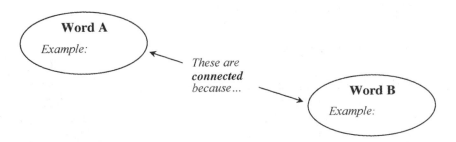

Your teacher may provide you with vocabulary cards to help you get started. If you use the cards to plan your concept map, be sure either to re-draw your concept map on your paper or to glue the vocabulary cards to a poster with all of the connections explained for others to see and understand.

While you are making your map, your team may think of related words or ideas that are not listed above. Be sure to include these ideas on your concept map.

③   SUMMARIZING MY UNDERSTANDING

This section gives you an opportunity to show what you know about certain math topics or ideas. Your teacher will direct you how to do this. Your teacher may give you a "GO" page to work on (or you can download this from www.cpm.org). "GO" stands for "Graphic Organizer," a tool you can use to organize your thoughts and communicate your ideas clearly.

④   WHAT HAVE I LEARNED?

This section will help you recognize those types of problems you feel comfortable with and those you need more help with. This section will appear at the end of every chapter to help you check your understanding. Even if your teacher does not assign this section, it is a good idea to try these problems and find out for yourself what you know and what you need to work on.

Solve each problem as completely as you can. The table at the end of this closure section has answers to these problems. It also tells you where you can find additional help and practice on similar problems.

CL 1-126. Trace the figures in parts (a) and (b) onto your paper and perform the indicated transformations. Copy the figure from part (c) onto graph paper and perform the indicated transformation. Label each image with prime notation ($A \rightarrow A'$).

a. Rotate *EFGHI* 90° clockwise ↻ about point *Z*

b. Reflect *JKLMN* over line *t*

c. Translate *ABCD* down 5 units and right 3 units

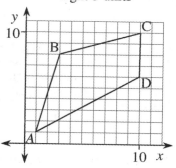

CL 1-127. Assume that all angles in the diagram at right are right angles and that all the measurements are in centimeters. Find the perimeter of the figure.

CL 1-128. Estimate the measures of the angles below. Are there any that you know for sure?

a.

b.

c.

d.

CL 1-129. **Examine** the angles in problem CL 1-128. If these four angles are placed in a bag, what is the probability of randomly selecting:

a. An acute angle

b. An angle greater than 60°

c. A 90° angle

d. An angle less than or equal to 180°

CL 1-130. **Examine** the shapes at right.

a.   Describe what you know about each shape based on the information provided in the diagram.

b.   Name the shape.

c.   Decide where each shape would be placed in the Venn diagram at right.

CL 1-131. Solve each equation below. Check your solution.

a. $3x - 12 + 10 = 8 - 2x$

b. $\frac{x}{7} = \frac{3}{2}$

c. $5 - (x + 7) + 4x = 7(x - 1)$

d. $x^2 + 11 = 36$

CL 1-132. Graph and connect the points in the table below. Then graph the equation in part (b) on the same set of axes. Also, find the equation for the data in the table.

a.

x	−4	−3	−2	−1	0	1	2	3	4	5	6
y	−5	−3	−1	1	3	5	7	9	11	13	15

b. $y = x^2 + x - 2$

CL 1-133. $\triangle ABC$ at right is equilateral. Use what you know about an equilateral triangle to write and solve an equation for x. Then find the perimeter of $\triangle ABC$.

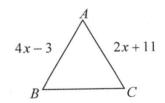

CL 1-134. Check your answers using the table at the end of this section. Which problems do you feel confident about? Which problems were hard? Have you worked on problems like these in math classes you have taken before? Use the table to make a list of topics you need help on and a list of topics you need to practice more.

HOW AM I THINKING?

This course focuses on five different **Ways of Thinking**: investigating, examining, reasoning and justifying, visualizing, and choosing a strategy/tool. These are some of the ways in which you think while trying to make sense of a concept or attempting to solve a problem (even outside of math class). During this chapter, you have probably used each Way of Thinking multiple times without even realizing it!

This closure activity will focus on one of these Ways of Thinking: **Investigating**. Read the description of this Way of Thinking at right.

Think about the **investigating** that you have done in this chapter. When have you tried something that you weren't specifically asked to do? What did you do when testing your idea did not work as you expected? You may want to flip through the chapter to refresh your memory about the problems that you have worked on. Discuss any of the **investigations** you have made with the rest of the class.

Once your discussion is complete, think about the way you think as you answer the following problems.

Investigating

Investigating is when you create your own questions and come up with something to do to answer those questions. You are often investigating when you ask questions for which you have not learned a formula or process. Common thoughts you might have when you are investigating are: "*I wonder what would happen if I . . .* " or, "*I might find the answer to my question if I . . .*" or, "*That didn't quite answer my question; now I'll try . . .* "

a. In the Shape Factory, you **investigated** what shapes you could create with four basic triangles. But **what if** you had started with quadrilaterals instead? **Investigate** this question as you find all shapes that could be made by rotating or reflecting the four quadrilaterals below. Remember that once rotated or reflected, the image should share a side with the original shape. Use tracing paper to help generate the new shapes. If you know the name of the new figure, state it.

PARALLELOGRAM   GENERAL TRAPEZOID   SQUARE   SPECIAL TRAPEZOID

Problem continues on next page →

Problem continued from previous page.

b.   Now write three "What if …?" questions that would extend your **investigation** in part (a).

c.   Now choose <u>one</u> question from part (b) to **investigate**. Decide how you will **investigate** your question. For example, will you need tracing paper? Do you need to make a table and record information?

After you have answered your question, write the results of your **investigation** clearly so that someone else can understand what question you selected, how you **investigated** your question, and any conclusions you made.

Answers and Support for Closure Activity #4
What Have I Learned?

Problem	Solutions	Need Help?	More Practice
CL 1-126.	a. (diagram with E', F', G', I', H', Z) b. (diagram with K', L', M', J', N', t)	Lesson 1.2.2, Lessons 1.2.2 and 1.2.3 Math Notes boxes, and Problem 1-50	Problems 1-50, 1-51, 1-61, 1-64, 1-68, 1-69, 1-70, 1-71, 1-73, 1-85, 1-86, 1-94, 1-96, 1-102

Problem	Solutions	Need Help?	More Practice
CL 1-126 continued	c.	Lesson 1.2.2, Lessons 1.2.2 and 1.2.3 Math Notes boxes, and Problem 1-50	Problems 1-50, 1-51, 1-61, 1-64, 1-68, 1-69, 1-70, 1-71, 1-73, 1-85, 1-86, 1-94, 1-96, 1-102
CL 1-127.	Perimeter = 30 centimeters	Lesson 1.1.3 Math Notes box	Problems 1-25, 1-44, 1-46, 1-65, 1-93
CL 1-128.	a. 90° b. ≈ 100° c. 180° d. ≈ 30°	Lesson 1.1.5 Math Notes box Problem 1-39	Problems 1-39, 1-42, 1-55
CL 1-129.	a. $\frac{1}{4}$ b. $\frac{3}{4}$ c. $\frac{1}{4}$ d. 1	Lesson 1.3.3 Math Notes box Problem 1-115	Problems 1-116, 1-118, 1-119, 1-122, 1-123
CL 1-130.	a. A: four sides make it a generic quadrilateral; B: Two pairs of equal sides make it a kite; C: Four right angles and a pair of parallel sides make it a rectangle; D: A quadrilateral with two parallel sides is a trapezoid. b.	Lesson 1.3.1 Math Notes box, Shapes Toolkit, catalog from problem 1-81, problem 1-107	Problems 1-3, 1-15, 1-86, 1-87, 1-94, 1-98, 1-99, 1-101, 1-104, 1-105, 1-108, 1-109, 1-110, 1-112, 1-113, 1-121, 1-123

Problem	Solutions	Need Help?	More Practice
CL 1-131.	a. $x = 2$ b. $x = \frac{21}{2}$ c. $x = \frac{5}{4}$ d. $x = \pm 5$	Lesson 1.1.4 Math Notes box	Problems 1-17, 1-25, 1-32, 1-34, 1-45, 1-57, 1-74, 1-100, 1-124
CL 1-132.	a. $y = 2x + 3$ 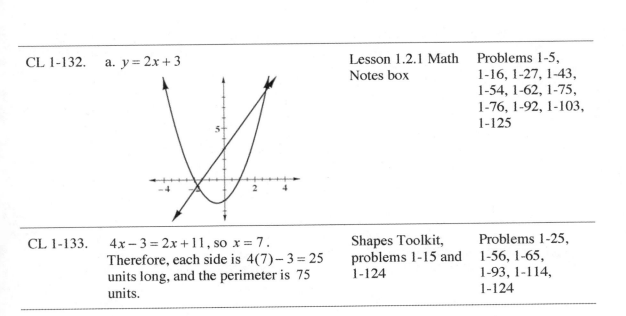	Lesson 1.2.1 Math Notes box	Problems 1-5, 1-16, 1-27, 1-43, 1-54, 1-62, 1-75, 1-76, 1-92, 1-103, 1-125
CL 1-133.	$4x - 3 = 2x + 11$, so $x = 7$. Therefore, each side is $4(7) - 3 = 25$ units long, and the perimeter is 75 units.	Shapes Toolkit, problems 1-15 and 1-124	Problems 1-25, 1-56, 1-65, 1-93, 1-114, 1-124

CHAPTER 2   Angles and Measurement

In Chapter 1, you studied many common geometric shapes and learned ways to describe a shape using its attributes. In this chapter, you will further **investigate** how to describe a complex shape by developing ways to accurately determine its angles, area, and perimeter. You will also use transformations from Chapter 1 to uncover special relationships between angles within a shape.

Throughout this chapter you will be asked to solve problems, such as those involving area or angles, in more than one way. This will require you to "see" shapes in multiple ways and to gain a broader understanding of problem solving.

Guiding Questions

Think about these questions throughout this chapter:

What is the relationship?

Can I generalize the process?

Is it always true?

What information do I need?

Is there another way?

In this chapter, you will learn:

➢ the relationships between pairs of angles formed by transversals and the angles in a triangle.

➢ how to find the area and perimeter of triangles, parallelograms, and trapezoids.

➢ the relationship among the three side lengths of a right triangle (the Pythagorean Theorem).

➢ how to estimate the value of square roots.

➢ how to determine when the lengths of three segments can and cannot form a triangle.

Chapter Outline

Section 2.1   You will broaden your understanding of angle, begun in Chapter 1, to include relationships between angles, such as those formed by intersecting lines or those inside a triangle.

Section 2.2   After examining how units of measure work, you will develop methods to find the areas of triangles, parallelograms, and trapezoids as well as more complicated shapes.

Section 2.3   You will discover a relationship among the sides of a right triangle called the Pythagorean Theorem. This will allow you to find the perimeter of triangles, parallelograms, and trapezoids, and to find the distance between two points on a graph.

2.1.1 What's the relationship?

Complementary, Supplementary, and Vertical Angles

In Chapter 1, you compared shapes by looking at similarities between their parts. For example, two shapes might have sides of the same length or equal angles. In this chapter you will **examine** relationships between parts within a *single* shape or diagram. Today you will start by looking at angles to identify relationships in a diagram that make angle measures equal. As you **examine** angle relationships today, keep the following questions in mind to guide your discussion:

How can we name the angle?

What is the relationship?

How do we know?

2-1. SOMEBODY'S WATCHING ME

Usually, to see yourself in a small mirror you have to be looking directly into it—if you move off to the side, you can't see your image any more. But Mr. Douglas knows a neat trick. He claims that if he makes a right angle with a hinged mirror, he can see himself in the mirror no matter from which direction he looks into it.

a. By forming a right angle with a hinged mirror, test Mr. Douglas's trick for yourself. Look into the place where the sides of the mirror meet. Can you see yourself? What if you look in the mirror from a different angle?

b. Does the trick work for *any* angle between the sides of the mirror? Change the angle between the sides of the mirror until you can no longer see your reflection where the sides meet.

c. At right is a diagram of a student trying out the mirror trick. What appears to be true about the lines of sight? Can you explain why Mr. Douglas's trick works? Talk about this with your team and be ready to share your ideas with the class.

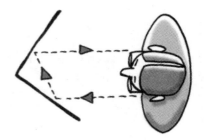

2-2.   To completely understand how Mr. Douglas's reflection trick
        works, you need to learn more about the relationships between
        angles. But in order to clearly communicate relationships
        between angles, you will need a convenient way to refer to and
        name them. **Examine** the diagram of equilateral $\triangle ABC$ at
        right.

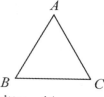

a.   The "top" of this triangle is usually referred to as "angle A," written $\angle A$.
        Point A is called the **vertex** of this angle. The *measure* of $\angle A$ (the number of
        degrees in angle A) is written $m\angle A$. Since $\triangle ABC$ is equilateral, write an
        equation showing the relationship between its angles.

b.   Audrey rotated $\triangle ABC$ around point A to form
        $\triangle AB'C'$. She told her teammate Maria, "I think the
        two angles at A are equal." Maria did not know
        which angles she was referring to. How many angles
        can you find at A? Are there more than three?

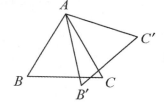

c.   Maria asked Audrey to be more specific. She
        explained, "One of my angles is $\angle BAB'$." At the
        same time, she marked her two angles with the
        same marking at right to indicate that they have the
        same measure.

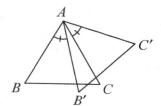

        Name her other angle. Be sure to use three letters
        so there is no confusion about which angle you
        mean.

2-3.   ANGLE RELATIONSHIPS

        When you know two angles have a certain **relationship**, learning
        something about one of them tells you something about the other.
        Certain angle relationships come up often enough in geometry that
        we give them special names.

a.   Two angles whose measures have a sum of 90° are called
        complementary angles. Since $\angle ABD$ is a right angle in
        the diagram at right, angles $\angle ABC$ and $\angle CBD$ are
        complementary. If $m\angle CBD = 76°$, what is $m\angle ABC$? Show how you got
        your answer.

b.   Another special angle is 180°. If the sum of the
        measures of two angles is 180°, they are called
        supplementary angles. In the diagram at right,
        $\angle LMN$ is a straight angle. If $m\angle LMP = 62°$,
        what is $m\angle PMN$?

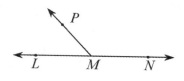

                                    Problem continues on next page →

2-3.   *Problem continued from previous page.*

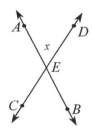

c. Now consider the diagram at right, which shows $\overrightarrow{AB}$ and $\overrightarrow{CD}$ intersecting at E. If $x = 23°$, find $m\angle AEC$, $m\angle DEB$, and $m\angle CEB$. Show all work.

d. When angles have equal measure, they are referred to as **congruent**. Which angle is congruent to $\angle AED$?

e. When two lines intersect, the angles that lie on opposite sides of the intersection point are called **vertical angles**. For example, in the diagram above, $\angle AED$ and $\angle CEB$ are vertical angles. Find another pair of vertical angles in the diagram.

2-4.   Travis noticed that the vertical angles in parts (c) and (d) of problem 2-3 are congruent and wondered if pairs of vertical angles always have the same measure.

a. Return to the diagram above and find $m\angle CEB$ if $x = 54°$. Show all work.

b. Based on your observations, write a **conjecture** (a statement based on an educated guess that is unproven). Start with, *"Vertical angles are ..."*

2-5.   In the problems below, you will use geometric relationships to find angle measures. Start by finding a special relationship between some of the sides or angles, and use that relationship to write an equation. Solve the equation for the variable, then use that variable value to answer the original question.

a. Find $m\angle MNP$.

b. Find $m\angle FGH$.

c. Find $m\angle DBC$.

d. Find $m\angle LPQ$ and $m\angle LPN$.

2-6.   When Jao answered part (b) of problem 2-4, he wrote the conjecture: *"Vertical angles are equal."* (Remember that a **conjecture** is an educated guess that has not yet been proven.)

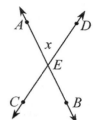

   a.   **Examine** the diagram at right. Express the measures of every angle in the diagram in terms of x.

   b.   Do you think your vertical angle conjecture holds for *any* pair of vertical angles? Be prepared to convince the rest of the class.

2-7.   Describe each of the angle relationships you learned about today in an entry in your Learning Log. Include a diagram, a description of the angles, and what you know about the relationship. For example, are the angles always equal? Do they have a special sum? Label this entry "Angle Relationships" and include today's date.

METHODS AND **M**EANINGS

MATH NOTES

Angle Relationships

If two angles have measures that add up to 90°, they are called **complementary angles**. For example, in the diagram at right, $\angle ABC$ and $\angle CBD$ are complementary because together they form a right angle.

If two angles have measures that add up to 180°, they are called **supplementary angles**. For example, in the diagram at right, $\angle EFG$ and $\angle GFH$ are supplementary because together they form a straight angle.

Two angles do not have to share a vertex to be complementary or supplementary. The first pair of angles at right are supplementary; the second pair of angles are complementary.

Supplementary

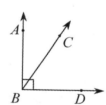

Complementary

When two angles have equal measure, they are called **congruent**. Their equality can be shown with matching markings, as shown in the diagram at right.

Congruent

2-8. Find the area of each rectangle below:

a.

11
cm

3 cm

b.

11

$3x$

c.

$3x$ -4

$11x$

-2

2-9. Mei puts the shapes at right into a bucket and asks Brian to pick one out.

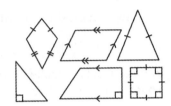

a. What is the probability that he pulls out a quadrilateral with parallel sides?

b. What is the probability that he pulls out a shape with rotation symmetry?

2-10. Camille loves guessing games. She is going to tell you a fact about her shape to see if you can guess what it is.

a. "My triangle has only one line of symmetry. What is it?"

b. "My triangle has three lines of symmetry. What is it?"

c. "My quadrilateral has no lines of symmetry but it does have rotation symmetry. What is it?"

2-11. Jerry has an idea. Since he knows that an isosceles trapezoid has reflection symmetry, he **reasons**, "That means that it must have two pairs of congruent angles." He marks the congruent parts on his diagram at right.

ISOSCELES
TRAPEZOID

Copy the shapes below onto your paper. Similarly mark which angles must be equal due to reflection symmetry.

a.

KITE

b.

ISOSCELES TRIANGLE

c.

REGULAR HEXAGON

d.

RHOMBUS

2-12. Larry saw Javon's incomplete Venn diagram at right, and he wants to finish it. However, he does not know the condition that each circle represents. Find a possible label for each circle, and place two more shapes into the diagram.

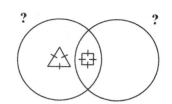

2.1.2 What's the relationship?

Angles Formed by Transversals

In Lesson 2.1.1, you **examined** vertical angles and found that vertical angles are always equal. Today you will look at another special relationship that guarantees angles are equal.

2-13. **Examine** the diagrams below. For each pair of angles marked on the diagram, quickly decide what relationship their measures have. Your responses should be limited to one of three relationships: congruent (equal measures), complementary (have a sum of 90°), and supplementary (have a sum of 180°).

a.

b.

c.

d.

2-14. Marcos was walking home after school thinking about special angle relationships when he happened to notice a pattern of parallelogram tiles on the wall of a building. Marcos saw lots of special angle relationships in this pattern, so he decided to copy the pattern into his notebook.

The beginning of Marcos's diagram is shown at right and provided on the Lesson 2.1.2 Resource Page. This type of pattern is sometimes called a **tiling**. In a tiling, a shape is repeated without gaps or overlaps to fill an entire page. In this case, the shape being tiled is a parallelogram.

Problem continues on next page →

Geometry Connections

2-14.   *Problem continued from previous page.*

a.   Consider the angles inside a single parallelogram. Are any angles congruent? On your resource page, use color to show which angles must have equal measure. If two angles are not equal, make sure they are shaded with different colors.

b.   Since each parallelogram is a translation of another, what can be stated about the angles in the rest of Marcos' tiling? Use a dynamic geometry tool, transparencies on an overhead, or tracing paper to find determine which angles must be congruent. Color all angles that must be equal the same color.

c.   What about relationships between lines? Can you identify any lines that must be parallel? Mark all the lines on your diagram with the same number of arrows to show which lines are parallel.

2-15.   Julia wants to learn more about the angles in Marcos's diagram and has decided to focus on just a part of his tiling. An enlarged view of that section is shown in the image below right, with some points and angles labeled.

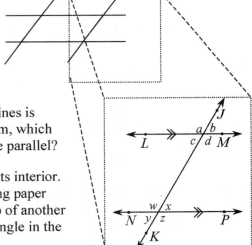

a.   A line that crosses two or more other lines is called a **transversal**. In Julia's diagram, which line is the transversal? Which lines are parallel?

b.   Trace ∡x on tracing paper and shade its interior. Then translate ∡x by sliding the tracing paper along the transversal until it lies on top of another angle and matches it exactly. Which angle in the diagram corresponds with x?

c.   What is the relationship between the measures of angles x and b? Must one be greater than the other, or must they be equal? Explain how you know.

d.   In this diagram, ∡x and ∡c are called **corresponding angles** because they are in the same position at two different intersections of the transversal. The corresponding angles in this diagram are equal because they were formed by translating a parallelogram. Name all the other pairs of equal corresponding angles you can find in Julia's diagram.

e.   Suppose b = 60°. Use what you know about vertical, supplementary, and corresponding angle relationships to find the measures of all the other angles in Julia's diagram.

2-16. Frank wonders whether corresponding angles are *always* equal. For parts (a) through (d) below, decide whether you have enough information to find the measures of x and y. If you do, find the angle measures and state the relationship. Use tracing paper to help you find corresponding angles.

a.

b.

c.

d.

e. Answer Frank's question: Are corresponding angles always equal?

f. Conjectures are often written in the form, "*If..., then...*". A statement in if-then form is called a **conditional statement**. Make a conjecture about corresponding angles by completing this conditional statement: "If ..., then corresponding angles are equal."

2-17. For each diagram below, find the value of x *if possible*. If it is not possible, explain how you know. State the relationships you use. Be prepared to **justify** every measurement you find to other members of your team.

a.

b.

c.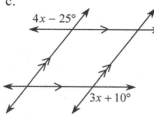

MĒTHODS AND MEANINGS

Naming Parts of Shapes

MATH NOTES

Part of geometry is the study of parts of shapes, such as points, line segments, and angles. To avoid confusion, standard notation is used to name these parts.

A point is named using a single capital letter. For example, the vertices (corners) of the triangle at right are named *A*, *B*, and *C*.

If a shape is transformed, the image shape is often named using **prime notation**. The image of point *A* is labeled *A'* (read as "A prime"), the image of *B* is labeled *B'* (read as "B prime"), etc. At right, $\triangle A'B'C'$ is the image of $\triangle ABC$.

The side of a polygon is a **line segment**. A line segment is named by naming its endpoints and placing a bar above them. For example, one side of the first triangle above is named $\overline{AB}$. When referring to the length of a segment, the bar is omitted. In $\triangle ABC$ above, $AB = 2$ cm.

A **line**, which differs from a segment in that it extends infinitely in either direction, is named by naming two points on the line and placing a bar with arrows above them. For example, the line below is named $\overleftrightarrow{DE}$. When naming a segment or line, the order of the letters is unimportant. The line below could also be named $\overleftrightarrow{ED}$.

D   E

An angle can be named by putting an angle symbol in front of the name of the angle's vertex. For example, the angle measuring 80° in $\triangle ABC$ above is named $\angle A$. Sometimes using a single letter makes it unclear which angle is being referenced. For example, in the diagram at right, it is unclear which angle is referred to by $\angle G$. When this happens, the angle is named with three letters. For example, the angle measuring 10° is called $\angle HGI$ or $\angle IGH$. Note that the name of the vertex must be the second letter in the name; the order of the other two letters is unimportant.

To refer to an angle's measure, an *m* is placed in front of the angle's name. For example, $m\angle HGI = 10°$ means "the measure of $\angle HGI$ is 10°."

2-18.   **Examine** the diagrams below. What is the geometric relationship between the labeled angles? What is the relationship of their measures? Then, use the relationship to write an equation and solve for x.

a.

b.

2-19.   In problem 2-11, you determined that because an isosceles triangle has reflection symmetry, then it must have two angles that are congruent.

a.   How can you tell which angles are congruent? For example, in the diagram at right, which angles must have equal measure? Name the angles and explain how you know.

b.   **Examine** the diagram for part (a). If you know that $m\angle B + m\angle C = 124°$, then what is the measure of $\angle B$? Explain how you know.

c.   Use this idea to find the value of x in the diagram at right. Be sure to show all work.

2-20.   On graph paper, draw the quadrilateral with vertices $(-1, 3)$, $(4, 3)$, $(-1, -2)$, and $(4, -2)$.

a.   What kind of quadrilateral is this?

b.   Translate the quadrilateral 3 units to the left and 2 units up. What are the new coordinates of the vertices?

2-21.   Find the equation for the line that passes through $(-1, -2)$ and $(4, 3)$. Is the point $(3, 1)$ on this line? Be sure to **justify** your answer.

2-22.   Juan decided to test what would happen if he rotated an angle.

a.   He copied the angle at right on tracing paper and rotated it 180°
about its vertex. What type of angle pair did he create? What
is the relationship of these angles?

b.   Juan then rotated the same angle 180° through a
different point (see the diagram at right). On your paper,
draw Juan's angle and the rotated image. Describe the
overall shape formed by the two angles.

2.1.3 What's the relationship?

More Angles Formed by Transversals

In Lesson 2.1.2, you looked at corresponding angles formed when a transversal intersects two
parallel lines. Today you will **investigate** other special angle relationships formed in this
situation.

2-23.   Suppose ∡*a* in the diagram at right measures 48°.

a.   Use what you know about vertical, corresponding, and
supplementary angle relationships to find the measure
of ∡*b*.

b.   Julia is still having trouble
seeing the angle relationships clearly in this
diagram. Her teammate, Althea explains,
"When I translate one of the angles along the
transversal, I notice its image and the other
given angle are a pair of vertical angles. That
way, I know that *a* and *b* must be congruent."

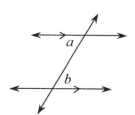

Use Althea's method and tracing paper to
determine if the following angle pairs are
congruent or supplementary. Be sure to state
whether the pair of angles created after the translation is a vertical pair or forms
a straight angle. Be ready to **justify** your answer for the class.

(1)   (2)   (3)

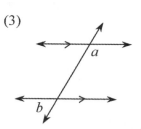

2-24.   In problem 2-23, Althea showed that the shaded angles in the diagram are congruent. However, these angles also have a name for their geometric relationship (their relative positions on the diagram). These angles are called **alternate interior** angles. They are called "alternate" because they are on opposite sides of the transversal, and "interior" because they are both inside the parallel lines.

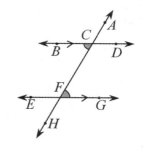

a.   On tracing paper, trace and shade in $\angle CFG$. How can you transform $\angle CFG$ so that it lands on $\angle BCF$? Be sure your team agrees.

b.   Find another pair of alternate interior angles in this diagram.

c.   Think about the relationship between the measures of alternate interior angles. If the lines are parallel, are they always congruent? Are they always supplementary? Complete the conjecture, "*If lines are parallel, then alternate interior angles are…*".

d.   Instead of writing conditional statements, Roxie likes to write **arrow diagrams** to express her conjectures. She expresses the conjecture from part (b) as

   Lines are parallel → alternate interior angles are congruent.

This arrow diagram says the same thing as the conditional statement you wrote in part (c). How is it different from your conditional statement? What does the arrow mean?

2-25.   The shaded angles in the diagram at right have another special angle relationship. They are called **same-side interior** angles.

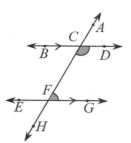

a.   Why do you think they have this name?

b.   What is the relationship between the angle measures of same-side interior angles? Are they always congruent? Supplementary? Talk about this with your team.

   Then write a conjecture about the relationship of the angle measures. Your conjecture can be in the form of a conditional statement or an arrow diagram. If you write a conditional statement, it should begin, "*If lines are parallel, then same-side interior angles are…*".

2-26.   THE REFLECTION OF LIGHT

You know enough about angle relationships now to start analyzing how light
bounces off mirrors. **Examine** the two diagrams below. Diagram A shows a beam
of light emitted from a light source at A. In Diagram B, someone has placed a
mirror across the light beam. The light beam hits the mirror and is reflected from its
original path.

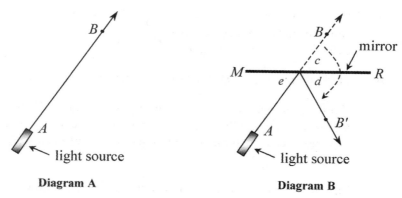

Diagram A   Diagram B

a.   What is the relationship between angles c and d? Why?

b.   What is the relationship between angles c and e? How do you know?

c.   What is the relationship between angles e and d? How do you know?

d.   Write a conjecture about the angle at which light hits a mirror and the angle at
      which it bounces off the mirror.

2-27. A CD player works by bouncing a laser off the surface of the CD, which acts like a mirror. An emitter sends out the light, which bounces off the CD and then is detected by a sensor. The diagram below shows a CD held parallel to the surface of the CD player, on which an emitter and a sensor are mounted.

a. The laser is supposed to bounce off the CD at a 64° angle as shown in the diagram above. For the laser to go directly into the sensor, at what angle does the emitter need to send the laser beam? In other words, what does the measure of angle x have to be? **Justify** your conclusion.

b. The diagram above shows two parts of the laser beam: the one coming out of the emitter and the one that has bounced off the CD. What is the angle ($\measuredangle y$) between these beams? How do you know?

2-28. ANGLE RELATIONSHIPS TOOLKIT

Obtain a Lesson 2.1.3 Resource Page ("Angle Relationships Toolkit") from your teacher. This will be a continuation of the Geometry Toolkit you started in Chapter 1. Think about the new angle relationships you have studied so far in Chapter 2. Then, in the space provided, add a diagram and a description of the relationship for each special angle relationship you know. Be sure to specify any relationship between the measures of the angle (such as whether or not they are always congruent). In later lessons, you will continue to add relationships to this toolkit, so be sure to keep this resource page in a safe place. At this point, your toolkit should include:

- Vertical angles

- Corresponding angles

- Same-side interior angles

- Straight angles

- Alternate interior angles

METHODS AND MEANINGS

MATH NOTES

Systems of Linear Equations

In a previous course, you learned that a **system of linear equations** is a set of two or more linear equations that are given together, such as the example at right. In a system, each variable represents the same quantity in both equations. For example, y represents the same quantity in *both* equations at right.

$$y = 2x$$
$$y = -3x + 5$$

To represent a system of equations graphically, you can simply graph each equation on the same set of axes. The graph may or may not have a **point of intersection**, as shown circled at right.

Sometimes two lines have *no* points of intersection. This happens when the two lines are parallel. It is also possible for two lines to have an *infinite* number of intersections. This happens when the graphs of two lines lie on top of each other. Such lines are said to **coincide**.

The **Substitution Method** is a way to change two equations with two variables into one equation with one variable. It is convenient to use when only one equation is solved for a variable. For example, to solve the system at right:

$$x = -3y + 1$$
$$4x - 3y = -11$$

- Use substitution to rewrite the two equations as one. In other words, replace x with $(-3y + 1)$ to get $4(-3y + 1) - 3y = -11$. This equation can then be solved to find y. In this case, $y = 1$.

$$x = \boxed{-3y + 1}$$
$$4(\quad) - 3y = -11$$
$$4(-3y + 1) - 3y = -11$$
$$-12y + 4 - 3y = -11$$
$$-15y + 4 = -11$$
$$-15y = -15$$
$$y = 1$$

- To find the point of intersection, substitute to find the other value.

- Substitute $y = 1$ into $x = -3y + 1$ and write the answer for x and y as an ordered pair.

- To test the solution, substitute $x = -2$ and $y = 1$ into $4x - 3y = -11$ to verify that it makes the equation true. Since $4(-2) - 3(1) = -11$, the solution $(-2, 1)$ must be correct.

$$x = -3(1) + 1 = -2$$
$$(-2, 1)$$

2-29.   The set of equations at right is an example of a **system of
         equations**. Read the Math Notes box for this lesson on how
         to solve systems of equations. Then answer the questions
         below.

$$y = -x + 1$$
$$y = 2x + 7$$

   a.   Graph the system on graph paper. Then write its solution (the point of
         intersection) in (x, y) form.

   b.   Now solve the system using the Substitution Method. Did your solution match
         your result from part (a)? If not, check your work carefully and look for any
         mistakes in your algebraic process or on your graph.

2-30.   On graph paper, graph the rectangle with vertices at $(2, 1)$, $(2, 5)$, $(7, 1)$, and $(7, 5)$.

   a.   What is the area of this rectangle?

   b.   Shirley was given the following points and asked to find the area, but her graph
         paper is not big enough. Find the area of Shirley's rectangle, and explain to
         her how she can find the area without graphing the points.

         Shirley's points: $(352, 150)$, $(352, 175)$, $(456, 150)$, and $(456, 175)$

2-31.   Looking at the diagram below, John says
         that $m\angle BCF = m\angle EFH$.

Note: This stoplight icon
will appear periodically
throughout the text.
Problems with this icon
display common errors
that can be made. Be
sure not to make the
same mistakes yourself!

   a.   Do you agree with John? Why or why not?

   b.   Jim says, "You can't be sure those angles are equal. An important piece of
         information is missing from the diagram!" What is Jim talking about?

Geometry Connections

2-32.   Use your knowledge of angle relationships to solve for x in the diagrams below.
Justify your solutions by naming the geometric relationship.

a.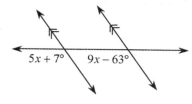

$5x + 7°$ $9x - 63°$

b.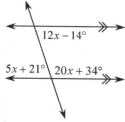

$12x - 14°$

$5x + 21°$ $20x + 34°$

2-33.   On graph paper, draw line segment $\overline{AB}$ if $A(6, 2)$ and $B(3, 5)$.

a.   Reflect $\overline{AB}$ across the line $x = 3$ and connect points B and B'. What shape is created by this reflection? Be as specific as possible.

b.   What polygon is created when $\overline{AB}$ is reflected across the line $y = -x + 6$ and all endpoints are connected to form a polygon?

2.1.4 How can I use it?

· ·
Angles in a Triangle

So far in this chapter, you have **investigated** the angle relationships created when two lines intersect, forming vertical angles. You have also **investigated** the relationships created when a transversal intersects two parallel lines. Today you will study the angle relationships that result when three non-parallel lines intersect, forming a triangle.

2-34.   Marcos decided to study the angle relationships in triangles by making another tiling. Find his pattern, shown at right, on the Lesson 2.1.4 Resource Page.

a.   Copy one of Marcos's triangles onto tracing paper. Use a colored pen or pencil to shade one of the triangle's angles on the tracing paper. Then use the same color to shade every angle on the resource page that is equal to the shaded angle.

b.   Repeat this process for the other two angles of the triangle, using a different color for each angle in the triangle. When you are done, every angle in your tiling should be shaded with one of the three colors.

Problem continues on next page →

2-34.   *Problem continued from previous page.*

c.   Now **examine** your colored tiling. What relationship can you find between the three different-colored angles? You may want to focus on the angles that form a straight angle. What does this tell you about the angles in a triangle? Write a conjecture in the form of a conditional statement or an arrow diagram. If you write a conditional statement, it should begin, "*If a polygon is a triangle, then the measure of its angles…*".

d.   How can you convince yourself that your conjecture is true for all triangles? If a dynamic geometry tool is available, use it to convince yourself that your conjecture is always true. If technology is not available, use the diagram above and your Angle Relationships Toolkit to write a convincing argument that your conjecture is true.

Then add this angle relationship to your Angle Relationships Toolkit from Lesson 2.1.3. This will be referred to as the **Triangle Angle Sum Theorem.** (A theorem is a statement that has been proven.)

2-35.   Use your conjecture from problem 2-34 about the angles in a triangle to find *x* in each diagram below. Show all work.

a.

b.

2-36.   What can the Triangle Angle Sum Theorem help you learn about special triangles?

a.   Find the measure of each angle in an equilateral triangle. **Justify** your conclusion.

b.   Consider the isosceles right triangle (also sometimes referred to as a "half-square") at right. Find the measures of all the angles in a half-square.

c.   What if you only know one angle of an isosceles triangle? For example, if $m\angle A = 34°$, what are the measures of the other two angles?

2-37. TEAM **REASONING** CHALLENGE

How much can you figure out about the figure at right using your knowledge of angle relationships? Work with your team to find the measures of all the labeled angles in the diagram at right. **Justify** your solutions with the name of the angle relationship you used. Carefully record your work as you go and be prepared to share your **reasoning** with the rest of the class.

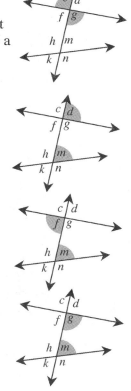

$\widehat{\mathbf{M}}$ETHODS AND $\mathbf{M}$EANINGS

More Angle Pair Relationships

MATH NOTES

Vertical angles are the two opposite (that is, non-adjacent) angles formed by two intersecting lines, such as angles ∡c and ∡g in the diagram at right. ∡c by itself is not a vertical angle, nor is ∡g, although ∡c and ∡g together are a pair of vertical angles. Vertical angles always have equal measure.

Corresponding angles lie in the same position but at different points of intersection of the transversal. For example, in the diagram at right, ∡m and ∡d form a pair of corresponding angles, since both of them are to the right of the transversal and above the intersecting line. Corresponding angles are congruent when the lines intersected by the transversal are parallel.

∡f and ∡m are **alternate interior angles** because one is to the left of the transversal, one is to the right, and both are between (inside) the pair of lines. Alternate interior angles are congruent when the lines intersected by the transversal are parallel.

∡g and ∡m are **same-side interior angles** because both are on the same side of the transversal and both are between the pair of lines. Same-side interior angles are supplementary when the lines intersected by the transversal are parallel.

2-38.   Find all missing angles in the diagrams below.

a.

b.
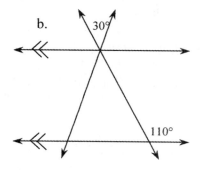

2-39.   Robert believes the lines graphed at right are perpendicular, but Mario is not convinced. Find the slope of each line, and explain how you know whether or not the lines are perpendicular.

2-40.   The diagram at right represents only half of a shape that has the graph of $y = 1$ as a line of symmetry. Draw the completed shape on your paper, and label the coordinates of the missing vertices.

2-41.   Janine measured the sides of a rectangle and found that the sides were 12 inches and 24 inches. Howard measured the same rectangle and found that the sides were 1 foot and 2 feet. When their math teacher asked them for the area, Janine said 288, and Howard said 2. Why did they get two different numbers for the area of the same rectangle?

2-42.   Graph the system of equations at right on graph paper. Then state the solution to the system. If there is not a solution, explain why.

$$y = -\frac{2}{5}x + 1$$

$$y = -\frac{2}{5}x - 2$$

2.1.5 What's the relationship?

Applying Angle Relationships

During Section 2.1, you have been learning about various special angle relationships that are created by intersecting lines. Today you will **investigate** those relationships a bit further, then apply what you know to explain how Mr. Douglas's mirror trick (from problem 2-1) works. As you work in your teams today, keep the following questions in mind to guide your discussion:

What's the relationship?

Are the angles equal? Are they supplementary?

How can I be sure?

2-43.   Use your knowledge of angle relationships to answer the questions below.

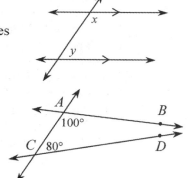

a.   In the diagram at right, what is the sum of angles *x* and *y*? How do you know?

b.   While looking at the diagram at right, Rianna exclaimed, "I think something is wrong with this diagram." What do you think she is referring to? Be prepared to share your thinking with the class.

2-44.   Maria is still not convinced that the lines in part (b) of problem 2-43 *must* be parallel. She decides to assume that they are not parallel and draws the diagram at right.

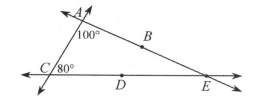

a.   Why must lines $\overleftrightarrow{AB}$ and $\overleftrightarrow{CD}$ intersect in Maria's diagram?

b.   What is $m\angle BED$? Discuss this question with your team and explain what it tells you about $\overleftrightarrow{AB}$ and $\overleftrightarrow{CD}$.

c.   **Examine** the diagram at right. In this diagram, must $\overleftrightarrow{FG}$ and $\overleftrightarrow{HI}$ be parallel? Explain how you know.

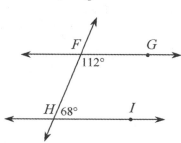

d.   Write a conjecture based on your conclusion to this problem.

2-45.   Use your conjecture from problem 2-44 to explain why lines must be parallel in the diagrams below.

a. 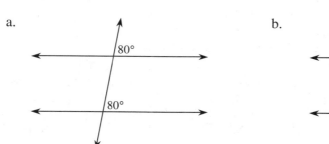   b.

c.   Looking back at the diagrams in parts (a) and (b), write two new conjectures that begin, "*If corresponding angles are equal, …*" and "*If the measures of alternate interior angles are equal, …*".

2-46.   SOMEBODY'S WATCHING ME, Part Two

Remember Mr. Douglas' trick from problem 2-1? You now know enough about angle and line relationships to analyze why a hinged mirror set so the angle between the mirrors is 90° will reflect your image back to you from any angle. Since your reflection is actually light that travels from your face to the mirror, you will need to study the path of the light. Remember that a mirror reflects light, and that the angle the light hits the mirror will equal the angle it bounces off the mirror.

Your task: Explain why the mirror bounces your image back to you from any angle. Include in your analysis:

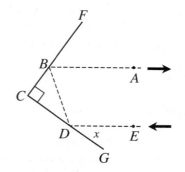

- Use angle relationships to find the measures of all the angles in the figure. (Each team member should choose a different *x* value and calculate all of the other angle measures using his or her selected value of *x*.)

- What do you know about the paths the light takes as it leaves you and as it returns to you? That is, what is the relationship between $\overline{BA}$ and $\overline{DE}$?

- Does Mr. Douglas' trick work if the angle between the mirrors is not 90°?

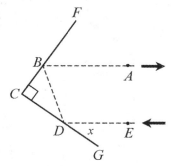

2-47. Since you are trying to show that the trick works for *any* angle at which the light could hit the mirror, each team will work with a different angle measure for *x* in this problem. Your teacher will tell you what angle *x* your team should use in the diagram at right.

a. Using angle relationships and what you know about how light bounces off mirrors, find the measure of every other angle in the diagram.

b. What is the relationship between $\angle ABD$ and $\angle EDB$? What does this tell you about the relationship between $\overline{BA}$ and $\overline{DE}$?

c. What if $m\angle C = 89°$? Does the trick still work?

2-48. Explain why the 90° hinged mirror always sends your image back to you, no matter which angle you look into it from.

————— *Further Guidance section ends here.* —————

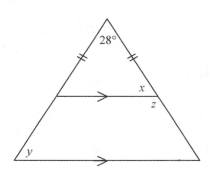

2-49. Use what you have learned in Section 2.1 to find the measures of *x*, *y*, and *z* at right. **Justify** each conclusion with the name of a geometric relationship from your Angle Relationships Toolkit.

2-50. EXTENSION

Hold a 90° hinged mirror at arm's length and find your own image. Now close your right eye. Which eye closes in the mirror? Look back at the diagram from problem 2-46. Can you explain why this eye is the one that closes?

METHODS AND MEANINGS

MATH NOTES

Proof by Contradiction

The kind of argument you used in Lesson 2.1.5 to **justify** "If same-side interior angles are supplementary, then lines are parallel" is sometimes called a **proof by contradiction**. In a proof by contradiction, you prove a claim by thinking about what the consequences would be if it were false. If the claim's being false would lead to an impossibility, this shows that the claim must be true.

For example, suppose you know Mary's brother is seven years younger than Mary. Can you argue that Mary is at least five years old? A proof by contradiction of this claim would go:

Suppose Mary is less than five years old.

Then her brother's age is negative!

But this is impossible, so Mary must be at least five years old.

To show that lines $\overrightarrow{AB}$ and $\overrightarrow{CD}$ must be parallel in the diagram at right, you used a proof by contradiction. You argued:

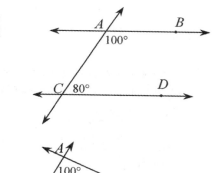

Suppose $\overrightarrow{AB}$ and $\overrightarrow{CD}$ intersect at some point E.

Then the angles in $\triangle AEC$ add up to more than 180°.

But this is impossible, so $\overrightarrow{AB}$ and $\overrightarrow{CD}$ must be parallel.

2-51.   Solve for x in the diagram at right.

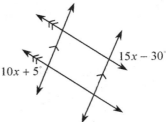

2-52.   For each diagram below, set up an equation
         and solve for x.

a.   Perimeter = 76 units

b.

c.

d.

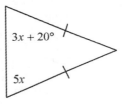

2-53.   Solve each system of equation below. Then verify that your solution makes each
         equation true. You may want to refer to the Math Notes box in Lesson 2.1.3.

a. $y = 5x - 2$
      $y = 2x + 10$

b. $x = -2y - 1$
      $2x + y = -20$

2-54.   Graph the line $y = \frac{3}{4}x$ on graph paper.

a.   Draw a slope triangle.

b.   Rotate your slope triangle 90° around the origin to get a new slope triangle.
      What is the new slope?

c.   Find the equation of a line perpendicular to $y = \frac{4}{3}x$.

2-55.   Mario has 6 shapes in a bucket. He tells you that the probability of pulling an
         isosceles triangle out of the bucket is $\frac{1}{3}$. How many isosceles triangles are in his
         bucket?

2.2.1 How can I measure an object?

Units of Measure

How tall are you? How large is the United States? How much water does your bathtub at home hold? All of these questions ask about the size of objects around you. How can we answer these questions more specifically than saying "big" or "small"? Today you will be **investigating** ways to answer these and other questions like them.

2-56. Your teacher will describe with words a figure he or she has drawn. Your job is to try to draw the **exact same figure** on your paper so that if you placed your drawing on top of your teacher's, the figures would match perfectly. Redraw your figure as many times as necessary.

2-57. Length often provides a direct way to answer the question, "How big?" In this activity, your teacher will give your team rulers with a unit of length to use to measure distances. For instance, if you have an object that has the same length as three of your units placed next to one another, then the object's length is "3 units."

    a. Common units you may have used before are inches or meters. However, your unit does not match any of the familiar units. Give your unit of measure a unique name. Then continue marking and labeling units on your ruler as accurately as possible.

    b. The **dimensions** of a figure are its measurements of length. For example, the measurements in each figure below describe the relative size of each object.

Dimensions can describe how long, wide, or tall the object is by measuring the lengths of the edges.

Or, dimensions can be found by measuring a length that is not a side.

Find the dimensions of the shape on the Lesson 2.2.1A Resource Page using your unit of length. That is, how wide is the shape? How tall? Compare your results with those of other teams. What happened?

    c. The local baseball club is planning to make a mural that is the same general shape as the one you measured in part (b) (but fortunately a much larger version!). The club plans to frame the mural with neon tubes. Approximately how many units of neon tube will they need to do this?

Geometry Connections

2-58.   To paint the mural, the wall must first be covered with a coat of primer. How much of the wall will need to be painted with the primer? Remember that the measurement of the region inside a shape is called the **area** of the shape.

   a.   Just as you were able to use your unit of length to measure distance, you need a unit of area to measure a surface. Use your team's ruler to make unit squares that are 1 unit long on each side. The area that your square unit covers is called "one square unit" and can be abbreviated as 1 sq. unit or $1 \ un^2$. What would you call this unit of measure, given the name you chose in problem 2-57?

   b.   What is the approximate area of the mural? That is, how many of your square units fit within your shape?

2-59.   Use your unit of measure to make a rectangle that has dimensions 3 units by 5 units.

   a.   What is the area of your rectangle? (That is, how many unit squares are there in your rectangle?)

   b.   When you answered part (a), did you count the squares? Did your team use a shortcut? If so, why does the shortcut work?

   c.   Compare your rectangle to rectangles that other teams made. What is the same about the rectangles and what is different?

2-60.   If you found out that your gym teacher is going to make you run 31,680 inches next period, how useful is this information? Or, if you knew that you were 0.003977 miles long at birth, do you have any idea how long that is?

   An important part of measurement is choosing an appropriate unit of measurement. With your team, suggest a unit of measurement that can best measure (and describe) each of these situations.

   a.   The distance you travel from home to get to school.

   b.   The surface of the school's soccer field.

   c.   The width of a strand of hair.

   d.   The length of your nose.

   e.   The amount of room in your locker.

METHODS AND MEANINGS

Triangle Angle Sum Theorem

The **Triangle Angle Sum Theorem** states that the measures of the angles in a triangle add up to 180°. For example, in $\triangle ABC$ at right:

$$m\angle A + m\angle B + m\angle C = 180°$$

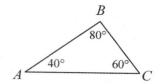

The Triangle Angle Sum Theorem can be verified by using a tiling of the given triangle (shaded at right). Because the tiling produces parallel lines, the alternate interior angles must be congruent. As seen in the diagram at right, the three angles of a triangle form a straight angle. Therefore, the sum of the angles of a triangle must be 180°.

Review & Preview

2-61.   **Examine** the shapes in your Shape Toolkit. Then name at least three shapes in the Shape Toolkit that share the following qualities.

- They have only one line of symmetry.

- They have fewer than four sides.

2-62.   **Examine** the diagram at right. Then use the information provided in the diagram to find the measures of angles a, b, c, and d. For each angle, name the relationship from your Angle Relationships Toolkit that helped **justify** your conclusion. For example, did you use vertical angles? If not, what type of angle did you use?

2-63.   **Examine** the triangle at right.

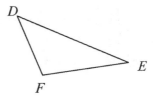

a.   If $m\angle D = 48°$ and $m\angle F = 117°$, then what is
$m\angle E$?

b.   Solve for x if $m\angle D = 4x + 2°$, $m\angle F = 7x - 8°$,
and $m\angle E = 4x + 6°$. Then find $m\angle D$.

c.   If $m\angle D = m\angle F = m\angle E$, what type of triangle is $\triangle FED$?

2-64.   Plot $\triangle ABC$ on graph paper if $A(6, 3)$, $B(2, 1)$, and $C(5, 7)$.

a. $\triangle ABC$ is rotated about the origin 180° to become $\triangle A'B'C'$. Name the
coordinates of A', B', and C'.

b.   This time $\triangle ABC$ is rotated 180° about point C to form $\triangle A''B''C''$. Name the
coordinates of B''.

c.   If $\triangle ABC$ is rotated 90° clockwise (↻) about the origin to form $\triangle A'''B'''C'''$,
what are the coordinates of point A'''?

2-65.   **Examine** the graph at right.

a.   Find the equation of the line.

b.   Is the line $y = \frac{3}{2}x + 1$ perpendicular to
this line? How do you know?

c.   On graph paper, graph $\overleftrightarrow{AB}$ if $A(-2, 4)$ and $B(4, 7)$.
Then find the equation of $\overleftrightarrow{AB}$.

d.   Find an equation of $\overleftrightarrow{AC}$ if $\overleftrightarrow{AC} \perp \overleftrightarrow{AB}$ from part (c).

2.2.2 How can I find the area?

Areas of Triangles and Composite Shapes

How much grass would it take to cover a football field? How much paint would it take to cover a stop sign? How many sequins does it take to cover a dress? Finding the area of different types of shapes enables us to answer many questions. However, different people will see a shape differently. Therefore, during this lesson, be especially careful to look for different **strategies** that can be used to find area.

As you solve these problems, ask yourself the following focus questions:

What shapes do I see in the diagram?

Does this problem remind me of one I have seen before?

Is there another way to find the area?

2-66.   **STRATEGIES** TO MEASURE AREA

In Lesson 2.2.1 you used a grid to measure area. But what if a grid is not available? Or what if we want an exact measurement?

Examine the variety of shapes below. Work with your team to find the area of each one. If a shape has shading, then find the area of the shaded region. Be sure to listen to your teammates carefully and look for different **strategies**. Be prepared to share your team's method with the class.

a.

b.

c.

d.

e.

f.

2-67.   Ismael claimed that he did not need to calculate the area for part (f) in problem 2-66 because it must be the same as the area for the triangle in part (e).

   a.   Is Ismael's claim correct? How do you know? Draw diagrams that show your thinking.

   b.   Do all triangles with the same base and height have the same area? Use your dynamic geometry tool to **investigate**. If no technology is available, obtain the Lesson 2.2.2 Resource Page and compare the areas of the given triangles.

   c.   Explain why the area of any triangle is half the area of a rectangle that has the same base and height. That is, show that the area of a triangle must be $\frac{1}{2}bh$.

2-68.   How do you know which dimensions to use when finding the area of a triangle?

   a.   Copy each triangle below onto your paper. Then find the area of each triangle. Draw any lines on the diagram that will help. Turning the triangles may help you discover a way to find their areas.

   b.   Look back at your work from part (a). Which numbers from each triangle did you use to find the area? For instance, in the center triangle, you probably used only the 6.8 and 6. Write an explanation and/or draw a diagram that would help another student understand how to **choose** which lengths to use when calculating the area.

   c.   Mario, Raquel, and Jocelyn are arguing about where the height is for the triangle at right. The three have written their names along the part they think should be the height. Determine which person is correct. Explain why the one you chose is correct and why the other two are incorrect.

2-69.   In a Learning Log entry, describe at least two different **strategies** that were used today to find the area of irregular shapes. For each method, be sure to include an example. Title this entry "Areas of Composite Figures" and include today's date.

METHODS AND MEANINGS

Multiplying Binomials

One method for multiplying binomials is to use a generic rectangle. That is, use each factor of the product as a dimension of a rectangle and find its area. If $(2x + 5)$ is the base of a rectangle and $(3x - 1)$ is the height, then the expression $(2x+5)(3x-1)$ is the area of the rectangle. See the example below.

Multiply: $(2x+5)(3x-1) = 6x^2 - 2x + 15x - 5$
$$= 6x^2 + 13x - 5$$

Review & Preview

2-70. Review how to multiply binomials by reading the Math Notes box for this lesson. Then rewrite each of the expressions below by multiplying binomials and simplifying the resulting expression.

a. $(4x+1)(2x-7)$

b. $(5x-2)(2x+7)$

c. $(4x-3)(x-11)$

d. $(-3x+1)(2x-5)$

2-71. The shaded triangle at right is surrounded by a rectangle. Find the area of the triangle.

2-72. For each diagram below, solve for x. Explain what relationship from your Angle Relationships Toolkit you used for each problem.

a. $6x$ $4x+10°$

b. $5x+13°$ $3x+7°$

c. $3x+5°$ $2x+18°$ $2x+17°$

d. x $30°$

2-73. Daniel and Mike were having an argument about where to place a square in the Venn diagram at right. Daniel wants to put the square in the intersection (the region where the two circles overlap).

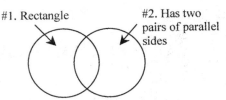

#1. Rectangle   #2. Has two pairs of parallel sides

Mike doesn't think that's right. *"I think it should go in the right region because it is a square, not a rectangle."*

"But a square IS a rectangle!" protests Daniel. Who is right? Explain your thinking.

2-74. What is the probability of drawing each of the following cards from a standard playing deck? Remember that a standard deck of cards includes: 52 cards of four suits. Two suits are black: clubs and spades; two are red: hearts and diamonds. Each suit has 13 cards: 2 through 10, Ace, Jack, Queen, and King.

a. P(Jack)

b. P(spade)

c. P(Jack of spades)

d. P(not spade)

2.2.3 What's the area?

Areas of Parallelograms and Trapezoids

In Lesson 2.2.2, you used your knowledge of the area of a rectangle to develop a method to find the exact area of a triangle that works for all triangles. How can your understanding of the area of triangles and rectangles help with the study of other shapes? As you work today, ask yourself and your team members these focus questions:

What do you see?

What shapes make up the composite figure?

Is there another way?

2-75. Find the areas of the figures below. Can you find more than one method for each shape?

a.

14
5
5   3

b.

4
6
5
9
4

2-76.   FINDING THE AREA OF A PARALLELOGRAM

One of the shape in your Shape Bucket is
shown at right. It is called a **parallelogram**: a
four-sided shape with two pairs of parallel
sides. How can you find the area of a
parallelogram? Consider this question as you
answer the questions below.

a.   Kenisha thinks that the rectangle and parallelogram below have the same area.
Her teammate Shaundra disagrees. Who is correct? **Justify** your conclusion.

Rectangle   **Parallelogram**

b.   In the parallelogram shown in part (a), the two lengths that you were given are
often called the **base** and **height**. Several more parallelograms are shown
below. In each case, find a related rectangle for which you know both the base
and height. Rotating your book might help. Use what you know about
rectangles to find the area of each parallelogram.

(1)   (2)

(3)   (4)

c.   Describe how to find the area of a parallelogram when given its base and
height.

d.   Does the angle at which the parallelogram slants matter? Does every
parallelogram have a related rectangle with equal area? Why or why not?
Explain how you know.

2-77.   Shaundra claims that the area of a parallelogram can be found by *only* using triangles.

   a.   Do you agree? Trace the parallelogram at right onto your paper. Then divide it into two triangles. (Do you see more than one way to do this? If you do, ask some team members to divide the parallelogram one way, and the others a second way.)

   b.   Use what you know about calculating the area of a triangle to find the area of the parallelogram. It may help to trace each triangle separately onto tracing paper so that you can rotate them and label any lengths that you know.

   c.   How does the answer to part (b) compare to the area you found in part (a) of problem 2-76?

2-78.   FINDING THE AREA OF A TRAPEZOID

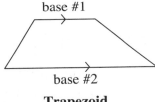

Trapezoid

Another shape you will study from the Shape Bucket is a **trapezoid**: a four-sided shape that has at least one pair of parallel sides. The sides that are parallel are called **bases**, as shown in the diagram at right. Answer the questions below with your team to develop a method to find the area of a trapezoid.

   a.   While playing with the shapes in her Shape Bucket, Shaundra noticed that two identical trapezoids can be arranged to form a parallelogram. Is she correct?

   Trace the trapezoid shown at right onto a piece of tracing paper. Be sure to label its bases and height as shown in the diagram. Work with a team member to move and rearrange the trapezoid on each piece tracing paper so that they create a parallelogram.

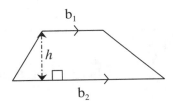

   b.   Since you built a parallelogram from two trapezoids, you can use what you know about finding the area of a parallelogram to find the area of the trapezoid. If the bases of each trapezoid are b_1 and b_2 and the height of each is h, then find the area of the parallelogram. Then use this area to find the area of the original trapezoid.

Problem continues on next page →

2-78.   *Problem continued from previous page.*

c.   Kenisha sees it differently. She sees two
triangles inside the trapezoid. If she divides a
trapezoid into two triangles, what area will she
get? Again assume that the bases of the
trapezoid are b_1 and b_2 and the height is h.

d.   Are the area expressions you created in parts (b) and (c)
equivalent? That is, will they calculate the same area? Use
your algebra skills to demonstrate that they are equivalent.

2-79.   Calculate the exact areas of the shapes below.

a.   b.   c.   d.

2-80.   EXTENSION

Examine the diagram of the kite at right. Work with your team to
find a way to show that its area must be half of the product of the
diagonals. That is, if the length of the diagonals are a and b, provide
a diagram or explanation of why the area of the kite must be $\frac{1}{2}ab$.

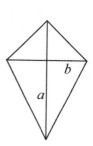

METHODS AND MEANINGS

Conditional Statements

MATH NOTES

A **conditional statement** is written in the form "**If ..., then ....**" Here
are some examples of conditional statements:

If a shape is a rhombus, then it has four sides of equal length.

If it is February 14th, then it is Valentine's Day.

If a shape is a parallelogram, then its area is $A = bh$.

2-81.   Solve for y in terms of x. That is, rewrite each equation so that it starts "$y =$ ".

   a. $6x + 5y = 20$ b. $4x - 8y = 16$

2-82.   Calculate the area of the shaded region at
   right.   Use the appropriate units.

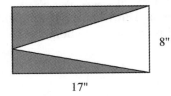

2-83.   How tall are you? How do you measure your height? Consider these questions as
   you answer the questions below.

   a.   Why do you stand up straight to measure your height?

   b.   Which diagram best represents how you would measure your height? Why?

   Diagram 1   **Diagram 2**

   c.   When you measure your height, do you measure up to your chin? Down to
   your knees? Explain.

2-84.   Read the Math Notes box for this lesson. Then rewrite each of the following
   statements as a conditional statement.

   a.   Mr. Spelling is always unhappy when it rains.

   b.   The sum of two even numbers is always even.

   c.   Marla has a piano lesson every Tuesday.

2-85.   Simplify the following expressions.

   a. $2x + 8 + 6x + 5$ b. $15 + 3(2x - 4) - 4x$

   c. $(x - 3)(3x + 4)$ d. $5x(2x + 7) + x(3x - 5)$

2.2.4 How can I find the height?

Heights and Area

In Lesson 2.2.2, you learned that triangles with the same base and height must have the same area. But what if multiple dimensions of a shape are labeled? How can you determine which dimension is the height?

2-86.   Candice missed the lesson about finding the area of the triangle. Not knowing where to start, she drew a triangle and measured its sides, as shown at right. After drawing her triangle, Candice said, "Well, I've measured all of the sides. I must be ready to find the area!"

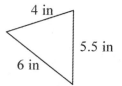

If you think she is correct, write a description of how to use the side lengths to find the area. If you think she needs to measure anything else, copy the figure on your paper and add a line segment to represent a measurement she needs.

2-87.   HEIGHT LAB

What is the height of a triangle? Is it like walking up any side of the triangle? Or is it like standing at the highest point and looking straight down? Today your team will build triangles with string and consider different ways height can be seen for triangles of various shapes.

a.   Use the materials given to you by your teacher to make a triangle like the one in the diagram below.

(1)   Tie one end of the short string to the weight and the other to the end of a pencil (or pen).

(2)   Tape a 15 cm section of the long string along the edge of a desk or table. Be sure to leave long ends of string hanging off each side.

(3)   Bring the loose ends of string up from the table and cross them as shown in the diagram. Then put the pencil with the weight over the crossing of the string. Cross the strings again on top of the pencil.

Problem continues on next page →

2-87.   *Problem continued from previous page.*

b.   Now, with your team, build and
sketch triangles that meet the three
conditions below. To organize your
work, assign each team member one
of the jobs described at right.

(1) The height of the triangle is inside
the triangle.

(2) The height of the triangle is a side
of the triangle.

(3) The height of the triangle is outside of the triangle.

c.   Now make sure that everyone in your team has sketches of the triangles that
you made.

2-88.   How can I find the height of a triangle if it is not a right triangle?

a.   On the Lesson 2.2.4 Resource Page there are four triangles labeled (1) through
(4). Assume you know the length of the side labeled "base." For each triangle,
draw in the height that would enable you to find the area of the triangle.
Note: You do not need to find the area.

b.   Find the triangle for part (b) at the bottom of the same resource page. For this
triangle, draw all three possible heights. First **choose** one side to be the base
and draw in the corresponding height. Then repeat the process of drawing in
the height for the other two sides, one at a time.

c.   You drew in three pairs of bases and heights for the triangle in part (b). Using
centimeters, measure the length of all three sides and all three heights. Find the
area three times using all three pairs of bases and heights. Since the triangle
remains the same size, your answers should match.

2-89.   AREA TOOLKIT

Over the past several days, you have explored how to find
the areas of triangles, parallelograms, and trapezoids. Today
you will start a new page of your Geometry Toolkit, called
the Area Toolkit. Keep this toolkit in a safe place. You will
want it for reference in class and when doing homework.

At this time, describe what you know about finding the areas of triangles, rectangles,
parallelograms, and trapezoids. Be sure to include an example for each shape.

METHODS AND MEANINGS

MATH NOTES

Areas of a Triangle, Parallelogram, and Trapezoid

The area of a triangle is half the area of a rectangle with the same base and height. If the base of the triangle is length b and the height length h, then the area of the triangle is:

$$A = \tfrac{1}{2}bh.$$

The area of a parallelogram is equal to a rectangle with the same base and height. If the base of the parallelogram is length b and the height length h, then the area of the parallelogram is:

$$A = bh.$$

Finally, the area of a trapezoid is found by averaging the two bases and multiplying by the height. If the trapezoid has bases b_1 and b_2 and height h, then the area is:

$$A = \tfrac{1}{2}(b_1 + b_2)h.$$

Review & Preview

2-90. Find the area of each figure below. Show all work. Remember to include units in your answer.

a. a square:

7 cm

b.

4 in   5 in

10 in

c.

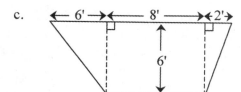

6'

2-91. Multiply the expressions below. Then simplify the result, if possible.

a. $3x(5x + 7)$

b. $(x + 2)(x + 3)$

c. $(3x + 5)(x - 2)$

d. $(2x + 1)(5x - 4)$

2-92.   Graph the following equations on the same set of axes. Label each line or curve with its equation. Where do the two curves intersect?

$$y = -x - 3 \qquad\qquad y = x^2 + 2x - 3$$

2-93.   On graph paper, plot quadrilateral $ABCD$ if $A(2, 7)$, $B(4, 8)$, $C(4, 2)$, and $D(2, 3)$.

   a.   What is the best name for this shape? **Justify** your conclusion.

   b.   Quadrilateral $A'B'C'D'$ is formed by rotating $ABCD$ 90° clockwise about the origin. Name the coordinates of the vertices.

   c.   Find the area of $ABCD$. Show all work.

2-94.   What is the probability of drawing each of the following cards from a standard playing deck? Refer to problem 2-74 if you need information about a deck of cards.

   a.   P(face card)   b.   P(card printed with an even number)

   c.   P(red ace)   d.   P(purple card)

2.3.1   How can I use a square?

Squares and Square Roots

You now have the tools to find the area of many complex shapes and are also able to use transformations to create new shapes. In this lesson you will combine these skills to explore the area of a square and to develop a method for finding the length of the longest side of a right triangle.

2-95.   What do you notice about the rectangle at right?

   a.   Elyse does not know how to solve for x. Explain to her how to find the missing dimension.

   b.   What if the area of the shape above is instead 66 ft²? What would x be in that case?

$A = 100 \text{ ft}^2$ x

2-96.   While Alexandria was doodling on graph
          paper, she made the design at right. She
          started with the shaded right triangle. She
          then rotated it 90° clockwise and translated
          the result so that the right angle of the image
          was at *B*. She continued this pattern until she
          completed the diagram.

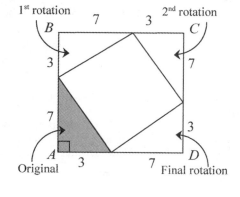

          a.   Draw Alexandria's design on graph
                 paper. What is the shape of *ABCD*?
                 How can you tell?

          b.   What is the shape of the inner
                 quadrilateral? How do you know?

          c.   What is the area of the inner quadrilateral? Show all work that leads to your
                 conclusion.

          d.   What's the length of the longest side of the shaded triangle?

2-97.   DONNA'S DILEMMA

          Donna needs help! She needs to find PQ (the length
          of $\overline{PQ}$) in $\triangle PQR$ shown at right.

          Alexandria realized that the
          triangle looked a lot like a piece
          of the square she drew earlier
          (shown in problem 2-96).
          Alexandria explained to Donna
          that if they could find the area
          of a square with side $\overline{PQ}$, then
          finding the length of $\overline{PQ}$ would
          be easy.

          a.   Draw $\triangle PQR$ on your paper.

          b.   Using the method from problem 2-96, help the students construct the square by
                 rotating the triangle 90° and translating it. Then find the length of $\overline{PQ}$. Is the
                 answer reasonable?

          c.   Find the perimeter of her triangle.

2-98.   Use Donna and Alexandria's method to find the length of side
          $\overline{AC}$ in the diagram at right. That is, draw a square on $\overline{AC}$
          using what you know about slope. Then use the area of the
          square to find $\overline{AC}$.

2-99. In a Learning Log entry, describe the process you developed today to find the length of the longest side of a right triangle when given the lengths of its legs. Label this entry "Finding the Length of the Hypotenuse" and include today's date.

METHODS AND MEANINGS

Square Root

The **square root** of a number x (written $\sqrt{x}$) is defined as the length of a side of a square with area x. For example, $\sqrt{16} = 4$. Therefore if the side of a square has a length of 4 units, then its area is 16 square units.

When the area of a square is not a "perfect square" such as 49, 25, or 9 un^2 then the square root is not an integer, and instead is an **irrational number.** Note that an irrational number cannot be written as a fraction of two integers. For example, $\sqrt{17} = 4.123\ldots$ is an irrational number because 17 is not a perfect square. The symbol "$\approx$" means "approximately equal to." Since 4.123 is an approximate value of $\sqrt{17}$, it can be stated that $\sqrt{17} \approx 4.123$.

The square root of a number can often be estimated by comparing the number under the square root with its closest perfect squares. For example, since $\sqrt{16} = 4$, then $\sqrt{17}$ must be a little bigger than 4. Therefore, a good estimation of $\sqrt{17}$ is 4.1. Likewise, if you want to estimate $\sqrt{97}$, you may want to start with $\sqrt{100} = 10$. Since 97 is smaller than 100, a good estimate of $\sqrt{97}$ would be 9.8 or 9.9.

2-100. Read the Math Notes box for this lesson.

a. What would be a reasonable estimate of $\sqrt{68}$? Explain your thinking. After you have made an estimate, check your estimation with a calculator.

b. Repeat this process to estimate the values below.

(1) $\sqrt{5}$ (2) $\sqrt{85}$ (3) $\sqrt{50}$ (4) $\sqrt{22}$

2-101. Draw the triangle at right on graph paper. Then draw a square on $\overline{KM}$ and use it to find the length of $\overline{KM}$.

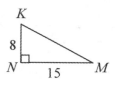

2-102. **Examine** the rectangle at right.

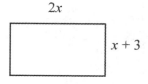

a. What is the perimeter in terms of x? In other words, find the perimeter.

b. If the perimeter is 78 cm, find the dimensions of the rectangle. Show all your work.

c. Verify that the area of this rectangle is 360 sq. cm. Explain how you know this.

2-103. **Examine** the arrow diagram below.

Polygon is a parallelogram → *area of the polygon equals base times height.*

a. Write this conjecture as a conditional ("If, then") statement.

b. Write a similar conjecture about triangles, both as a conditional statement and as an arrow diagram.

2-104. Berti is the Shape Factory's top employee. She has received awards every month for having the top sales figures so far for the year. If she stays on top, she'll receive a $5000 bonus for excellence. She currently has sold 16,250 shapes and continues to sell 340 per month.

Since there are eight months left in the sales year, Sarita is working hard to catch up. While she has only sold 8,830 shapes, she is working overtime and on weekends so that she can sell 1,082 per month. Will Sarita catch up with Berti before the end of the sales year? If so, when?

2.3.2 Is the answer reasonable?

Triangle Inequality

You now have several tools for describing triangles (lengths, areas, and angle measures), but can **any** three line segments create a triangle? Or are there restrictions on the side lengths of a triangle? And how can you know that the length you found for the side of a triangle is accurate? Today you will **investigate** the relationship between the side lengths of a triangle.

2-105. Roiri (pronounced "ROAR-ree") loves right triangles and has provided the one at right to analyze. He wants your team to find the length of the **hypotenuse** ($\overline{AC}$) using the method from problem 2-97.

a. Estimate the length of $\overline{AC}$.

b. Draw Roiri's triangle on graph paper and then construct a square on the hypotenuse. Use the area of the square to find the length of the hypotenuse.

c. Was your result for the hypotenuse close to your estimate? Why or why not?

d. For a different triangle $\triangle ABC$ where $AB = 3$ units and $BC = 4$ units, Roiri found that $AC = 25$. Donna is not sure that is possible. What do you think? **Visualize** this triangle and explain if you think this triangle is possible or not.

2-106.   PINK SLIP

Oh no! During your last shift at the Shape
Factory everything seemed to be going fine-
-until the machine that was producing
triangles made a huge CLUNK and then
stopped. Since your team was on duty, all
of you will be held responsible for the
machine's breakdown.

Luckily, your boss has informed you that if
you can figure out what happened and how
to make sure it will not happen again, you
will keep your job. The last order the
machine was processing was for a triangle
with sides 3 cm, 5 cm, and 10 cm.

a.   Use the manipulative (such as a dynamic geometry tool or pasta)
      provided by your teacher to **investigate** what happened today at
      the factory. Can a triangle be made with <u>any</u> three side lengths?
      If not, what condition(s) would make it impossible to build a
      triangle? Try building triangles with the side lengths listed
      below:

      (1)   3 cm, 5 cm, and 10 cm   (2)   4 cm, 9 cm, and 12 cm

      (3)   2 cm, 4 cm, and 5 cm   (4)   3 cm, 5 cm, and 8 cm

b.   For those triangles that could not be built, what happened? Why were they
      impossible?

c.   Use your dynamic geometry tool (or dry pasta) to **investigate** the restrictions
      on the three side lengths that can form a triangle. For example, if two sides of
      a triangle are 5 cm and 12 cm long, respectively, what is the longest side that
      could join these two sides to form a triangle? (Could the third side be 12 cm
      long? 19 cm long?) What is the shortest possible length that could be used to
      form a triangle? (Does 5 cm work? 9 cm?)

d.   Write a memo to your boss explaining what happened. If you can convince
      your boss that the machine's breakdown was not your fault **and** show the
      company how to fix the machine so that this does not happen again, you might
      earn a promotion!

2-107.   The values you found in parts (a) and (c) of problem 2-106 were the **minimum** and **maximum limits** for the length of the third side of any triangle with two sides of lengths 5 cm and 12 cm. The fact that there are restrictions on the side lengths that may be used to create a triangle is referred to as the **Triangle Inequality.**

Determine the minimum and maximum limits for each missing side length in the triangles below.

a.

b.

c.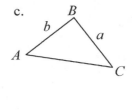

2-108.   In a Learning Log entry, explain how you can tell if three sides will form a triangle or not. Draw diagrams to support your statements. Title this entry, "Triangle Inequality" and include today's date.

ETHODS AND MEANINGS

Right Triangle Vocabulary

All of the triangles that we have been working with in this section are right triangles, that is, triangles that contain a 90° angle. The two shortest sides of the right triangle (the sides that meet at the right angle) are called the **legs** of the triangle and the longest side (the side opposite the right angle) is called the **hypotenuse** of the triangle.

2-109.   Draw a right triangle with legs of length 6 and 8 units, respectively, onto graph paper. Construct a square on the hypotenuse and use the square's area to find the length of the hypotenuse.

2-110.   Write the equation of each line described below in slope-intercept form ($y = mx + b$).

   a. $m = \frac{6}{5}$ and $b = -3$ b. $m = -\frac{1}{4}$ and $b = 4.5$

   c. $m = \frac{1}{3}$ and the line passes   d. $m = 0$ and $b = 2$
        through the origin $(0, 0)$

2-111.   **Examine** the diagram at right. Based on the information in the diagram, which angles can you determine? Copy the diagram on your paper and find only those angles that you can **justify**.

2-112.   Hannah's shape bucket contains an equilateral triangle, an isosceles right triangle, a regular hexagon, an isosceles trapezoid, a rhombus, a kite, a parallelogram and a rectangle. If she reaches in and selects a shape at random, what is the probability that that the shape will meet the criterion described below?

   a.   At least two sides congruent.

   b.   Two pairs of parallel sides.

   c.   At least one pair of parallel sides.

2-113.   On graph paper, plot $ABCD$ if $A(-1, 2)$, $B(0, 5)$, $C(2, 5)$, and $D(6, 2)$.

   a.   What type of shape is $ABCD$? **Justify** your answer.

   b.   If $ABCD$ is rotated $90°$ counterclockwise ($\circlearrowleft$) about the origin, name the coordinates of the image $A'B'C'D'$.

   c.   On your graph, reflect $ABCD$ across the y-axis to find $A''B''C''D''$. Name the coordinates of A''' and C'''.

   d.   Find the area of $ABCD$. Show all work.

2.3.3 Is there a shortcut?

The Pythagorean Theorem

During Lessons 2.3.1 and 2.3.2, you have learned a method to find the length of a hypotenuse of a right triangle by finding the area of the square built on the hypotenuse, as shown in the diagram at right. However, what if the sides of the triangle make it difficult to draw (such as very large numbers or decimal values)? Or what if you do not even know one of the lengths of the legs?

Today, you will work with your team to find the relationship between the legs and hypotenuse of a right triangle. By the end of this lesson, you should be able to find the side of <u>any</u> right triangle, when given the lengths of the other two sides.

2-114.   Roiri complained that while the method
from problem 2-97 works, it seems like
too much work! He remembers that
rearranging a shape does not change its
area and thinks he can find a shortcut
by rearranging Donna's square. Obtain
a Lesson 2.3.3 Resource Page for your
team and cut out the shaded triangles.
Note that the lengths of the sides of the
triangles are *a*, *b*, and *c* units
respectively.

a.   First, arrange the triangles to look like Donna's in the
diagram at right. Draw this diagram on your paper.
What is the area of the unshaded square?

b.   Roiri claims that moving the triangles within the outer
square won't change the area of the unshaded square.
Is Roiri correct? Why or why not?

c.   Move the shaded triangles to match the diagram at
right. In this configuration, what is the total area that
is unshaded?

d.   Write an equation that relates the two ways that you
found to represent the unshaded area in the figure.

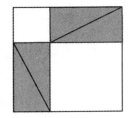

2-115.   The relationship you found in problem 2-114 (between the square of the lengths of the legs and the square of the length of the hypotenuse in a right triangle) is known as the **Pythagorean Theorem**. This relationship is a powerful tool because once you know the lengths of any two sides of a right triangle, you can find the length of the third side. But does this relationship always hold true?

   a.   Use a dynamic geometry tool to test whether the square of the hypotenuse always equals the sum of the squares of the legs of a right triangle.

   b.   Add an entry in your Learning Log for the Pythagorean Theorem, explaining what it is and how to use it. Be sure to include a diagram.

2-116.   Apply the Pythagorean Theorem to answer the questions below.

   a.   For each triangle below, find the value of the variable.

   (1)   (2)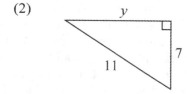

   b.   **Examine** the rectangle shown at right. Find its perimeter and area.

   c.   On graph paper, draw $\overline{AC}$ if $A(2, 6)$ and $B(5, -1)$. Then draw a slope triangle. Use the slope triangle to find the length of $\overline{AC}$.

2-117.   The Garcia family took a day trip from Cowpoke Gulch. Their online directions told them to drive four miles north, six miles east, three miles north, and then one mile east to Big Horn Flat. Draw a diagram and calculate the direct distance (straight) from Cowpoke Gulch to Big Horn Flat.

Geometry Connections

METHODS AND MEANINGS

The Pythagorean Theorem

The **Pythagorean Theorem** states that in a right triangle,

$$(\text{length of leg \#1})^2 + (\text{length of leg \#2})^2 = (\text{length of hypotenuse})^2$$

The Pythagorean Theorem can be used to find a missing side length in a right triangle. See the example below.

$$5^2 + x^2 = 8^2$$
$$25 + x^2 = 64$$
$$x^2 = 39$$
$$x = \sqrt{39} \approx 6.24$$

In the example above, $\sqrt{39}$ is an example of an **exact** answer, while 6.24 is an **approximate** answer.

Review & Preview

2-118.   One of the algebra topics you have reviewed during this chapter is solving systems of equations. Assess what you know about solving systems as you answer the questions below.

   a.   Find the points of intersection of the lines below using any method. Write your solutions as a point (x, y).

   (1) $y = -x + 8$
          $y = x - 2$

   (2) $2x - y = 10$
          $y = -4x + 2$

   b.   Find the equation for each line on the graph at right. Remember, the general form of any line in the **slope-intercept form** is $y = mx + b$.

   c.   Solve the system of equations you found in part (b) algebraically. Verify that your solution matches the one shown in the graph at right.

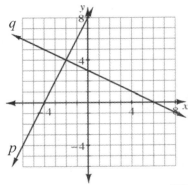

2-119.   Lines *p* and *q* graphed in problem 2-118 form a triangle with the *x*-axis.

a.   How can you describe this triangle? In other words, what is the most appropriate name for this triangle? How do you know?

b.   Find the area of the triangle.

c.   What is the perimeter?

2-120.   Find the area of the trapezoid at right. What **strategies** did you use?

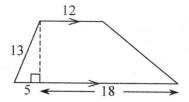

2-121.   Use the relationships in the diagrams below to solve for *x*, if possible. If it is not possible, state how you know. If it is possible, **justify** your solution by stating which geometric relationships you use.

a.

b.

c.

2-122.   Find the minimum and maximum limits for the length of a third side of a triangle if the other two sides are 8" and 13".

Chapter 2 Closure   What have I learned?

Reflection and Synthesis

The activities below offer you a chance to reflect on
what you have learned in this chapter. As you
work, look for concepts that you feel very
comfortable with, ideas that you would like to learn
more about, and topics you need more help with.
Look for connections between ideas as well as
connections with material you learned previously.

① TEAM BRAINSTORM

With your team, brainstorm a list for each of the following two subjects. Be as
detailed as you can. How long can you make your list? Challenge yourselves. Be
prepared to share your team's ideas with the class.

Topics: What have you studied in this chapter? What ideas and
words were important in what you learned? Remember to
be as detailed as you can.

Connections: How are the topics, ideas, and words that you learned in
previous courses connected to the new ideas in this
chapter? Again, make your list as long as you can.

② MAKING CONNECTIONS

The following is a list of the vocabulary used in this chapter. The words that appear
in bold are new to this chapter. Make sure that you are familiar with all of these
words and know what they mean. Refer to the glossary or index for any words that
you do not yet understand.

alternate interior angles	area	**arrow diagram**
base	**complementary angles**	**conditional statement**
conjecture	**corresponding angles**	**dimension**
height	**hypotenuse**	**leg**
line	**parallelogram**	perimeter
proof by contradiction	**Pythagorean Theorem**	**rectangle**
right angle	**same-side interior angles**	**square**
square root	straight angle	**supplementary angles**
theorem	**transversal**	**trapezoid**
triangle inequality	**unit of measure**	**vertical angles**

Problem continues on next page →

② *Problem continued from previous page.*

Make a concept map showing all of the connections you can find among the key words and ideas listed above. To show a connection between two words, draw a line between them and explain the connection, as shown in the example below. A word can be connected to any other word as long as there is a justified connection. For each key word or idea, provide a sketch of an example.

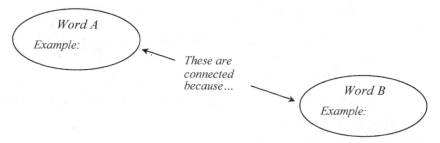

Your teacher may provide you with vocabulary cards to help you get started. If you use the cards to plan your concept map, be sure to either re-draw your concept map on your paper or glue the vocabulary cards to a poster with all of the connections explained for others to see and understand.

While you are making your map, your team may think of related words or ideas that are not listed above. Be sure to include these ideas on your concept map.

③ SUMMARIZING MY UNDERSTANDING

This section gives you an opportunity to show what you know about certain math topics or ideas. Your teacher will direct you how to do this.

④ WHAT HAVE I LEARNED?

This section will help you recognize those types of problems you feel comfortable with and those you need more help with. This section will appear at the end of every chapter to help you check your understanding. Even if your teacher does not assign this section, it is a good idea to try these problems and find out for yourself what you know and what you need to work on.

Solve each problem as completely as you can. The table at the end of this closure section has answers to these problems. It also tells you where you can find additional help and practice on similar problems.

CL 2-123. Sandra's music bag contains:

3 CDs of country music

6 CDs of rock and roll

4 CDs of rap music

5 cassette tapes of country music

1 cassette tape of rock and roll

3 cassette tapes of rap music

a.   As Sandra drives, she often reaches into her bag and randomly pulls out some music (she does not want to take her eyes off the road). What is the probability that she will select some rap music?

b.   Find P(CD), that is, the probability that she will randomly select a CD (of any type of music).

c.   Find P(cassette of country music).

d.   Find P(not rock and roll), the probability that the music she randomly selects is **not** rock and roll.

CL 2-124. Find the area of each figure.

a.

b.

c.

d.

CL 2-125. Find the perimeter of each figure.

a.

b.

CL 2-126. Graph the segment that connects the points $A(-4,8)$ and $B(7,3)$.

    a.   What is the slope of $\overline{AB}$?   b.   How long is $\overline{AB}$?

CL 2-127. Identify the geometric angle relationship(s) in each diagram. Use what you know about those relationships to write an equation and solve for x.

    a.   b.   c.   d.

CL 2-128. **Examine** the system of equations at right.

$$y = -2x + 6$$
$$y = \tfrac{1}{2}x - 9$$

    a.   Solve the system below <u>twice</u>: graphically and algebraically. Verify that your solutions from the different methods are the same.

    b.   What is the relationship between the two lines? How can you tell?

CL 2-129. Charlotte was transforming the hexagon $ABCDEF$.

    a.   What single transformation did she perform in Diagram #1?

Diagram #1

    b.   What single transformation did she perform in Diagram #2?

    c.   What transformation didn't she do? Write directions for this type of transformation for hexagon $ABCDEF$ and perform it.

Diagram #2

CL 2-130. Explain what you are doing when you find the perimeter of a shape. How is that different than finding the area?

CL 2-131. Check your answers using the table at the end of this section. Which problems do you feel confident about? Which problems were hard? Have you worked on problems like these in math classes you have taken before? Use the table to make a list of topics you need help on and a list of topics you need to practice more.

This course focuses on five different **Ways of Thinking**: investigating, examining, reasoning and justifying, visualizing, and choosing a strategy/tool. These are some of the ways in which you think while trying to make sense of a concept or to solve a problem (even outside of math class). During this chapter, you have probably used each Way of Thinking multiple times without even realizing it!

This closure activity will focus on one of these Ways of Thinking: **examining**. Read the description of this Way of Thinking at right.

Think about the diagrams that you have looked at or drawn during this chapter. When have you had to understand information from a diagram or picture? What helps you to see what is in the diagram? What diagrams or parts of diagrams have you seen in a previous math class? You may want to flip through the chapter to refresh your memory about the problems that you have worked on. Discuss any of the methods you have developed to **examine** the problem in order to identify what is important or what information is conveyed in a diagram.

Once your discussion is complete, think about the way you think as you answer the following problems.

Examining

To **examine** means to look at a diagram and recognize its geometric properties. As you develop this way of thinking you will learn what specifically to look for in a diagram depending on the problem you are solving. Often, examining is what you do to answer to the question, "How does this diagram help me?" When you catch yourself thinking, "I can see from the diagram that... ", you are examining.

a.   Sometimes, **examining** a shape means you have to disregard how it *looks* and concentrate on the information provided by the markings.

For example, **examine** the shape at right. This shape looks like a square, but is it? Make as many statements as you can state about this shape based on the markings. What shape is *ABCD*? Which statements are obvious from the diagram and which did you have to think about?

Problem continues on next page →

⑤   *Problem continued from previous page.*

b.   At other times, examining a diagram suggests that you notice different parts that contribute to the entire diagram. For example, look at the diagram at right. Assuming that the diagram is drawn to scale, what shapes can you find in the diagram?

c.   In part (a), you looked for attributes of a shape, while in part (b), you looked for shapes within a shape.

However, another aspect of examining a diagram is to look for relationships between parts of the diagram. For example, **examine** the diagram at right. What relationships do you see between the angles in the diagram? What relationships can you find between the lines and/or line segments? List as many relationships as you can based on the information in the diagram.

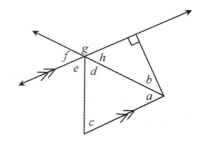

Answers and Support for Closure Activity #4
What Have I Learned?

Problem	Solutions	Need Help?	More Practice
CL 2-123.	a. $\frac{7}{22} \approx 0.32$ b. $\frac{13}{22} \approx 0.59$ c. $\frac{5}{22} \approx 0.23$ d. $\frac{15}{22} \approx 0.68$	Lesson 1.3.3 Math Notes box	Problems 2-9, 2-55, 2-74, 2-94, 2-112
CL 2-124.	a. 140 sq. in. b. 12 sq. cm. c. 117 sq. ft. d. 57 sq. m.	Lesson 2.2.4 Math Notes box	Problems 2-66, 2-68, 2-71, 2-75, 2-76, 2-78, 2-79, 2-82, 2-83, 2-90, 2-120
CL 2-125.	a. $x = 13$ units; $p = 30$ units b. $p = 34$ units	Lessons 1.1.3 and 2.3.3 Math Notes boxes	Problems 1-44, 1-65, 1-93, 2-52(a), 2-57, 2-97, 2-102, 2-116(b), 2-119

Problem	Solutions	Need Help?	More Practice
CL 2-126.	a. $m = -\frac{5}{11}$ b. length $= \sqrt{146} \approx 12.1$ units	Lessons 1.2.5 and 2.3.3 Math Notes boxes	Problems 1-36, 1-76, 2-116, 2-117
CL 2-127.	a. $x + 15° = 102°$; $x = 87°$; corresponding angles b. $7x - 3° = x + 21°$; $x = 4°$; vertical angles c. $2x + 2° + 3x + 8° = 180°$; $x = 34°$; supplementary angles d. $x + x + 2x - 6° = 180°$; $x = 46.5°$; sum of angles in a triangle is $180°$	Lessons 2.1.1 and 2.1.4 Math Notes boxes	Problems 2-13, 2-16, 2-17, 2-18, 2-19, 2-23, 2-31, 2-32, 2-35, 2-36, 2-37, 2-38, 2-49, 2-51, 2-52, 2-62, 2-63, 2-72, 2-111, 2-121
CL 2-128.	a. $(6, -6)$ b. They are perpendicular because the slopes are opposite reciprocals.	Lessons 2.1.3, 1.2.1, and 1.2.5 Math Notes boxes	Problems 1-62, 1-92, 2-29, 2-39, 2-42, 2-53, 2-54(c), 2-65, 2-92, 2-118
CL 2-129.	a. Reflection (flip) b. Rotation (turn counterclockwise 90°) c. Translation (slide). Answers will vary, and example is provided below:	Lessons 1.2.2 Math Notes box	Problems 1-50, 1-51, 1-59, 1-60, 1-61, 1-64, 1-69, 1-73, 1-85, 1-96, 2-11, 2-19, 2-20, 2-33, 2-64, 2-113
CL 2-130.	The perimeter of a shape is the length of that shape's boundary. While to find the area, consider everything *inside* the boundary.	Lesson 1.1.3 Math Notes box	Problems 1-65, 1-66, 1-74, 1-84, 2-57, 2-116

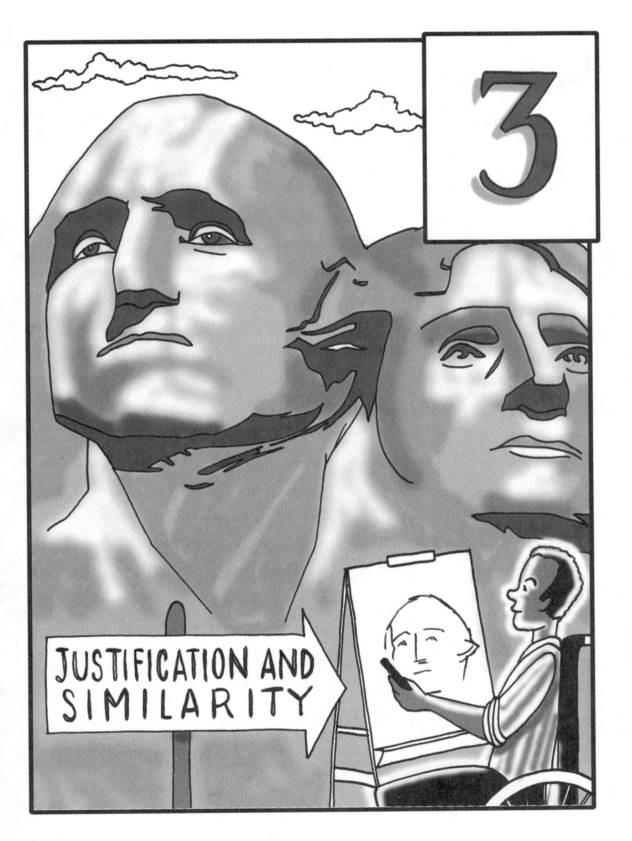

CHAPTER 3 Justification and Similarity

Measuring, describing, and transforming: these are three major skills in geometry that you have been developing. In this chapter, you will focus on comparing; you will explore ways to determine if two figures have the same shape (called **similar**). You will also develop ways to use the information about one figure to learn more about another that has the same shape.

Making logical and convincing arguments that support specific ideas about the shapes you are studying is another important skill. In this chapter you will learn how you can document facts to support a conclusion in a flowchart.

In this chapter, you will learn:

> ➤ how to support a mathematical statement using flowcharts and conditional statements.

> ➤ about the special relationships between shapes that are similar or congruent.

> ➤ how to determine if triangles are similar or congruent.

Guiding Questions

Think about these questions throughout this chapter:

Is it still the same shape?

How did the shape grow or shrink?

What do I need to show for it to be similar?

How can I justify that?

What evidence can I state?

Chapter Outline

Section 3.1 Through an exploration with rubber bands, students will generate similar figures, which will launch a focus on similarity for Sections 3.1 and 3.2. During these lessons, students will determine what common qualities similar shapes have.

Section 3.2 As students discover the conditions that cause triangles to be similar or congruent, they will learn about using a flowchart to organize facts and support their conclusions.

3.1.1 What do these shapes have in common?

Similarity

In Section 1.3, you organized shapes into groups based on their size, angles, sides, and other characteristics. You identified shapes using their characteristics and investigated relationships between different kinds of shapes, so that now you can tell if two shapes are both parallelograms or trapezoids, for example. But what makes two figures look alike?

Today you will be introduced to a new transformation that enlarges a figure while maintaining its shape, called a **dilation**. After creating new enlarged shapes, you and your team will explore the interesting relationships that exist between figures that have the same shape.

In your teams, you should keep the following questions in mind as you work together today:

What do the shapes have in common?

How can you demonstrate that the shapes are the same?

What specifically is different about the shapes?

3-1. WARM-UP STRETCH

Before computers and copy machines existed, it sometimes took hours to enlarge documents or to shrink text on items such as jewelry. A pantograph device (like the one below) was often used to duplicate written documents and artistic drawings. You will now employ the same geometric principles by using rubber bands to draw enlarged copies of a design. Your teacher will show you how to do this.

3-2.   In problem 3-1, you created designs that were
        similar, meaning that they have the same shape.
        But how can you determine if two figures are
        similar? What do similar shapes have in common?
        To find out, your team will need to create similar
        shapes that you can measure and compare.

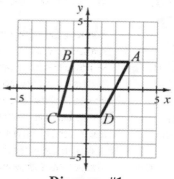

Diagram #1

a.   Obtain a Lesson 3.1.1
      Resource Page from your
      teacher (or download it from
      www.cpm.org). On it, find
      the quadrilateral shown in
      Diagram #1 at right.

      Dilate (stretch) the
      quadrilateral from the origin
      by a factor of 2, 3, 4, or 5 to
      form $A'B'C'D'$. Each team
      member should pick a
      different enlargement factor.
      You may want to imagine that
      your rubber band chain is
      stretched from the origin so
      that the knot traces the
      perimeter of the original
      figure.

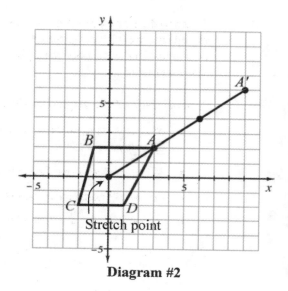

Diagram #2

      For example, if your job is to
      stretch *ABCD* by a factor of 3,
      then A' would be located as
      shown in Diagram #2 at right.

b.   Carefully cut out your enlarged shape and compare it to your teammates'
      shapes. How are the four shapes different? How are they the same? As you
      investigate, make sure you record what qualities make the shapes different and
      what qualities make the shapes the same. Be ready to report your conclusions
      to the class.

3-3.   WHICH SHAPE IS THE EXCEPTION?

Sometimes shapes look the same and
sometimes they look very different.
What characteristics make figures alike
so that we can say that they are the same
shape? How are shapes that look the
same but are different sizes related to
each other? Understanding these
relationships will allow us to know if
shapes that appear to have the same
shape actually do have the same shape.

Your task: For each set of shapes below, three shapes are similar, and one is an
exception, which means that it is not like the others. Find the exception in each set
of shapes. Your teacher may give you tracing paper to help you in your
investigation.

Answer each of these questions for both sets of shapes below:

- Which shape appears to be the exception? What makes that shape different
  from the others?

- What do the other three shapes have in common?

- Are there commonalities in the angles? Are there differences?

- Are there commonalities in the sides? Are there differences?

a.

b.

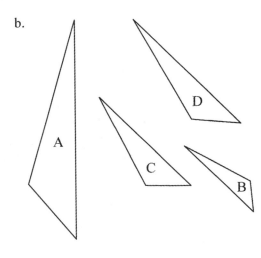

3-4.   Write an entry in your Learning Log about the characteristics that
        figures with different sizes need to have in order to maintain the same
        shape. Add your own diagrams to illustrate the description. Title this
        entry "Same Shape, Different Size" with today's date.

METHODS AND MEANINGS

Dilations

The transformations you studied in Chapter 1 (translations, rotations, and reflections) are called rigid transformations because they all maintain the size and shape of the original figure.

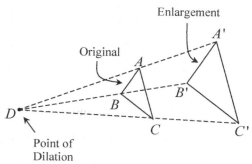

However, a **dilation** is a transformation that maintains the shape of a figure but multiplies its dimensions by a chosen factor. In a dilation, a shape is stretched proportionally from a particular point, called the **point of dilation** or **stretch point**. For example, in the diagram at right, $\triangle ABC$ is dilated to form $\triangle A'B'C'$. Notice that while a dilation changes the size and location of the original figure, it does not rotate or reflect the original.

Note that if the point of dilation is located inside a shape, the enlargement encloses the original, as shown at right.

Review & Preview

3-5. Plot the rectangle *ABCD* formed with the points $A(-1, -2)$, $B(3, -2)$, $C(3, 1)$, and $D(-1, 1)$ onto graph paper. Use the method used in problem 3-2 to enlarge it from the origin by a factor of 2 (using two "rubber bands"). Label this new rectangle $A'B'C'D'$.

    a. What are the dimensions of the enlarged rectangle, $A'B'C'D'$?

    b. Find the area and the perimeter of $A'B'C'D'$.

    c. Find AC (the length of $\overline{AC}$).

3-6. Solve each equation below for x. Show all work and check your answer by substituting it back into the equation and verifying that it makes the equation true.

    a. $\frac{x}{3} = 6$ b. $\frac{5x+9}{2} = 12$ c. $\frac{x}{4} = \frac{9}{6}$ d. $\frac{5}{x} = \frac{20}{8}$

3-7.   **Examine** the triangle at right.

   a.   Estimate the measure of each angle
         of the triangle at right.

   b.   Given only its shape, what is the best name for this triangle?

3-8.   On graph paper, graph line $\overleftrightarrow{MU}$ if $M(-1, 1)$ and $U(4, 5)$.

   a.   Find the slope of $\overleftrightarrow{MU}$.

   b.   Find MU (the distance from M to U).

   c.   Are there any similarities to the calculations used in parts (a) and (b)? Any
         differences?

3-9.   Rewrite the statements below into conditional ("If …, then …") form.

   a.   All equilateral triangles have 120° rotation symmetry.

   b.   A rectangle is a parallelogram.

   c.   The area of a trapezoid is half the sum of the bases multiplied by the height.

3.1.2 How can I maintain the shape?

Proportional Growth and Ratios

So far you have studied several shapes that appear to be **similar** (exactly the same shape but not
necessarily the same size). But how can we know for sure that two shapes are similar? Today
you will focus on the relationship between the lengths of sides of similar figures by enlarging
and reducing shapes and looking for patterns.

3-10.   Find your work from problem 3-5. The graph you
        created should resemble the graph at right.

   a.   In problem 3-5, you dilated (stretched) $ABCD$
         to create rectangle $A'B'C'D'$, which is similar
         to $ABCD$. Which side of $A'B'C'D'$
         corresponds to $\overline{CB}$? Which side corresponds to
         $\overline{AB}$?

   b.   Compare the lengths of each pair of
         corresponding sides. What do you notice?
         How could you get the lengths of $A'B'C'D'$ from the dimensions of $ABCD$?

Problem continues on next page →

3-10.   *Problem continued from previous page.*

c.   Could you get the dimensions of $A'B'C'D'$ by adding the same amount to each side of $ABCD$? Try this and explain what happened.

d.   Monica enlarged $ABCD$ to get a different rectangle $A''B''C''D''$ which is similar to $ABCD$. She knows that $\overline{A''B''}$ is 20 units long. How many times larger than $ABCD$ is $A''B''C''D''$? (That is, how many "rubber bands" did she use?) And how long is $\overline{B''C''}$? Show how you know.

3-11.   In problem 3-10, you learned that you can create similar shapes by multiplying each side length by the same number. This number is called the **zoom factor**. You may have used a zoom factor before when using a copy machine. For example, if you set the zoom factor on a copier to 50%, the machine shrinks the image in half (that is, multiplies it by 0.5) but keeps the shape the same. In this course, the zoom factor will be used to describe the ratio of the new figure to the original figure.

Original

Enlarged

What zoom factor was used to enlarge the puppy shown at right?

3-12.   Casey decided to enlarge her favorite letter: C, of course! Your team is going to help her out. Have each member of your team choose a different zoom factor below. Then on graph paper, enlarge (or reduce) the block "C" at right by your zoom factor.

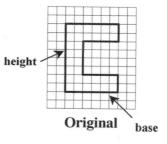

height

Original   base

a.   3   b.   2

c.   1   d. $\frac{1}{2}$

3-13.   Look at the different "C's" that were created in problem 3-12.

a.   What happened when the zoom factor was 1?

b.   When two shapes are the same shape <u>and</u> the same size (that is, the zoom factor is 1), they are called **congruent**. Compare the shapes below with tracing paper and determine which shapes are congruent.

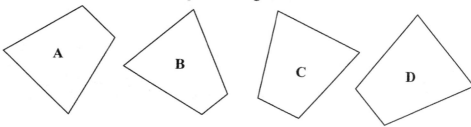

A   B   C   D

3-14.   EQUAL RATIOS OF SIMILARITY

Casey wants to learn more about her enlarged "C"s. Return to your work from problem 3-12.

a.   Since the zoom factor multiplies each part of the original shape, then the **ratio** of the widths must equal the ratio of the lengths.

Casey decided to show these ratios in the diagram at right. Verify that her ratios are equal.

b.   When looking at Casey's work, her brother wrote the equation $\frac{8}{6} = \frac{24}{18}$. Are his ratios, in fact, equal? And how could he show his work on his diagram? Copy his diagram at right and add arrows to show what sides Casey's brother compared.

c.   She has decided to create an enlarged "C" for the door of her bedroom. To fit, it needs to be 20 units tall. If x is the width of this "C", write and solve an equation to find out how wide the "C" on Casey's door must be. Be ready to share your equation and solution with the class.

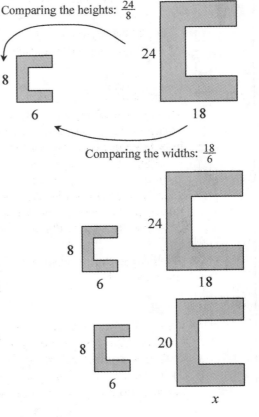

Comparing the heights: $\frac{24}{8}$

Comparing the widths: $\frac{18}{6}$

3-15.   Use your observations about ratios between similar figures to answer the following questions.

a.   Are the triangles above similar? How do you know?

b.   If the pentagons at right are similar, what are the values of x and y?

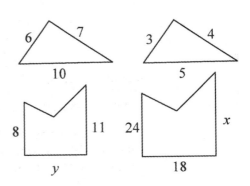

3-16.   In a new entry of your Learning Log, explain what you know about the ratio of similar figures. If you know the dimensions of one shape, how can you figure out the dimensions of another shape that is similar to it? Title this entry, "Common Ratios of Similar Figures" and include today's date.

METHODS AND **M**EANINGS

MATH NOTES

Ratio of Similarity and Zoom Factor

The term "ratio" was introduced in Chapter 1 in the context of probability. But ratios are very important when comparing two similar figures. Review what you know about ratios below.

A comparison of two quantities (numbers or measures) is called a **ratio**. A ratio can be written as:

$$a{:}b \quad \text{or} \quad \tfrac{a}{b} \quad \text{or} \quad \text{"a to b"}$$

Each ratio has a numeric value that can be expressed as a fraction or a decimal. For the two similar right triangles below, the ratio of the small triangle's hypotenuse to the large triangle's hypotenuse is $\frac{6}{10}$ or $\frac{3}{5}$. This means that for every three units of length in the small triangle's hypotenuse, there are five units of length in the large triangle's hypotenuse.

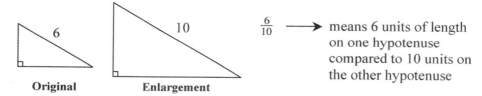

Original	**Enlargement**

$\frac{6}{10} \longrightarrow$ means 6 units of length on one hypotenuse compared to 10 units on the other hypotenuse

The ratio between any pair of corresponding sides in similar figures is called the **ratio of similarity**.

When a figure is enlarged or reduced, each side is multiplied (or divided) by the same number. While there are many names for this number, this text will refer to this number as the **zoom factor**. To help indicate if the figure was enlarged or reduced, the zoom factor is written as the ratio of the new figure to the original figure. For the two triangles above, the zoom factor is $\frac{10}{6}$ or $\frac{5}{3}$.

3-17.   Enlarge the shape at right on graph paper using a zoom factor of 4.

3-18.   The ratios Casey wrote from the table in part (a) of problem 3-14 are **common ratios between corresponding sides** of the two shapes. That is, they are ratios between the matching sides of two shapes.

   a.   Look at the two similar shapes below. Which sides correspond? Write common ratios with the names of sides and lengths, just like Bernhard did.

   b.   Find the hypotenuse of each triangle above. Is the ratio of the hypotenuses equal the ratios you found in part (a)?

3-19.   The temperature in San Antonio, Texas is currently 77°F and is increasing by 3° per hour. The current temperature in Bombay, India is 92°F and the temperature is dropping by 2° per hour. When will it be as hot in San Antonio as it is in Bombay? What will the temperature be?

3-20.   **Examine** the relationships in the diagram at right. Then solve for x and y, if possible.

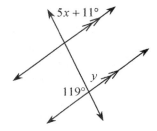

3-21.   Read the following statements and decide if, when combined, they present a *convincing* argument. You may need to refer back to your Shape Toolkit as you consider the following statements and decide if the conclusion is correct. Be sure to **justify** your reasoning.

   Fact #1: A square has four sides of equal length.

   Fact #2: A square is a rectangle because it has four right angles.

   Fact #3: A rhombus also has four sides of equal length

   Conclusion: Therefore, a rhombus is a rectangle.

3.1.3 How are the shapes related?

Using Ratios of Similarity

You have learned that when we enlarge or reduce a shape so that it remains similar (that is, it maintains the same shape), each of the side lengths have been multiplied by a common zoom factor. We can also set up ratios within shapes and make comparisons to other similar shapes. Today you will learn about what effect changing the size of an object has on its perimeter. You will also learn how ratios can help solve similarity problems when drawing the figures is impractical.

3-22.   **Examine** the rectangles at right.

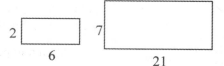

a.   Use ratios to show that these shapes are similar (figures that have the same shape, but not necessarily the same size).

b.   What other ratios could you use?

c.   Linh claims that these shapes are not similar. When she compared the heights, she wrote $\frac{2}{7}$. Then she compared the bases and got $\frac{21}{6}$. Why is Linh having trouble? Explain completely.

3-23.   Each pair of figures below is similar. Review what you have learned so far about similarity as you solve for x.

a.

b.

c.

perimeter = 60

3-24.   Casey's back at it! Now she wants you to enlarge the block "U" for her spirit flag.

a.   Copy her "U" onto graph paper.

b.   Now draw a larger "U" with a zoom factor of $\frac{3}{2} = 1.5$. What is the height of the new "U"?

c.   Find the ratio of the perimeters. That is, find $\frac{\text{Perimeter New}}{\text{Perimeter Original}}$. What do you notice?

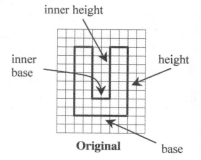

d.   Casey enlarged "U" proportionally so that it has a height of 10. What was her zoom factor? What is the base of this new "U"? **Justify** your conclusion.

144

3-25.   After enlarging his "U" in problem
3-24, Al has an idea. He drew a 60°
angle, as shown in Diagram #1 at
right. Then, he extended the sides of
the angle so that they are twice as
long, as shown in Diagram #2.
"Therefore, the new angle must have
measure 120°," he explained. Do
you agree? Discuss this with your
team and write a response to Al.

Diagram #1   **Diagram #2**

3-26.   Al noticed that the ratio of the perimeters of two similar
figures is equal to the ratio of the side lengths. *"What about
the area? Does it grow the same way?"* he wondered.

3

7

a.   Find the area and perimeter of the rectangle above.

b.   Test Al's question by enlarging the rectangle by a zoom factor of 2. Then find
the new area and perimeter.

c.   Answer Al's question: Does the perimeter double? Does the area double?
Explain what happened.

(M)ETHODS AND MEANINGS

Proportional Equations

MATH NOTES

    A **proportional equation** is one that compares two or more ratios.
Proportional equations can express comparisons between two similar objects
or compare two corresponding parts of an object.

For example, the following
equations can be written for the
similar triangles at right:

$$\frac{a}{c} = \frac{b}{d} \quad or \quad \frac{a}{b} = \frac{c}{d}.$$

3-27.   Rakisha is puzzled. She is working with the parallelogram drawn at right and wants to make it smaller instead of bigger.

a.   What should she do if she wants the sides of her new shape to be *half as long* as the original sides? What zoom factor should she use? Find the dimensions of her new shape.

b.   While drawing some other shapes, Rakisha ended up with a shape congruent to the original parallelogram. What is the common ratio between pairs of corresponding sides?

3-28.   Enlarge the shape at right on graph paper using a zoom factor of 2. Then find the perimeter and area of both shapes. What do you notice when you compare the perimeters? The areas?

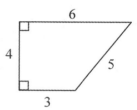

3-29.   Solve each equation below. Show all work and check your answer.

a. $\frac{14}{5} = \frac{x}{3}$ b. $\frac{10}{m} = \frac{5}{11}$ c. $\frac{t-2}{12} = \frac{7}{8}$ d. $\frac{x+1}{5} = \frac{x}{3}$

3-30.   **Examine** the graph of line $\overleftrightarrow{AB}$ at right.

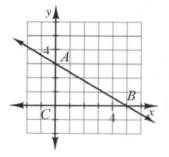

a.   Find the equation of $\overleftrightarrow{AB}$.

b.   Find the area and perimeter of $\triangle ABC$.

c.   Write an equation of the line through A that is perpendicular to $\overleftrightarrow{AB}$.

3-31.   **Examine** the diagram at right. Name the geometric relationships of the angles below.

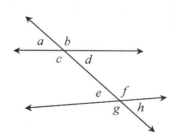

a. d and e b. e and h

c. a and e d. c and d

3.1.4 How can I use equivalent ratios?

Applications and Notation

Now that you have a good understanding of how to use ratios in similar figures to solve problems, how can you extend these ideas to situations outside the classroom? You will start by considering a situation for which we want to find the length of something that would be difficult to physically measure.

3-32. GEORGE WASHINGTON'S NOSE

On her way to visit Horace Mann University, Casey stopped by Mount Rushmore in South Dakota. The park ranger gave a talk that described the history of the monument and provided some interesting facts. Casey could not believe that the carving of George Washington's face is 60 feet tall from his chin to the top of his head!

However, when a tourist asked about the length of Washington's nose, the ranger was stumped! Casey came to her rescue by measuring, calculating and getting an answer. How did Casey get her answer?

Your task: Figure out the length of George Washington's nose on the monument. Work with your study team to come up with a **strategy**. Show all measurements and calculations on your paper with clear labels so anyone could understand your work.

Discussion Points

What is this question asking you to find?

How can you use similarity to solve this problem?

Is there something in this room that you can use to compare to the monument?

What parts do you need to compare?

Do you have any math tools that can help you gather information?

3-33. Solving problem 3-32, you may have written a proportional equation like the one below. When solving proportional situations, is very important that parts be labeled to help you follow your work.

$$\frac{Length\ of\ George's\ Nose}{Length\ of\ George's\ Head} = \frac{Length\ of\ Student's\ Nose}{Length\ of\ Student's\ Head}$$

Likewise, when working with geometric shapes such as the similar triangles below, it is easier to explain which sides you are comparing by using notation that everyone understands.

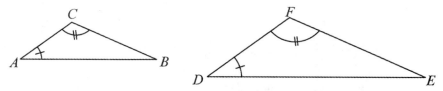

a. One possible proportional equation for these triangles is $\frac{AC}{AB} = \frac{DF}{DE}$. Write at least three more proportional equations based on the similar triangles above.

b. Jeb noticed that $m\angle A = m\angle D$ and $m\angle C = m\angle F$. But what about $m\angle B$ and $m\angle E$? Do these angles have the same measure? Or is there not enough information? **Justify** your conclusions.

3-34. The two triangles at right are similar. Read the Math Notes box for this lesson to learn about how to write a statement to show that two shapes are similar.

Then **examine** the two triangles below. Which of the following statements are correctly written and which are not? Note that more than one statement may be correct. Discuss your answers with your team.

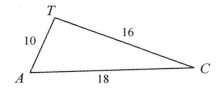

a. $\triangle DOG \sim \triangle CAT$

b. $\triangle DOG \sim \triangle CTA$

c. $\triangle OGD \sim \triangle ATC$

d. $\triangle DGO \sim \triangle CAT$

3-35. Find the value of the variable in each pair of similar figures below. You may want to set up tables to help you write equations.

a. *ABCD* ~ *JKLM*

b. △*NOP* ~ △*XYZ*

c. △*GHI* ~ △*PQR*

d. △*ABC* ~ △*XYZ*

3-36. Rochida was given the diagram at right and told that the two triangles are similar.

a. Rochida knows that to be similar, all corresponding angles must be equal. Are all three sets of angles equal? How can you tell?

b. Rochida decides to redraw the shape as two separate triangles, as shown at right. Write a proportional equation using the corresponding sides.

c. Solve the equation for *x*. How long is $\overline{AB}$? How long is $\overline{AC}$?

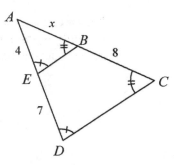

3-37.   Write a Learning Log entry describing the different ways you can compare two similar objects or quantities with equivalent ratios. Title this entry "Comparing With Ratios" and include today's date.

METHODS AND **M**EANINGS

Writing a Similarity Statement

To represent the fact that two shapes are **similar**, use the symbol "~". For example, if the triangles below are similar, this can be stated as $\triangle ABC \sim \triangle DEF$. The order of the letters in the name of each triangle determines which sides and angles correspond. For example, in the statement $\triangle ABC \sim \triangle DEF$, you can determine that angle A corresponds to angle D and that side $\overline{BC}$ corresponds to side $\overline{EF}$.

3-38.   Solve for the missing lengths in the sets of similar figures below. You may want to set up tables to help you write equations.

a. $\triangle ABC \sim \triangle OPQ$

b. $EFGHI \sim STUVW$

c. $JKLM \sim WXYZ$

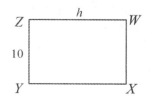

Geometry Connections

3-39.   In recent lessons, you have learned that similar triangles have equal corresponding angles. Is it possible to have equal corresponding angles when the triangles do not appear to match? What if you are not given all three angle measures? Consider the two cases below.

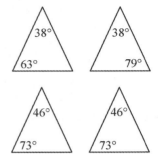

a.   Find the measure of the third angle in the first pair of triangles at right. Compare the two triangles. What do you notice?

b.   **Examine** the second pair of triangles at right. Without calculating, do you know that the unmarked angles must be equal? Why or why not?

3-40.   Sandy has a square, equilateral triangle, rhombus, and regular hexagon in her Shape Bucket, while Robert has a scalene triangle, kite, isosceles trapezoid, non-special quadrilateral, and obtuse isosceles triangle in his. Sandy will randomly select a shape from her Shape Bucket, while Robert will randomly select a shape from his.

a.   Who has a greater probability of selecting a quadrilateral? **Justify** your conclusion.

b.   Who has a greater probability of selecting an equilateral shape? **Justify** your conclusion.

c.   What is more likely to happen: Sandy selecting a shape with at least two sides that are parallel or Robert selecting a shape with at least two sides that are equal?

3-41.   Frank and Alice are penguins. At birth, Frank's beak was 1.95 inches long, while Alice's was 1.50 inches long. If Frank's beak grows by 0.25 inches per year and Alice's grows by 0.40 inches per year, how old will they be when their beaks are the same length?

3-42.   Plot *ABCDE* formed with the points $A(-3, -2)$, $B(5, -2)$, $C(5, 3)$, $D(1, 6)$, and $E(-3, 3)$ onto graph paper.

a.   Use the method from problem 3-2 to enlarge it from the origin by a factor of 2. Label this new shape $A'B'C'D'E'$.

b.   Find the area and the perimeter of both figures.

3.2.1 What information do I need?

Conditions for Triangle Similarity

Now that you know what similar shapes have in common, you are ready to turn to a related question: How much information do I need to know that two triangles are similar? As you work through today's lesson, remember that similar polygons have corresponding angles that are congruent and corresponding sides that are proportional.

3-43.   ARE THEY SIMILAR?

Erica thinks the triangles below might be similar. However, she knows not to trust the way figures look in a diagram, so she asks for your help.

a.   If two shapes are similar, what must be true about their angles and sides?

b.   Obtain the Lesson 3.2.1 Resource Page from your teacher. Measure the angles and sides of Erica's triangles and help her decide if the triangles are similar or not.

3-44. **HOW MUCH IS ENOUGH?**

Jovan is tired of measuring all the angles and sides to determine if
two triangles are similar. "There must be an easier way," he
thinks. "What if I know that all of the side lengths have a
common ratio? Does that mean that the triangles are similar?"

a.   Before experimenting, make a prediction. Do you think that the triangles have
to be similar if the pairs of corresponding sides share a common ratio?

b.   Experiment with Jovan's idea. To do this, use a dynamic geometry tool to test
triangles with proportional side lengths. If you do not have access to a
dynamic tool, cut straws or strands of linguini into the lengths below and create
two triangles. Can you create two triangles that are not similar? **Investigate**,
sketch your shapes, and write down your conclusion.

Triangle #1: side lengths 3, 5, and 6

Triangle #2: side lengths 6, 10, and 12

c.   Jovan then asks, "Is it enough to know that each pair of corresponding angles
are congruent? Does that mean the triangles are similar?" Again use a
dynamic geometry tool to test triangles with equal corresponding angles or use
linguini with protractors to create three angles that form a triangle. Can you
create two triangles with the same three angle measures that are not similar?
Investigate, sketch your shapes, and write down your conclusion.

3-45. Scott is looking at the set of shapes at right.
He thinks that $\triangle EFG \sim \triangle HIJ$ but he is
not sure that the shapes are drawn to scale.

a.   Are the corresponding angles
equal? Convince Scott that
these triangles are similar.

b.   How many pairs of angles need to be
congruent to be sure that triangles are
similar?

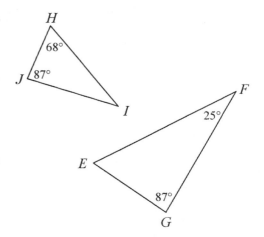

3-46.   Based on your conclusions from problems 3-44 and 3-45, decide if each pair of triangles below is similar. Explain your **reasoning**.

a.

b.

c.

d.

3-47.   Read the Math Notes box for this lesson, which introduces new names for the observations you made in problems 3-44 and 3-45. Then write a Learning Log entry about what you learned today. Be sure to address the question: *how much information do I need about a pair of triangles in order to be sure that they are similar?* Title this entry "AA ~ and SSS ~" and include today's date.

☉ETHODS AND MEANINGS

Conditions for Triangle Similarity

For two shapes to be similar, corresponding angles must have equal measure and corresponding sides must be proportional.

However, if you are testing for similarity between two triangles, then it is sufficient to know that all three corresponding side lengths share a common ratio.

This guarantees similarity and is referred to as the **SSS Triangle Similarity Conjecture** (which can be abbreviated as "SSS Similarity" or "SSS ~" for short.)

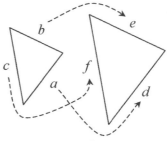

Also, for two triangles it is sufficient to know that two pairs of corresponding angles have equal measures because then the third pair of angles must have equal measure.

SSS ~ : If $\frac{a}{d} = \frac{b}{e} = \frac{c}{f}$, then the triangles are similar.

This is known as the **AA Triangle Similarity Conjecture** (which can be abbreviated as "AA Similarity" or "AA ~" for short).

AA ~ : If 2 pairs of angles have equal measure, then the triangles are similar.

Review & Preview

3-48.   Assume that all trees are green.

a.   Does this statement mean that an oak tree must be green? Explain why or why not.

b.   Does this statement mean that anything green must be a tree? Explain why or why not.

c.   Are the statements "All trees are green" and "All green things are trees" saying the same thing? Explain why or why not.

3-49.   Decide if each pair of triangles below is similar. If the triangles are similar, **justify** your conclusion by stating the similarity conjecture you used. If the triangles are not similar, explain how you know.

a.

b.

Equilateral Triangles

c.

d.

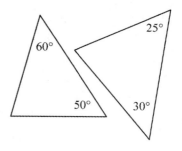

3-50.   Consider the following arrow diagram:

Lines are parallel → *alternate interior angles are equal.*

a.   Write this arrow diagram as a conditional ("If…, then…") statement.

b.   Write a similar conditional statement about corresponding angles, then write it as an arrow diagram.

3-51.   Find the area and perimeter of the shape at right. Show all work.

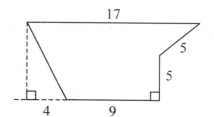

3-52.   Assume that each pair of figures below is similar. Write a similarity statement to illustrate which parts of each shape correspond. Remember: letter order is important!

a. $ABCD \sim ?$

b. $RIGHT \sim ?$

c.   △____ ~△____

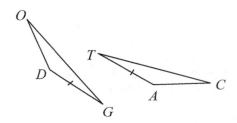

3.2.2 How can I organize my information?

Creating a Flowchart

In Lesson 3.2.1, you developed the AA ~ and SSS ~ conjectures to help confirm that triangles are similar. Today you will continue working with similarity and will learn how to use flowcharts to organize your **reasoning**.

3-53.   **Examine** the triangles at right.

a.   Are these triangles similar? Use full sentences to explain your **reasoning**.

b.   Julio decided to use a diagram (called a **flowchart**) to explain his reasoning.

Compare your explanation to Julio's flowchart. Did Julio use the same **reasoning** you used?

JULIO'S FLOWCHART

3-54. Besides showing your **reasoning**, a flowchart can be used to organize your work as you determine whether or not triangles are similar.

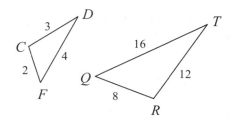

a. Are these triangles similar? Which triangle similarity conjecture (see the Math Notes box from Lesson 3.2.1) did you use?

b. What facts must you know to use the triangle similarity conjecture you chose? Julio started to list the facts in a flowchart at right. Copy them on your paper and complete the third oval.

Facts:

c. Once you have the needed facts in place, you can conclude that you have similar triangles. Add to your flowchart by making an oval and filling in your conclusion.

Conclusion:

d. Finally, draw arrows to show the flow of the facts that lead to your conclusion and record the similarity conjecture you used, following Julio's example from problem 3-53.

3-55. Now **examine** the triangles at right.

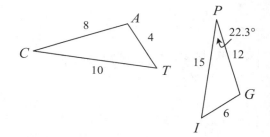

a. Are these triangles similar? **Justify** your conclusion using a flowchart.

b. What is $m\angle C$? How do you know?

3-56. Lindsay was solving a math problem and drew the flowchart below:

a. Draw and label two triangles that could represent Lindsay's problem. What question did the problem ask her? How can you tell?

b. Lindsay's teammate was working on the same problem and made a mistake in his flowchart:

How is this flowchart different from Lindsay's? Why is this the wrong way to explain the **reasoning** in Lindsay's problem?

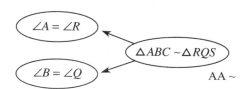

3-57. Ramon is **examining** the triangles at right. He suspects they may be similar by SSS ~.

a. Why is SSS ~ the best conjecture to test for these triangles?

b. Set up ovals for the facts you need to know to show that the triangles are similar. Complete any necessary calculations and fill in the ovals.

c. Are the triangles similar? If so, complete your flowchart using an appropriate similarity statement. If not, explain how you know.

3-58. In your Learning Log, explain how to set up a flowchart. For example, how do you know how many ovals you should use? How do you know what to put inside the ovals? Provide an example. Label this entry "Using Flowcharts" and include today's date.

(M)ETHODS AND MEANINGS

Congruent Shapes

MATH NOTES

If two figures have the same shape and are the same size, they are **congruent**. Since the figures must have the same shape, they must be similar.

Two figures are congruent if they meet both of the following conditions:

- the two figures are similar, and

- their side lengths have a common ratio of 1.

3-59.   Solve for the missing lengths in the sets of similar figures below. You may want to set up tables to help you write equations.

a.   *ABCD ~ JKLM*

b.   △*NOP ~*△*XYZ*

3-60.   **Examine** each diagram below. Which diagrams are possible? Which are impossible? **Justify** each conclusion.

a.

b.

c.

3-61.   Decide which transformations were used on each pair of shapes below. Note that there may have been more than one transformation.

a.

b.

c.

d.

3-62.   Determine whether or not the
         reasoning in the flowchart at
         right is correct. If it is wrong,
         redo the flowchart to make it
         correct.

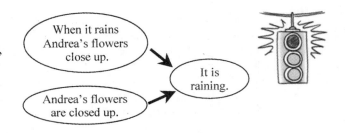

When it rains
Andrea's flowers
close up.

It is
raining.

Andrea's flowers
are closed up.

3-63.   Sketch each triangle if possible. If not possible, explain why not.

         a.   Right isosceles triangles   b.   Right obtuse triangles

         c.   Scalene equilateral triangles   d.   Acute scalene triangles

3.2.3   How can I use equivalent ratios?

Triangle Similarity and Congruence

By looking at side ratios and at angles, you are now able to determine whether two figures are
similar. But how can you tell if two shapes are the same shape *and* the same size? In this
lesson you will **examine** properties that guarantee that shapes are exact replicas of one another.

3-64.   Decide if each pair of triangles below is similar. Use a flowchart to organize your
         facts and conclusion for each pair of triangles.

a.

b.

c.

d.

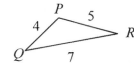

3-65.   For the diagrams in problem 3-64, find the lengths of the sides listed below, if possible. If it is not possible, explain why not.

a. $\overline{BC}$ b. $\overline{AC}$ c. $\overline{VT}$ d. $\overline{TN}$

3-66.   **Examine** the triangles at right.

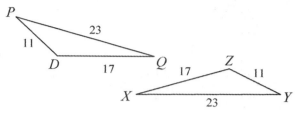

a.   Are these triangles similar? How do you know? Use a flowchart to organize your explanation.

b.   Kamraan says, "These triangles aren't just similar—they're congruent!" Is Kamraan correct? What special value in your flowchart indicates that the triangles are congruent?

c.   Write a conjecture (in "If…, then…" form) that explains how you know when two shapes are congruent.

3-67.   Flowcharts can also be used to represent real-life situations. For example, yesterday Joe found out that three people in his family (including Joe) wanted to see a movie, so he went to the theater and bought three tickets. Unfortunately, while he was gone, three more family members decided to go. When everyone arrived at the theater, Joe did not have enough tickets.

Joe sat down later that night and tried to create a flowchart to describe what had happened. Here are the three possibilities he came up with:

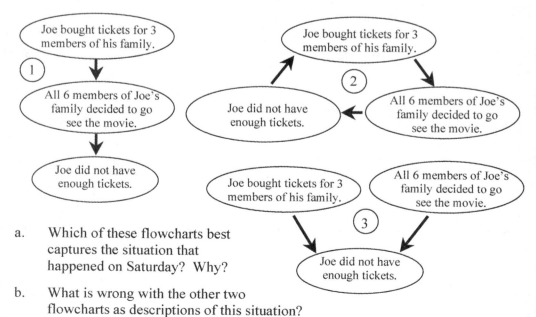

a.   Which of these flowcharts best captures the situation that happened on Saturday? Why?

b.   What is wrong with the other two flowcharts as descriptions of this situation?

METHODS AND MEANINGS

MATH NOTES

Solving a Quadratic Equation

In a previous course, you learned how to solve **quadratic equations** (equations that can be written in the form $ax^2 + bx + c = 0$). Review two methods for solving quadratic equations below.

Some quadratic equations can be solved by **factoring** and using the **Zero Product Property**. For example, because $x^2 - 3x - 10 = (x - 5)(x + 2)$, the quadratic equation $x^2 - 3x - 10 = 0$ can be rewritten as $(x - 5)(x + 2) = 0$. The Zero Product Property states that if $ab = 0$, then $a = 0$ or $b = 0$. So, if $(x - 5)(x + 2) = 0$, then $x - 5 = 0$ or $x + 2 = 0$. Therefore, $x = 5$ or $x = -2$.

Another method for solving quadratic equations is the **Quadratic Formula.** This method is particularly helpful for solving quadratic equations that are difficult or impossible to factor. Before using the Quadratic Formula, the quadratic equation you want to solve must be in standard form, that is, written as $ax^2 + bx + c = 0$.

In this form, a is the coefficient of the x^2 term, b is the coefficient of the x term, and c is the constant term. The Quadratic Formula states:

$$x = \frac{-b \pm \sqrt{b^2 - 4ac}}{2a}$$

This formula gives two possible answers due to the "$\pm$" symbol. This symbol (read as "plus or minus") is shorthand notation that tells us to calculate the formula twice: once using addition and once using subtraction. Therefore, every Quadratic Formula problem must be simplified twice to give:

$$x = \frac{-b + \sqrt{b^2 - 4ac}}{2a} \quad \text{or} \quad x = \frac{-b - \sqrt{b^2 - 4ac}}{2a}$$

To solve $x^2 - 3x - 10 = 0$ using the Quadratic Formula, substitute $a = 1$, $b = -3$, and $c = -10$ into the formula, as shown below.

$$x = \frac{-(-3) \pm \sqrt{(-3)^2 - 4(1)(-10)}}{2(1)} \rightarrow \frac{3 \pm \sqrt{49}}{2} \rightarrow \frac{3 \pm 7}{2} \rightarrow x = 5 \text{ or } x = -2$$

3-68.   On graph paper, graph the parabola $y = 2x^2 - 5x - 3$.

    a.   What are the roots (*x*-intercepts) of the parabola?

    b.   Read the Math Notes box for this lesson. Then solve the equation $2x^2 - 5x - 3 = 0$ algebraically. Did you solutions match your roots from part (a)?

3-69.   On graph paper, plot *ABCD* if $A(0, 3)$, $B(2, 5)$, $C(6, 3)$, and $D(4, 1)$.

    a.   Rotate *ABCD* 90° clockwise (↻) about the origin to form $A'B'C'D'$. Name the coordinates of B'.

    b.   Translate $A'B'C'D'$ up 8 units and left 7 units to form $A''B''C''D''$. Name the coordinates of C''.

    c.   After rotating *ABCD* 180° to form $A'''B'''C'''D'''$, Arah noticed that $A'''B'''C'''D'''$ position and orientation was the same as *ABCD*. What was the point of rotation? How did you find it?

3-70.   Use the relationships in each diagram below to solve for *x*. **Justify** your solution by stating which geometry relationships you used.

    a.

    b.

    c.
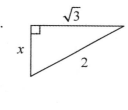

3-71.   Solve for the missing lengths in the sets of similar figures below. Show all work.

    a. $\triangle GHI \sim \triangle PQR$

    b. $\triangle ABC \sim \triangle XYZ$

3-72. Explain how you know that the shapes at right are similar.

9 un

4 un

Perimeter = 26 un.

Area = 36 sq. un.

3.2.4 What information do I need?

More Conditions for Triangle Similarity

So far, you have worked with two methods for determining that triangles are similar: the AA ~ and the SSS ~ Conjectures. Are these the only ways to determine if two triangles are similar? Today you will **investigate** similar triangles and complete your list of triangle similarity conjectures.

Keep the following questions in mind as you work together today:

How much information do you need?

Are the triangles similar? How can you tell?

Can I find a triangle with this information that is not similar?

3-73. Robel's team is using the SSS ~ Conjecture to show that two triangles are similar. "This is too much work," Robel says. "When we're using the AA ~ Conjecture, we only need to look at two angles. Let's just calculate the ratios for *two* pairs of corresponding sides to determine that triangles are similar."

Is SS ~ a valid similarity conjecture for triangles? That is, if two pairs of corresponding side lengths share a common ratio, must the triangles be similar?

In this problem, you will **investigate** this question using a dynamic geometry tool or another manipulative (such as linguini) provided by your teacher.

a. Robel has a triangle with side lengths 4 cm and 5 cm. If your triangle has two sides that share a common ratio with Robel's, does your triangle have to be similar to his? Use a dynamic geometry tool or straws or linguini to **investigate** this question.

Problem continues on next page →

3-73.   *Problem continued from previous page.*

    b.   Kashi asks, "What if the angles between the two sides have the same measure? Would that be enough to know the triangles are similar?" Use the dynamic geometry tool or straws and linguini to answer Kashi's question.

    c.   Kashi calls this the "SAS ~ Conjecture," placing the "A" between the two "S"s because the angle is *between* the two sides. He knows it works for Robel's triangle, but does it work on all other triangles? Test this method on a variety of triangles using the dynamic geometry tool or straws and linguini.

3-74.   What other triangle similarity conjectures involving sides and angles might there be? List the names of every other possible triangle similarity conjecture you can think of that involves sides and angles.

3-75.   Cori's team put "SSA ~" on their list of possible triangle similarity conjectures. Use a dynamic geometry tool or straws or linguini to **investigate** whether SSA ~ is a valid triangle similarity conjecture. If a triangle has two sides sharing a common ratio with Robel's, and has the same angle "outside" these sides as Robel's, must it be similar to Robel's triangle? If you determine SSA ~ is not a valid similarity conjecture, cross it off your list!

3-76.   Betsy's team came up with a similarity conjecture they call "AAS ~," but Betsy thinks they should cross it off their list. Betsy says, "This similarity conjecture has extra, unnecessary information. There's no point in having it on our list."

    a.   What is Betsy talking about? Why does the AAS ~ method contain more information than you need?

    b.   Go through your list of possible triangle similarity conjectures, crossing off all the invalid ones and all the ones that contain unnecessary information.

    c.   How many valid triangle similarity conjectures (without extra information) are there? List them.

3-77.   Reflect on what you have learned today. In your Learning Log, write down the triangle similarity conjectures that help to determine if triangles are similar. You can write these conjectures as conditional statements (in "If..., then..." form) or as arrow diagrams. Title this entry "Triangle Similarity Conjectures" and include today's date.

METHODS AND MEANINGS

MATH NOTES

Writing a Flowchart

A **flowchart** helps to organize facts and indicate which facts lead to a conclusion. The bubbles contain facts, while the arrows point to a conclusion that can be made from a fact or multiple facts.

For example, in the flowchart at right, two independent (unconnected) facts are stated: *"All squares are rectangles"* and *"ABCD is a square."* However, these facts lead to the conclusion that *ABCD* must be a rectangle. Note that the arrows point toward the conclusion.

3-78.   If possible, draw a triangle that has exactly the following number of lines of symmetry. Then name the kind of triangle drawn.

a.   0   b.   1   c.   2   d.   3

3-79.   Do two lines always intersect? Consider this as you answer the questions below.

a.   Write a system of linear equations that does not have a solution. Write each equation in your system in **slope-intercept form** ($y = mx + b$). Graph your system on graph paper and explain why it does not have a solution.

b.   How can you tell algebraically that a system of linear equations has no solution? Solve your system of equations from part (a) algebraically and demonstrate how you know that the system has no solution.

3-80.   Determine which of the following pairs of triangles are similar. Explain your work.

a.

b.

c.

3-81.   The dashed line at right represents the line of symmetry of the shaded figure. Find the area and perimeter of the shaded region. Show all work.

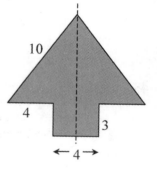

3-82.   **Examine** the diagrams below. For each one, write and solve an equation to find x. Show all work.

a.

b.

c.

d.

3.2.5 Are the triangles similar?

Determining Similarity

You now have a complete list of the three Triangles Similarity Conjectures (AA ~, SSS ~, and SAS ~) that can be used to verify that two triangles are similar. Today you will continue to practice applying these conjectures and using flowcharts to organize your **reasoning**.

3-83.   Lynn wants to show that the triangles at right are similar.

    a.   What similarity conjecture should Lynn use?

    b.   Make a flow chart showing that these triangles are similar.

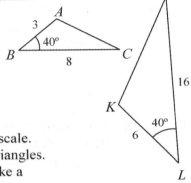

3-84.   Below are six triangles, none of which is drawn to scale. Among the six triangles are three pairs of similar triangles. Identify the similar triangles, then for each pair make a flowchart **justifying** the similarity.

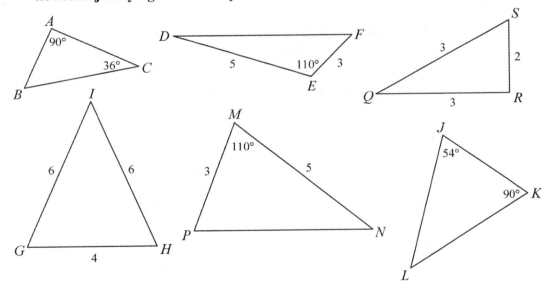

3-85.   Revisit the similar triangles from problem 3-84.

    a.   Which pair of triangles are congruent? How do you know?

    b.   Suppose that in problem 3-84, $AB = 3$ cm, $AC = 4$ cm, and $KJ = 12$ cm. Find all the other side lengths in $\triangle ABC$ and $\triangle JKL$.

3-86.   **Examine** the triangles at right.

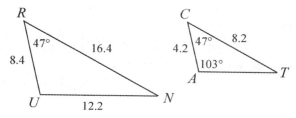

a.   Are these triangles similar? If so, make a flowchart **justifying** their similarity.

b.   Charles has $\triangle CAT \sim \triangle RUN$ as the conclusion of his flowchart. Leesa has $\triangle NRU \sim \triangle TCA$ as her conclusion. Who is correct? Why?

c.   Are $\triangle CAT$ and $\triangle RUN$ congruent? Explain how you know.

d.   Find all the missing side lengths and all the angle measures of $\triangle CAT$ and $\triangle RUN$.

3-87.   THE FAMILY FORTUNE, Part Two

In Lesson 1.1.4, you had to convince city officials that you were a relative of Molly "Ol' Granny" Marston, who had just passed away leaving a sizable inheritance. Below is the evidence you had available:

Family Portrait — a photo showing three young children. On the back you see the date 1968.

Newspaper Clipping — from 1972 titled "Triplets Make Music History." The first sentence catches your eye: "Jake, Judy, and Jeremiah Marston, all eight years old, were the first triplets ever to perform a six-handed piano piece at Carnegie Hall."

Jake Marston's Birth Certificate — showing that Jake was born in 1964, and identifying his parents as Phillip and Molly Marston.

Your Learner's Permit — signed by your father, Jeremiah Marston.

Wilbert Marston's Passport — issued when Wilbert was fifteen.

As their answer to this problem, one team wrote the following argument for the city officials:

> *The birth certificate shows that Jake Marston was Molly Marston's son. The newspaper clipping shows that Jeremiah Marston was Jake Marston's brother. Therefore, Jeremiah Marston was Molly Marston's son. The learner's permit shows that Jeremiah Marston is my father. Therefore, I am Molly Marston's grandchild.*

Your task: Make a flowchart showing the **reasoning** in this team's argument. This flowchart will have more levels than the ones you have made in the past, because certain conclusions will be used as facts to support other conclusions. So plan carefully before you start to draw your chart.

MINOR METHODS AND MEANINGS

Complete Conditions for Triangle Similarity

There are exactly three valid, non-redundant triangle similarity conjectures that use only sides and angles. (A conjecture is "redundant" if it includes more information than is necessary to establish triangle similarity.) They are abbreviated as: SSS ~, AA ~, and SAS ~. In the SAS ~ Conjecture, the "A" is placed between the two "S"s to indicate that the angle must be *between* the two sides used.

For example, $\triangle RUN$ and $\triangle CAT$ below are similar by SAS ~. $\frac{RU}{CA} = 2$ and $\frac{UN}{AT} = 2$, so two pairs of corresponding side lengths share a common ratio. The measure of the angle between $\overline{RU}$ and $\overline{UN}$, $\angle U$,

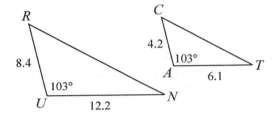

equals the measure of the angle between $\overline{CA}$ and $\overline{AT}$, $\angle A$, so the conditions for SAS ~ are met.

3-88. Sketch each triangle described below, if possible. If not possible, explain why it is not possible.

a. Equilateral obtuse triangle

b. Right scalene triangle

c. Obtuse isosceles triangle

d. Acute right triangle

3-89.   Determine which similarity conjectures (AA ~, SSS ~, or SAS ~) could be used to establish that the following pairs of triangles are similar. List as many as you can.

a.

b.
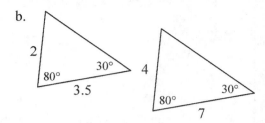

c.

3-90.   Solve each equation to find the value of x. Leave your answers in decimal form accurate to the thousandths place.

a. $\frac{3.2}{x} = \frac{7.5}{x^2}$

b. $4(x-2)+3(-x+4)=-2(x-3)$

c. $2x^2 + 7x - 15 = 0$

d. $3x^2 - 2x = -1$

3-91.   On graph paper, sketch a rectangle with side lengths of 15 units and 9 units. Shrink the rectangle by a zoom factor of $\frac{1}{3}$. Make a table showing the area and perimeter of both rectangles.

3-92.   Susan lives 20 miles northeast of Matt. Simone lives 15 miles dues south of Susan. If Matt lives due west of Simone, approximately how many miles does he live from Simone? Draw a diagram and show all work.

3.2.6 What can I do with similar triangles?

Applying Similarity

In previous lessons, you have learned methods for finding similar triangles. Once you find triangles are similar, how can that help you? Today you will apply similar triangles to analyze situations and solve new applications. As you work on today's problems, ask the following questions in your team:

What is the relationship?

Are any triangles similar? What similarity conjecture can we use?

3-93. YOU ARE GETTING SLEEPY…

Legend has it that if you stare into a person's eyes in a special way, you can hypnotize them into squawking like a chicken. Here's how it works.

Place a mirror on the floor. Your victim has to stand exactly 200 cm away from the mirror and stare into it. The only tricky part is that you need to figure out where you have to stand so that when you stare into the mirror, you are also staring into your victim's eyes.

If your calculations are correct and you stand at the *exact* distance, your victim will squawk like a chicken!

a. Choose a member of your team to hypnotize. Before heading to the mirror, first analyze this situation. Draw a diagram showing you and your victim standing on opposite sides of a mirror. Measure the heights of both yourself and your victim (heights to the eyes, of course), and label all the lengths you can on the diagram. (Remember: your victim will need to stand 200 cm from the mirror.)

b. Are there similar triangles in your diagram? **Justify** your conclusion. (Hint: Remember what you know about how light reflects off mirrors.) Then calculate how far you will need to stand from the mirror to hypnotize your victim.

c. Now for the moment of truth! Have your teammate stand 200 cm away from the mirror, while you stand at your calculated distance from the mirror. Do you make eye contact? If not, check your measurements and calculations and try again.

3-94.   LESSONS FROM ABROAD

Latoya was trying to take a picture of her family in front of the
Big Ben clock tower in London. However, after she
snapped the photo, she realized that the top of
her father's head exactly blocked the top
of the clock tower!

While disappointed with the picture,
Latoya thought she might be able to
estimate the height of the tower
using her math knowledge. Since
Latoya took the picture while
kneeling, the camera was 2 feet
above the ground. The camera was
also 12 feet from her 6-foot tall father, and he was standing about 930 feet from the
base of the tower.

a.   Sketch the diagram above on your paper and locate as many triangles as you
can. Can you find any triangles that must be similar? If so, explain how you
know they are similar.

b.   Use the similar triangles to determine the height of the Big Ben clock tower.

3-95.   TRIANGLE CHALLENGE

Use what you know about triangles and angle relationships to answer these questions
about the diagram below. As you work, make a careful record of your **reasoning**
(including a flowchart for any similarity arguments) and be ready to share it with the
class.

a.   First challenge: Find y.

b.   Second challenge: Is $\overline{HR}$ parallel to
$\overline{AK}$? How do you know?

3-96.   Use the relationships in the diagram at right to
solve for x and y. **Justify** your solutions.

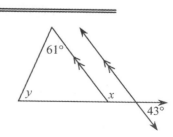

3-97.   The area of the triangle at right is 25 square units. Find the value of h. Then find the perimeter of the entire triangle. Show all work.

3-98.   **Examine** the graph of the line at right.

a.   Find the slope of this line using slope triangle A.

b.   Find the slope using slope triangle B.

c.   Without calculating, what does the slope ratio for slope triangle C have to be?

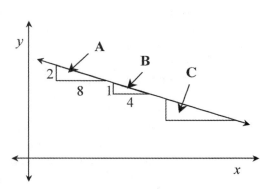

3-99.   If $ABCD \sim WXYZ$, find x, y, and z.

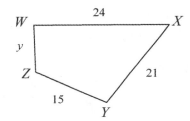

3-100.   The area of the rectangle shown at right is 40 square units. Write and solve an equation to find x. Then find the dimensions of the rectangle.

Chapter 3 Closure   What have I learned?

Reflection and Synthesis

The activities below offer you a chance to reflect on what you have learned in this chapter. As you work, look for concepts that you feel very comfortable with, ideas that you would like to learn more about, and topics you need more help with. Look for connections between ideas as well as connections with material you learned previously.

①   TEAM BRAINSTORM

With your team, brainstorm a list for each of the following two subjects. Be as detailed as you can. How long can you make your list? Challenge yourselves. Be prepared to share your team's ideas with the class.

Topics: What have you studied in this chapter? What ideas and words were important in what you learned? Remember to be as detailed as you can.

Connections: How are the topics, ideas, and words that you learned in previous courses connected to the new ideas in this chapter? Again, make your list as long as you can.

②   MAKING CONNECTIONS

The following is a list of the vocabulary used in this chapter. The words that appear in bold are new to this chapter. Make sure that you are familiar with all of these words and know what they mean. Refer to the glossary or index for any words that you do not yet understand.

AA ~	angle	conditional
congruent	conjecture	**corresponding sides**
dilation	**enlarge**	**flowchart**
hypotenuse	**logical argument**	original
perimeter	**proportional equation**	ratio
relationship	**SAS ~**	**sides**
similarity	**SSS ~**	**statement**
translate	vertex	**zoom factor**

Problem continues on next page →

②　　*Problem continued from previous page.*

Make a concept map showing all of the connections you can find among the key words and ideas listed above. To show a connection between two words, draw a line between them and explain the connection, as shown in the example below. A word can be connected to any other word as long as there is a justified connection. For each key word or idea, provide a sketch of an example.

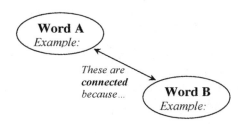

Your teacher may provide you with vocabulary cards to help you get started. If you use the cards to plan your concept map, be sure either to re-draw your concept map on your paper or to glue the vocabulary cards to a poster with all of the connections explained for others to see and understand.

While you are making your map, your team may think of related words or ideas that are not listed above. Be sure to include these ideas on your concept map.

③　　SUMMARIZING MY UNDERSTANDING

This section gives you an opportunity to show what you know about certain math topics or ideas. Your teacher will direct you how to do this. Your teacher may give you a "GO" page to work on. "GO" stands for "Graphic Organizer," a tool you can use to organize your thoughts and communicate your ideas clearly.

④　　WHAT HAVE I LEARNED?

This section will help you evaluate which types of problems you feel comfortable with and which types you need more help with. This section will appear at the end of every chapter to help you check your understanding. Even if your teacher does not assign this section, it is a good idea to try these problems and find out for yourself what you know and what you need to work on.

Solve each problem as completely as you can. The table at the end of this closure section has answers to these problems. It also tells you where you can find additional help and practice on problems like these.

CL 3-101. **Examine** the shape at right.

a.　　On graph paper, enlarge this shape by a factor of 3.

b.　　Now redraw the enlarged shape from part (a) using a zoom factor of $\frac{1}{2}$.

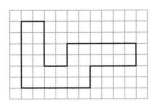

CL 3-102. Jermaine has a triangle with sides 8, 14, and 20. Sadie and Aisha both think that they have triangles that are similar to Jermaine's triangle. The sides of Sadie's triangle are 2, 3.5, and 5. The sides of Aisha's triangle are 4, 10, and 16. Decide who, if anyone, has a triangle similar to Jermaine's triangle. Be sure to explain how you know.

CL 3-103. Each pair of figures below is similar. Find the lengths of all unknown sides.

a.

b.
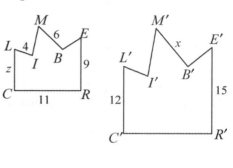

CL 3-104. Draw an example for each geometric term below. Diagrams should be clearly marked with all necessary information. You should also include a brief description of the qualities of each term.

a. supplementary angles

b. alternate interior angles

c. parallel lines

d. complementary angles

CL 3-105. Find the perimeter and area of the shape at right.

CL 3-106. Create a flowchart that represents the story:

Marcelle and Harpo live at Apt. I, 8 Logic St. Marcelle took his guitar to band practice across town and isn't back yet. Harpo hears guitar music in the hallway. He decides that someone else in the building also plays guitar.

CL 3-107. For each pair of triangles below, determine whether or not the triangles are similar. If they are similar, show your **reasoning** in a flowchart. If they are not similar, explain how you know.

a.

b.

c.

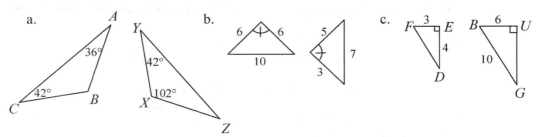

CL 3-108. Use the relationships in the diagrams below to find the values of the variables, if possible. The diagrams are not drawn to scale.

a.

b.

c.

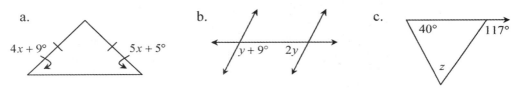

CL 3-109. Among the triangles below are pairs of similar triangles. Find the pairs of similar triangles and state the triangle similarity conjecture that you used to determine that the triangles are similar.

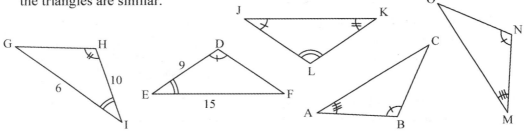

CL 3-110. Check your answers using the table at the end of this section. Which problems do you feel confident about? Which problems were hard? Have you worked on problems like these in math classes you have taken before? Use the table to make a list of topics you need help on and a list of topics you need to practice more.

HOW AM I THINKING?

This course focuses on five different **Ways of Thinking**: investigating, examining, reasoning and justifying, visualizing, and choosing a strategy/tool. These are some of the ways in which you think while trying to make sense of a concept or to solve a problem (even outside of math class). During this chapter, you have probably used each Way of Thinking multiple times without even realizing it!

This closure activity will focus on one of these Ways of Thinking: **reasoning and justifying**. Read the description of this Way of Thinking at right.

Think about the problems you have worked on in this chapter. When did you need to make sense out of multiple pieces of information? What helps you to determine what makes sense? Were there times when you made assumptions instead of relying on facts? How have you used **reasoning** in a previous math class? You may want to flip through the chapter to refresh your memory about the problems that you have worked on. Discuss any of the methods you have developed to help you **reason**.

Once your discussion is complete, think about the way you think as you answer the questions below.

a. At right is a crossword puzzle and a list of words that fit within the puzzle. Do you know where all of the words MUST go or is there more than one possible solution? Write an argument that will convince your teacher of your answer.

Reasoning and Justifying

To use logical **reasoning** means to organize facts with the purpose of making and communicating a convincing argument. As you develop this way of thinking, you will learn what pieces of information are facts and how you can combine facts to make convincing (uncontestable) arguments. You think this way when you answer questions like *"Is that always true?"* When you catch yourself defending a statement or idea, you are using logical reasoning.

IRON
SODIUM
HELIUM
OXYGEN

Problem continues on next page →

⑤　*Problem continued from previous page.*

b.　**Examine** the Venn diagram at right. What shape(s) can go in the intersection? **Justify** your statements so that they are convincing.

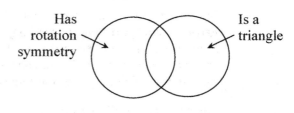

Has rotation symmetry

Is a triangle

c.　Being able to **justify** your thinking is especially important when you are working in a study team. While you may have a correct idea, if you cannot convince your team that your ideas are valid, your teammates may not agree.

Consider the diagram above. Assume that your teammates think angles *a* and *b* must be congruent. Do you agree? How can you explain your **reasoning** so that your team is convinced? Use a diagram to support your argument.

d.　What if someone else is trying to convince <u>you</u> of something? How do you think as you follow someone else's argument? Consider this as you read Lila's **reasoning** below. Then decide if you agree with her statement or not. If you agree, what helped convince you?

I know that the sum of the angles of a triangle is 180°, but I don't think that is true for a quadrilateral. If I draw a diagonal, I split my quadrilateral into two triangles. I know that the angles of each of these triangles add up to 180°. Therefore, I think the angles of the quadrilateral must add up to 360°.

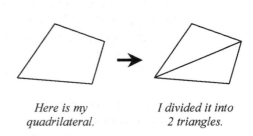

Here is my quadrilateral.

I divided it into 2 triangles.

Answers and Support for
Closure Activity #4
What Have I Learned?

Problem	Solutions	Need Help?	More Practice
CL 3-101.	a. b.	Lessons 3.1.1 and 3.1.2 Math Notes boxes, problem 3-11	Problems 3-12, 3-24, 3-26, 3-27, 3-28, 3-91
CL 3-102.	Sadie's triangle is similar to Jermaine by SSS ~ ; The ratio of the corresponding sides is $\frac{1}{4}$.	Lessons 3.2.1 and 3.2.5 Math Notes boxes	Problems 3-46, 3-24, 3-54, 3-55, 3-57, 3-66, 3-80, 3-83, 3-84, 3-86, 3-89
CL 3-103.	a. $w = 8$, $y = \frac{21}{4} = 5.25$ b. $x = 10$, $z = \frac{36}{5} = 7.2$	Lessons 3.1.2 and 3.1.3 Math Notes boxes	Problems 3-23, 3-35, 3-36, 3-38, 3-59, 3-65, 3-71, 3-99
CL 3-104.	a. $a + b = 180$ b. c. d. $a + b = 90$	Lessons 2.1.1 and 2.1.4 Math Notes boxes, Problem 2-3	Problems 2-13, 2-16, 2-17, 2-18, 2-23, 2-24, 2-25, 2-62, 2-72, 3-20, 3-31, 3-60

Problem	Solutions	Need Help?	More Practice
CL 3-105.	Perimeter = 26 un., Area = 34 un.^{2}	Lessons 1.1.3, 2.2.4, and 2.3.3 Math Notes boxes	Problems 2-66, 2-75, 2-79, 2-90, 2-120, 3-5, 3-42, 3-51, 3-81
CL 3-106.		Lesson 3.2.4 Math Notes box	Problems 3-62, 3-56, 3-67, 3-87
CL 3-107.	a. b. Not similar because corresponding sides do not have the same ratio. c.	Lessons 3.2.1 and 3.2.5 Math Notes Boxes	Problems 3-46, 3-49, 3-53, 3-54, 3-55, 3-57, 3-64, 3-66, 3-80, 3-83, 3-84, 3-89
CL 3-108.	a. $x = 4°$ b. Cannot determine because the lines are not marked parallel. c. $z = 77°$	Lessons 2.1.1 and 2.1.4 Math Notes boxes, Problem 2-3	Problems 2-13, 2-16, 2-17, 2-18, 2-23, 2-24, 2-25, 2-31, 2-32, 2-38, 2-49, 2-51, 2-62, 2-72, 2-111, 3-20, 3-31, 3-60, 3-70, 3-96
CL 3-109.	$\triangle ABC \sim \triangle MNO$, by AA ~ $\triangle EDF \sim \triangle IGH$, by SAS ~ $\triangle EDF \sim \triangle LJK$, by AA ~ $\triangle IGH \sim \triangle LJK$, by AA ~	Lessons 3.2.1 and 3.2.4 Math Notes boxes	Problems 3-46, 3-49, 3-53, 3-54, 3-55, 3-57, 3-64, 3-66, 3-80, 3-83, 3-84, 3-89

CHAPTER 4 Trigonometry and Probability

In Chapter 3, you **investigated** similarity and discovered that similar triangles have special relationships. In this chapter, you will discover that the side ratios in a right triangle can serve as a powerful mathematical tool that allows you to find missing side lengths and missing angle measures for any right triangle. You will also learn how these ratios (called trigonometric ratios) can be used in solving problems.

You will also develop additional skills in prediction as you extend your understanding of probability. You will **examine** different models to represent possibilities and to assist you in calculating probabilities.

Guiding Questions

Think about these questions throughout this chapter:

Are they similar?

What is the ratio?

What is the probability?

How can I represent it?

In this chapter, you will learn:

> how the tangent ratio is connected to the slope of a line.

> the trigonometric ratio of tangent.

> how to apply trigonometric ratios to find missing measurements in right triangles.

> how to model real world situations with right triangles and use trigonometric ratios to solve problems.

> several ways to model probability situations, such as tree diagrams and area models.

Chapter Outline

Section 4.1 Students will **investigate** the relationship between the slope of a line and the slope angle. The slope ratio will be used to find missing measurements of a right triangle and to solve real world problems.

Section 4.2 Students will continue with their study of probability by studying different models (systematic lists, tree diagrams and area models) used to represent situations involving chance.

4.1.1 What patterns can I use?

. . . .

Constant Ratios in Right Triangles

In Chapter 3, you looked for relationships and patterns among shapes such as triangles, parallelograms, and trapezoids. Now we are going to focus our attention on slope triangles, which were used in algebra to describe linear change. Are there geometric patterns within slope triangles themselves that we can use to answer other questions? In this lesson, you will look closely at slope triangles on different lines to explore their patterns.

4-1.   LEANING TOWER OF PISA

For centuries, people have marveled at the Leaning Tower of Pisa due to its slant and beauty. Ever since construction of the tower started in the 1100's, the tower has slowly tilted south and has increasingly been at risk of falling over. It is feared that if the angle of slant ever falls below 83°, the tower will collapse.

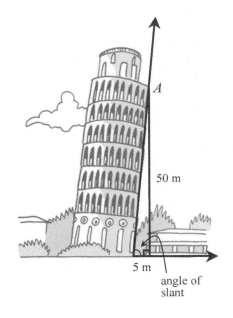

Engineers closely monitor the angle at which the tower leans. With careful measuring, they know that the point labeled A in the diagram at right is now 50 meters off the ground. Also, they determined that when a weight is dropped from point A, it lands five meters from the base of the tower, as shown in the diagram.

a.   With the measurements provided above, what can you determine?

b.   Can you determine the angle at which the tower leans? Why or why not?

c.   At the end of Section 4.1, you will know how to find the angle for this situation and many others. However, at this point, how else can you describe the "lean" of the leaning tower?

4-2.   PATTERNS IN SLOPE TRIANGLES

In order to find an angle (such as the angle at which the Leaning Tower of Pisa leans), you need to **investigate** the relationship between the angles and the sides of a right triangle. You will start by studying slope triangles. Obtain the Lesson 4.1.1 Resource Pages (two in all) from your teacher and find the graph shown below. Notice that one slope triangle has been drawn for you. **Note:** For the next several lessons angle measures will be rounded to the nearest degree.

a.   Draw three new slope triangles on the line. Each should be a different size. Label each triangle with as much information as you can, such

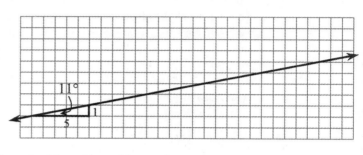

as its horizontal and vertical lengths and its angle measures.

b.   What do these triangles have in common? How are these triangles related to each other?

c.   Write the slope ratio for each triangle as a fraction, such as $\frac{\Delta y}{\Delta x}$. (Note: Δy represents the vertical change or "rise," while Δx represents the horizontal change or "run.") Then change the slope ratio into decimal form.

d.   What do you notice about the slope ratios written in fraction form? What do you notice about the decimals?

4-3.   Tara thinks she sees a pattern in these slope triangles, so she decides to make some changes in order to **investigate** whether or not the patterns remain true.

a.   She asks, "What if I draw a slope triangle on this line with $\Delta y = 6$? What would be the Δx of my triangle?" Answer her question and explain how you figured it out.

b.   "What if Δx is 40?" she wonders. "Then what is Δy?" Find Δy, and explain your **reasoning**.

c.   Tara wonders, "What if I draw a slope triangle on a different line? Can I still use the same ratio to find a missing Δx or Δy value?" Discuss this question with your team and explain to Tara what she could expect.

4-4.   CHANGING LINES

In part (c) of problem 4-3, Tara asked, "What if I draw my triangle on a different line?" With your team, **investigate** what happens to the slope ratio and slope angle when the line is different. Use the graph grids provided on your Lesson 4.1.1 Resource Pages to graph the lines described below. Use the graphs and your answers to the questions below to respond to Tara's question.

a.   On graph A, graph the line $y = \frac{2}{5}x$. What is the slope ratio for this line? What does the slope angle appear to be? Does the information about this line support or change your conclusion from part (c) of problem 4-3? Explain.

b.   On graph B, you are going to create $\angle QPR$ so that it measures 18°. First, place your protractor so that point P is the vertex. Then find 18° and mark and label a new point, R. Draw ray $\overrightarrow{PR}$ to form $\angle QPR$. Find an approximate slope ratio for this line.

c.   Graph the line $y = x + 4$ on graph C. Draw a slope triangle and label its horizontal and vertical lengths. What is $\frac{\Delta y}{\Delta x}$ (the slope ratio)? What is the slope angle?

4-5.   TESTING CONJECTURES

The students in Ms. Coyner's class are writing conjectures based on their work today. As a team, decide if you agree or disagree with each of the conjectures below. Explain your **reasoning**.

- All slope triangles have a ratio $\frac{1}{5}$.

- If the slope ratio is $\frac{1}{5}$, then the slope angle is approximately 11°.

- If the line has an 11° slope angle, then the slope ratio is approximately $\frac{1}{5}$.

- Different lines will have different slope angles and different slope ratios.

METHODS AND **M**EANINGS

Slope and Angle Notation

Slope is the ratio of the vertical distance to the horizontal distance in a slope triangle. The vertical part of the triangle is called Δy, (read "change in y"), while the horizontal part of the triangle is called Δx (read "change in x").

When we are missing a side length in a triangle, we often assign that length a variable from the English alphabet such as x, y, or z. However, sometimes we need to distinguish between an unknown side length and an unknown angle measure. With that in mind, mathematicians sometimes use Greek letters as variables for angle measurement. The most common variable for an angle is the Greek letter θ (*theta*), pronounced "THAY-tah." Two other Greek letters commonly used include α (*alpha*), and β (*beta*), pronounced "BAY-tah."

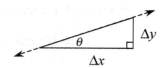

When a right triangle is oriented like a slope triangle, such as the one in the diagram above, the angle the line makes with the horizontal side of the triangle is called a **slope angle.**

Review & Preview

4-6.   Use what you know about the angles of a triangle to find the value of x and the angles in each triangle below.

a.

b.

c.

d.
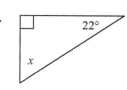

Geometry Connections

4-7.   Use the triangles at right to answer the following questions.

   a. Are the triangles at right similar? How do you know?
       Show your **reasoning** in a flowchart.

   b. **Examine** your work from part (a).
       Are the triangles also congruent?
       Explain why or why not.

4-8.   As Randi started to solve for x in the diagram at right,
        she wrote the equation $7^2 + x^2 = (x+1)^2$.

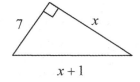

   a. Is Randi's equation valid? Explain your thinking.

   b. To solve her equation, first rewrite $(x+1)^2$ by multiplying $(x+1)(x+1)$. You
       may want to review the Math Notes box for Lesson 2.2.2.

   c. Now solve your equation for x.

   d. What is the perimeter of Randi's triangle?

4-9.   Assume that the shapes at right are
        similar. Find the values of x, y, and z.

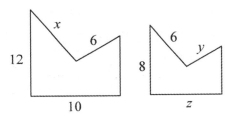

4-10.   Are the lines represented by the equations at
        right parallel? Support your **reasoning** with
        convincing evidence.

$$y = -\tfrac{3}{5}x + 2$$
$$y = -\tfrac{3}{5}x - 3$$

4.1.2 How important is the angle?

Connecting Slope Ratios to Specific Angles

In Lesson 4.1.1, you started **trigonometry**, the study of the measures of triangles. As you continue to **investigate** right triangles with your team today, use the following questions to guide your discussion:

What do we know about this triangle?

How does this triangle relate to other triangles?

Which part is Δx? Which part is Δy?

4-11.   What do you know about this triangle? To what other triangles does it relate? Use any information you have to solve for x.

4-12.   For each triangle below, find the missing angle or side length. Use your work from Lesson 4.1.1 to help you.

a.

b.

c.

d.

e.

f.

4-13.   Sheila says the triangle in part (f) of problem 4-12 is the
         same as her drawing at right.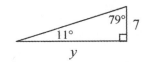

    a.   Do you agree? Use tracing paper to convince you of
          your conclusion.

    b.   Use what you know about the slope ratio of 11° to find the slope ratio for 79°.

    c.   What is the relationship of 11° and 79°? Of their slope ratios?

4-14.   For what other angles can you find the slope ratios based on the work you did in
         Lesson 4.1.1?

    a.   For example, since you know the slope ratio for 22°, what other angle do you
          know the slope ratio for? Use tracing paper to find a slope ratio for the
          complement of each slope angle you know. Use tracing paper to help re-orient
          the triangle if necessary.

    b.   Use this information to find x in the diagram at right.

    c.   Write a conjecture about the relationship of the slope ratios for
          complementary angles. You may want to start with, "*If one
          angle of a right triangle has the slope ratio $\frac{a}{b}$, then ...*"

4-15.   BUILDING A TRIGONOMETRY TABLE

         So far you have looked at several similar slope
         triangles and their corresponding slope ratios.
         These relationships will be very useful for finding
         missing side lengths or angle measures of right
         triangles for the rest of this chapter.

         Before you forget this valuable information, organize information about the triangles
         and ratios you have discovered so far in the table on the Lesson 4.1.2 ("Trig Table")
         Resource Page provided by your teacher or download from www.cpm.org. Keep it
         in a safe place for future reference. Include all of the angles you have studied up to
         this point. An example for 11° is filled in on the table to get you started.

METHODS AND MEANINGS

Slope Ratios and Angles

In Lesson 4.1.1, you discovered that certain slope angles produce slope triangles with special ratios. Below are the triangles you have studied so far. Note that the angles below are rounded to the nearest degree.

Review & Preview

4-16. Use your Trig Table from problem 4-15 to help you find the value of each variable below.

a.

b.

c.

4-17. The triangles shown at right are similar.

a. What is the ratio of side length NE to side length AK?

b. Use a ratio to compare the perimeters of $\triangle ENC$ and $\triangle KAR$. How is the perimeter ratio related to the side length ratio?

c. If you have not already done so, find the length of $\overline{EC}$.

4-18.   **Examine** each pair of figures below. Are they similar? Explain how you know.

a.

b.

c.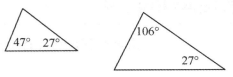

4-19.   Find the equation of the line with a slope of $\frac{1}{3}$ that goes through the point (0, 9).

4-20.   **Examine** the figure at right, which is not drawn to scale. Which is longer, $\overline{AB}$ or $\overline{BC}$? Explain your answer.

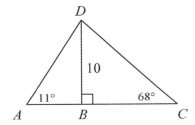

4.1.3   What if the angle changes?

Expanding the Trig Table

In the last few lessons, you found the slope ratios for several angles. However, so far you are limited to using the slope angles that are currently in your Trig Table. How can we find the ratios for other angles? And how are the angles related to the ratio?

Today your goal is to determine ratios for more angles and to find patterns. As you work today, keep the following questions in mind:

> What happens to the slope ratio when the angle increases? Decreases?

> What happens to the slope ratio when the angle is 0°? 90°?

> When is a slope ratio more than 1? When is it less than 1?

4-21.   On your paper, draw a slope triangle with a slope angle of 45°.

a.   Now **visualize** what would happen to the triangle if the slope angle increased to 55°. Which would be longer? Δy? Or Δx? Explain your **reasoning**.

b.   Using your dynamic geometry tool, create a triangle with a slope angle measuring 55°. Then use the resulting slope ratio to help you solve for x in the triangle at right. (Note: the triangle at right is not draw to scale.)

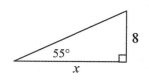

4-22.   Copy each of the following triangles onto your paper. Decide whether or not the given measurements are possible. If the triangle is possible, find the value of x or θ. Use the dynamic geometry tool to find the appropriate slope angles or ratios. If technology is not available, your teacher will provide a Lesson 4.1.3 Resource Page with the needed ratios. Round angle measures to the nearest degree. If a triangle's indicated measurement is not possible, explain why.

a.

b.

c.

d.

e.

f.

g.

4-23.   If you have not already, add these new slope ratios with their corresponding angles to your Trig Table. Be sure to draw and label the triangle for each new angle. Summarize your findings—which slope triangles did not work? Do you see any patterns?

4-24. What statements can you make about the connections between slope angle and slope ratio? In your Learning Log, write down all of your observations from this lesson. Be sure to answer the questions given at the beginning of the lesson (reprinted below). Title this entry, "Slope Angles and Slope Ratios" and include today's date.

What happens to the slope ratio when the angle increases? Decreases?

What happens to the slope ratio when the angle is 0°? 90°?

When is a slope ratio more than 1? When is it less than 1?

4-25. Ben thinks that the slope ratio for this triangle is $\frac{7}{10}$. Carlissa thinks the ratio is $\frac{10}{7}$. Who is correct? Explain your thinking fully.

4-26. Use your observations from problem 4-24 to answer the following questions:

a. Thalia did not have a tool to help her find the slope angle in the triangle at right. However, she claims that the slope angle has to be more than 45°. Do you agree with Thalia? Why?

b. Lyra was trying to find the slope ratio for the triangle at right, and she says the answer is $\frac{\Delta y}{\Delta x} = 2.675$. Isiah claims that cannot be correct. Who is right? How do you know?

c. Without finding the actual value, what information do you know about x in the diagram at right?

4-27. An airplane takes off and climbs at an angle of 11°. If the plane must fly over a 120-foot tower with at least 50 feet of clearance, what is the minimum distance between the point where the plane leaves the ground and the base of the tower?

a. Draw and label a diagram for this situation.

b. What is the minimum distance between the point where the plane leaves the ground and the tower? Explain completely.

4-28. Edwina has created her own Shape Bucket and has provided the clues below about her shapes. List one possible group of shapes that could be in her bucket.

$$P(\text{equilateral}) = 1$$
$$P(\text{triangle}) = \tfrac{1}{3}$$

4-29. Use what you know about the sum of the angles of a triangle to find $m\angle ABC$ and $m\angle BAC$. Are these angles acute or obtuse? Find the sum of these two angles. How can we describe the relationship of these two angles?

4.1.4 What about other right triangles?

The Tangent Ratio

In Lesson 4.1.2 you started a Trig Table of angles and their related slope ratios. Unfortunately, you only have the information for a few angles. How can you quickly find the ratios for other angles when a computer is not available or when an angle is not on your Trig Table? Do you have to draw each angle to get its slope ratio? Or is there another way?

4-30. WILL IT TOPPLE?

In problem 4-1, you learned that the Leaning Tower of Pisa is expected to collapse once its angle of slant is less than 83°. Currently, the top of the seventh story (point A in the diagram at right) is 50 meters above the ground. In addition, when a weight is dropped from point A, it lands 5 meters from the base of the tower, as shown in the diagram.

a. What is the slope ratio for the tower?

b. Use your Trig Table to determine the angle at which the Leaning Tower of Pisa slants. Is it in immediate danger of collapse?

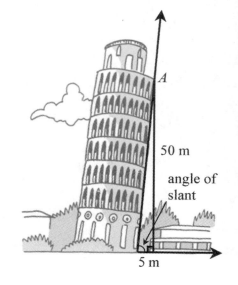

4-31.   Solve for the variables in the triangles below. It may be helpful to first orient the triangle (by rotating your paper or by using tracing paper) so that the triangle resembles a slope triangle. Use your Trig Table for reference.

a.

b.

c.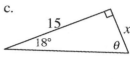

4-32.   MULTIPLE METHODS

Tiana, Mae Lin, Eddie, and Amy are looking at the triangle at right and trying to find the missing side length.

a.   Tiana declares, "Hey! We can rotate the triangle so that 18° looks like a slope angle, and then $\Delta y = 4$." Will her method work? If so, use her method to solve for a. If not, explain why not.

b.   Mae Lin says, "I see it differently. I can tell $\Delta y = 4$ without turning the triangle." How can she tell? Explain one way she could know.

c.   Eddie replies, "What if we use 72° as our slope angle? Then $\Delta x = 4$." What is he talking about? Discuss with your team and explain using pictures and words.

d.   Use Eddie's observation in part (c) to confirm your answer to part (a).

4-33.   USING A SCIENTIFIC CALCULATOR

Examine the triangle at right.

a.   According to the triangle at right, what is the slope ratio for 32°? Explain how you decided to set up the ratio. Write the ratio in both fraction and decimal form.

b.   What is the slope ratio for the 58° angle? How do you know?

c.   Scientific calculators have a button that will give the slope ratio when the slope angle is entered. In part (a), you calculated the slope ratio for 32° as 0.625. Use the "tan" button on your calculator to verify that you get ≈ 0.625 when you enter 32°. Does that button give you ≈ 1.600 when you enter 58°? Be ready to help your teammates find the button on their calculator.

d.   The ratio in a right triangle that you have been studying is referred to as the **tangent ratio**. When you want to find the slope ratio of an angle, such as 32°, it is written "tan 32°." So, an equation for this triangle can be written as $\tan 32° = \frac{5}{8}$. Read more about the tangent ratio in the Math Notes box for this lesson.

4-34.   For each triangle below, trace the triangle on tracing paper. Label its legs Δy and Δx based on the given slope angle. Then write an equation (such as $\tan 14° = \frac{x}{5}$), use your scientific calculator to find a slope ratio for the given angle, and solve for x.

a.

x

8

38°

b.

x

73°

9

c.

45°

14

x

4-35.   How do you set up a tangent ratio equation? How can you know which side is Δy? How can you use your scientific calculator to find a slope ratio? Write a Learning Log entry about what you learned today. Be sure to include examples or refer to your work from today. Title this entry "The Tangent Ratio" and include today's date.

METHODS AND MEANINGS

MATH NOTES

The Tangent Ratio

For any slope angle in a slope triangle, the ratio that compares the Δy to Δx is called the **tangent ratio**. The ratio for any angle is constant, regardless of the size of the triangle. It is written:

$$\tan (\text{slope angle}) = \frac{\Delta y}{\Delta x}$$

hypotenuse

Δy

slope angle

Δx

One way to identify which side is Δy and Δx is to first reorient the triangle so that it looks like a slope triangle, as shown at right.

For example, when the triangle at right is rotated, the resulting slope triangle helps to show that the tangent of θ is $\frac{p}{r}$, since θ is the slope angle, p is Δy and r is Δx. This is written:

$$\tan \theta = \frac{p}{r}$$

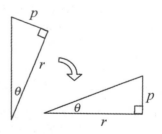

p

r

θ

θ

p

r

Whether the triangle is oriented as a slope triangle or not, you can identify Δy as the leg that is always opposite (across the triangle from) the angle, while Δx is the leg closest to the angle.

$$\tan \theta = \frac{opposite\ leg}{adjacent\ leg} = \frac{p}{r}$$

p

θ

r

Geometry Connections

4-36.   Find the missing side length for each triangle. Use the tangent button on your calculator to help.

a.

b.

c.
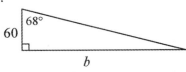

4-37.   Use the relationships in the diagrams below to write an equation and solve for *x*.

a.

b.

c.
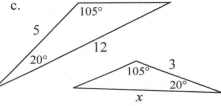

4-38.   What is the relationship of the triangles at right?
Justify your conclusion.

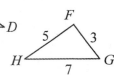

4-39.   Mr. Singer made the flowchart at right about a student named Brian.

a.   What is wrong with Mr. Singer's flowchart?

b.   Rearrange the ovals so the flowchart makes more sense.

4-40.   When she was younger, Mary had to look up at a 68° angle to see into her father's eyes whenever she was standing 15 inches away. How high above the flat ground were her father's eyes if Mary's eyes were 32″ above the ground?

4.1.5 What if I can't measure it?

Applying the Tangent Ratio

In this section so far, you have learned how to find the legs of a right triangle using an angle. But how can you use this information? Today you and your team will use the tangent ratio to solve problems and answer questions.

4-41.   STATUE OF LIBERTY

Lindy gets nose-bleeds whenever she is 300 feet above ground. During a class fieldtrip, her teacher asked if she wanted to climb to the top of the Statue of Liberty. Since she does not want to get a nose-bleed, she decided to take some measurements to figure out how high the torch of the statue is. She found a spot directly under the torch and then measured 42 feet away and determined that the angle up to the torch was 82°. Her eyes are 5 feet above the ground.

Should she climb to the top or will she get a nose-bleed? Draw a diagram that fits this situation. **Justify** your conclusion.

4-42.   HOW TALL IS IT?

How tall is Mount Everest? How tall is the White House? Often we want to know a measurement of something we cannot easily measure with a ruler or tape measure. Today you will work with your team to measure the height of something inside your classroom or on your school's campus in order to apply your new tangent tool.

Your Task: Get a **clinometer** (a tool that measures a slope angle) and a meter stick (or tape measure) from your teacher. As a team, decide how you will use these tools to find the height of the object selected by your teacher. Be sure to record all measurements carefully on your Lesson 4.1.6A Resource Page and include a diagram of the situation.

Discussion Points

What should the diagram look like?

What measurements would be useful?

How can you use your tools effectively to get accurate measurements?

4-43.   The trapezoids at right are similar.

a.   What is the ratio of the heights?

b.   Compare the areas. What is the ratio of the areas?

4-44.   For each diagram below, write an equation and solve for *x*, if possible.

a.

$3x + 3°$

$x + 7°$

b.

$9x + 4°$

$3x + 14°$

4-45.   Joan and Jim are planning a dinner menu including a main dish and dessert. They have 4 main dish choices (steak, tuna casserole, turkey burgers, and lasagna) and 3 dessert choices (brownies, ice cream, and chocolate chip cookies.) How many different dinner menus do they have to choose from? List all of the possible menus.

4-46.   Leon is standing 60 feet from a telephone pole. As he looks up, a red-tailed hawk lands on the top of the pole. Leon's angle of sight up to the bird is 22° and his eyes are 5.2 feet above the ground.

a.   Draw a detailed picture of this situation. Label with all of the given information.

b.   How tall is the pole? Show all of your work.

4-47.   Find the value of *x* in the triangle at right. Refer to problem 4-8 for help. Show all work.

$x + 3$ 26

10

4.2.1 How can I make a list?

• •

Introduction to Probability Models

In Chapter 1 you began to study probability, which is a measure of the chance that a particular event will occur. In the next few lessons you will encounter a variety of situations that require probability calculations. In many cases you will have to develop new probability tools to help you analyze these situations. Today's lesson focuses on tools for listing *all* the possible outcomes of a probability situation.

4-48.   THE RAT RACE, Part One

Ryan has a pet rat Romeo that he boasts is the smartest rat in the county. Sammy overheard Ryan at the county fair claiming that Romeo could learn to run a particular maze and find the cheese at the end.

"I don't think Romeo's that smart!" Sammy declares, "I think the rat just chooses a random path through the maze."

Ryan has built a maze with the floor plan shown at right. Ryan places the cheese in an airtight container (so Romeo can't smell the cheese!) in room A.

Ryan runs Romeo through the maze 100 times, and Romeo finds the cheese 66 times. "See how smart Romeo is?" Ryan asks, "He clearly learned something and got better at the maze as he went along." Sammy isn't so sure.

a.   Does the fact that Romeo ends up in Room A mean that he has learned the route and improved his ability to return to the same room over time? Or do you think he would achieve the same results by moving randomly throughout the maze? Discuss this question with your team.

b.   Predicting what will happen requires you to analyze the **probability** of possible outcomes. To accurately decide if Romeo is randomly guessing or if he is learning the route, you will need to learn more about probability. We will return to this problem at the end of Section 4.2. At this point, review the Math Notes box from Lesson 1.3.3 and then move on to problem 4-49.

4-49.   TOP OF THE CHARTS

Renae's MP3 player can be programmed to randomly play songs from her playlist without repeating a single song. Currently, Renae's MP3 player has 5 songs loaded on it, which are listed at right. As she walks between class, she only has time to listen to one song.

PLAYLIST
a. **I Love My Mama** (country) by the Strings of Heaven
b. **Don't Call Me Mama** (country) Duet by Sapphire and Hank Tumbleweed
c. **Carefree and Blue** (R & B) by Sapphire and Prism Escape
d. **Go Back To Mama** (Rock) Duet by Bjorn Free and Sapphire
e. **Smashing Lollipops** (Rock) by Sapphire

a.   What is the probability that her MP3 player will select a country song?

b.   What is the probability that Renae will listen to a song with "Mama" in the title?

c.   What is the probability she listens to a duet with Hank Tumbleweed?

d.   What is the probability she listens to a song that is not R & B?

4-50.   While waiting for a bus after school, Renae programmed her MP3 player to randomly play two songs. Assume that the MP3 player will not play the same song twice.

a.   List all the combinations of two songs that Renae could select. The order that she hears the songs does not matter for your list. How can you be sure that you listed all of the song combinations?

b.   Find the probability that Renae will listen to two songs with the name "Mama" in the title.

c.   What is the probability that at least one of the songs will have the name "Mama" in the title?

d.   Why does it make sense that the probability in part (d) is higher than the probability in part (c)?

4-51.　When a list is created by following a system (an orderly process), it is called a **systematic list**. Using a systematic list to answer questions involving probability can help you determine **all** of the possible outcomes. There are different **strategies** that may help you make a systematic list, but what is most important is that you methodically follow your system until it is complete. For the problem below, create a systematic list. Be prepared to share your **strategy**.

To get home, Renae can take one of four busses: #41, #28, #55, or #81. Once she is on a bus, she will randomly select one of the following equally likely activities: listening to her MP3 player, writing a letter, or reading a book.

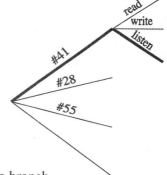

a.　List all the possible ways Renae can get home. Use a systematic list to make sure you find all the combinations of a bus and an activity.

b.　Use your list to find the following probabilities:

(1)　P(Renae takes an odd-numbered bus)

(2)　P(Renae does not write a letter)

(3)　P(Renae catches the #28 bus and then reads a book)

c.　Does her activity depend on which bus she takes? Explain why or why not.

4-52.　Sometimes writing an entire systematic list seems unnecessarily repetitive. However, creating a **tree diagram**, like the one started at right, is one way to avoid the repetition. This structure organizes the list by connecting each bus with each activity.

In this tree, the first set of branches represents the bus options. At the end of each of these branches are branches representing the activities. This system reduces some of the writing repetition.

Renae can then read the possible scenarios by following a branch across the diagram. For example, if you follow the bold branches, Renae will take the #41 bus and will listen to her MP3 player.

On your paper, complete this tree diagram to show all of the different travel options that Renae could take.

4-53. For the evening, Renae has programmed her MP3 player to play all five songs in a random order.

a. What is the probability that the first song is a country song?

b. If the first song is a country song, does that affect the probability that the second song is a country song? Explain your thinking.

c. As songs are playing, the number of songs left to play decreases. Therefore, the probability of playing each of the remaining songs is dependent on which songs that have played before it. This is an example of **dependent events.** If Renae has already listened to "Don't Call Me Mama," "Carefree and Blue," and "Smashing Lollipops," what is the probability that one of the singers of the fourth song will be Sapphire? Explain your **reasoning**.

d. In problem 4-51, you considered a situation of **independent events**, when the bus that Renae took did not affect which activity she chose. For example, what is the probability that Renae writes a letter if she takes the #41 bus? What if she takes the #55 bus?

> **PLAYLIST**
>
> a. **I Love My Mama** (country) by the Strings of Heaven
>
> b. **Don't Call Me Mama** (country) Duet by Sapphire and Hank Tumbleweed
>
> c. **Carefree and Blue** (R & B) by Sapphire and Prism Escape
>
> d. **Go Back To Mama** (Rock) Duet by Bjorn Free and Sapphire
>
> e. **Smashing Lollipops** (Rock) by Sapphire

Review & Preview

4-54. When Ms. Shreve randomly selects a student in her class, she has a $\frac{1}{3}$ probability of selecting a boy.

a. If her class has 36 students, how many boys are in Ms. Shreve's class?

b. If there are 11 boys in her class, how many girls are in her class?

c. What is the probability that she will select a girl?

d. Assume that Ms. Shreve's class has a total of 24 students. She selected one student (who was a boy) to attend a fieldtrip and then was told she needed to select one more student to attend. What is the probability that the second randomly selected student will also be a boy?

4-55.   What is wrong with the
         argument shown in the
         flow chart at right?
         What assumption does
         the argument make?

4-56.   For each diagram below, solve for *x*. Name the relationship(s) you used. Show all
         work.

         a.   b.

4-57.   Kamillah decided to find the height of the Empire State Building. She walked 1 mile
         away (5280 feet) from the tower and found that she had to look up 15.5° to see the
         top. Assuming Manhattan is flat, if Kamillah's eyes are 5 feet above the ground how
         tall is the Empire State Building?

4-58.   Renae wonders, "What if I program my MP3 player to randomly play 3 songs?"

         a.   Assuming that her MP3 player is still programmed as described in problem
               4-53, how many combinations of 3 songs could she listen to? Make a list of
               all the combinations. Remember that the order of the songs is not important.

         b.   Compare your answer to part (a) with the number of combinations that she
               could have with 2 songs in problem 4-50. Why does it make sense that these
               are the same?

4.2.2   How can I test my prediction?

Theoretical and Experimental Probability

In Lesson 4.2.1, you organized situations using systematic lists and tree diagrams in order to calculate the probability that an event would occur. How can you verify that your calculated probabilities are accurate? Today you will analyze a couple of games. For each game, you will calculate the chance of winning. Then you will play the game to decide if your probability analysis is accurate.

4-59.   Luis is going to spin the spinner at right.

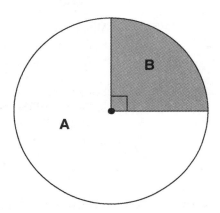

a.   What are the possible results of his spin?

b.   What do you predict Luis' result will be after one spin? **Justify** your prediction.

c.   If Luis spun this spinner four times, what do you predict his results would be?

d.   A paperclip with one end extended can be spun around the center of a spinner to collect data, as shown at right. With your team, spin a paperclip four times about the spinner above and record the results. Did your **experimental results** match your prediction in part (c)? Why or why not?

e.   What if the spinner is spun 40 times? 400 times? Would you predict the result to be closer to the expected results? Why or why not?

f.   What if Luis has spun the spinner 400 times and landed on region A every time? What would be the probability that the next spin would land on region B? Explain.

4-60.   Congratulations! You are going to be a
        contestant on a new game show with a chance to
        win some money. You will spin two spinners to
        see how much money you will win. The first
        spinner has an equal chance of coming out
        $100, $300, or $1500. The second spinner is
        equally divided between "Keep your winnings,"
        and "Double your winnings."

   a.   Make a systematic list <u>and</u> tree
        diagram of all the possible outcomes.

   b.   What is the probability that you will take
        home $200? What is the probability that
        you will take home more than $500?

   c.   What is the probability that you will double
        your winnings? Does the probability that
        you will double your winnings depend on
        the result of the first spinner?

   d.   Does your answer for part (c) mean that you are guaranteed to double your
        winnings half the time you play the game?

   e.   What if the amounts on the first spinner were $100, $200, and $1500? What is
        the probability that you would take home $200? Justify your conclusion.

4-61.   ROLL AND WIN

        Now consider a game that is played with two regular dice, each numbered 1 through
        6. First, each player chooses a number. The two dice are rolled and the numbers
        that come up are **added** together. If the sum is the number you chose, you win a
        point. For example, if a 2 and a 5 are rolled, the sum is 7, so the person who chose
        the number 7 would get a point.

   a.   First, use your intuition. Which number do you think will be the most common
        sum? In other words, which number would you pick to play?

   b.   What are the possible results when two dice are rolled and their numbers
        added?

   c.   Are the results from the separate dice dependent or
        independent? Does the result from one die affect the
        other? Explain.

   d.   What about the separate rolls? When the two dice are
        rolled, does the sum depend on the previous rolls? Why
        or why not?

   e.   Now play Roll and Win to see which sum occurs the most often. Have each
        member of your team choose a different number. Roll the dice 36 times and
        record the results. Which sum occurred most often?

Geometry Connections

4-62. One way to analyze this situation is to **make a table** like the one at right. Copy and complete this table of sums on your paper.

Dice #1

	1	2	3	4	5	6
1				5		
2		4				
3						
4			7			
5						
6						

Dice #2

 a. What is the probability the outcome will be odd? P(even)?

 b. Which sum is the most likely result? What is the probability of rolling that sum?

 c. What is the probability of rolling the sum of 2? 10? 15?

 d. Compare your data from the table with that from problem 4-61. Did your experimental results match your theoretical probability? If not, explain what you could do to get results that are closer to the predicted results.

Review & Preview

4-63. What are the possible lengths for side $\overline{ML}$ in the triangle at right? Show how you know.

4-64. Alexis, Bart, Chuck, and Dariah all called in to a radio show to get free tickets to a concert. List all the possible orders in which their calls could have been received.

4-65. **Examine** the diagram at right. If $\overline{AC}$ passes through point B, then answer the questions below.

 a. Are the triangles similar? If so, make a flowchart **justifying** your answer.

 b. Are the triangles congruent? Explain how you know.

4-66. **Examine** pentagon *SMILE* at right. Do any of its sides have equal length? How do you know? Be sure to provide convincing evidence. You might want to copy the figure onto graph paper.

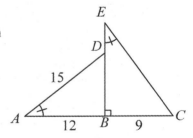

4-67. Find the area of the triangle at right. Show all work.

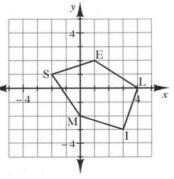

4.2.3 How can I represent it?

Using an Area Model

So far in this chapter, you have studied several different ways to represent situations involving chance. You have analyzed games using systematic lists, tree diagrams, and tables. In these games, each outcome you listed had an equal probability of occurring. But what if a game is biased so that some outcomes are more likely than others? How can you represent biased games? Today you will learn a new tool to analyze more complicated situations of chance, called an area model.

4-68.   IT'S IN THE GENES

Can you bend your thumb backwards at the middle joint to make an angle, like the example at right? Or does your thumb remain straight? The ability to bend your thumb back is thought to rely on a single gene.

Example of a thumb that can bend backwards at the joint.

What about your tongue? If you can roll your tongue into a "U" shape, you probably have a special gene that enables you to do this.

Assume that half of the U.S. population can bend their thumbs backwards and that half can roll their tongues. Also assume that these genes are independent (in other words, having one gene does not affect whether or not you have the other) and randomly distributed (spread out) throughout the population. Then the possible outcomes of these genetic traits can be organized in a table like the one below.

a.   According to this table, what is the probability that a random person from the U.S. has both special traits? That is, what is the chance that he or she can roll his or her tongue <u>and</u> bend his or her thumb back?

b.   According to this table, what is the probability that a random person has only one of these special traits? **Justify** your conclusion.

c.   This table is useful because every cell in the table is equally likely. Therefore, each possible outcome, such being able to bend your thumb but not roll your tongue, has a $\frac{1}{4}$ probability.

However, this table assumes that half the population can bend their thumbs backwards. In actuality, only a small percentage (about $\frac{1}{4}$) of the U.S. population has this special trait. It also turns out that a majority (about $\frac{7}{10}$) of the population can roll their tongues. How can this table be adjusted to represent these percentages? Discuss this with your team and be prepared to share your ideas with the class.

4-69.   USING AN AREA MODEL

One way to represent a probability situation that has outcomes with unequal
probabilities is by using an **area model**. An area model uses a square with an area
of 1 to represent all possible outcomes. The square is subdivided to represent the
different possible outcomes. The area of each outcome is the probability that the
outcome will occur.

For example, if $\frac{1}{4}$ of the U.S. population
can bend their thumbs back, then the
column representing this ability should
take only one-fourth of the square's
width, as shown at right.

BEND THUMB?

YES $\frac{1}{4}$ NO $\frac{3}{4}$

ROLL TONGUE?

a   How should the diagram be altered
to that show that $\frac{7}{10}$ of the U.S. can
roll their tongues? Copy this
diagram on your paper and add two
rows to represent this probability.

b.   The relative probabilities of the
different outcomes are represented
by the areas of the regions. For
example, the portion of the area
model representing people with both special traits is a rectangle with a width of
$\frac{1}{4}$ and a height of $\frac{7}{10}$. What is the area of this rectangle? This area tells you
the probability that a random person in the U.S. has both traits.

c.   What is the probability that a randomly selected person can roll his or her
tongue but not bend his or her thumb back? Show how you got this
probability.

4-70.   PROBABILITIES IN VEIN

You and your best friend may not only look
different, you may also have different types of
blood! For instance, members of the American
Navajo population can be classified into two
groups: 73% percent (73 out of 100) of the
Navajo population has type "O" blood, while
27% (27 out of 100) has type "A" blood.
(Blood types describe certain chemicals, called
"antigens," that are found in a person's blood.)

Navajo Person #1

	O $\frac{73}{100}$	A $\frac{27}{100}$
O $\frac{73}{100}$		
A $\frac{27}{100}$		

Navajo Person #2

a.   Suppose you select two Navajo individuals at random. What is the probability
that both individuals have type "A" blood? This time, drawing an area model
that is exactly to scale would be challenging. Therefore, a **generic area model**
(like the one above) is useful because it will still allow you to calculate the
individual areas. Copy and complete this generic area model.

Problem continues on next page →

4-70.   *Problem continued from previous page.*

   b.   What is the probability that two Navajo individuals selected at random have the same blood type?

4-71.   SHIPWRECKED!

You and your best friend (both from the U.S.) are shipwrecked on a desert island! You have been injured and are losing blood rapidly, and your best friend is the only person around to give you a transfusion.

Unlike the Navajo you learned of in problem 4-70, most populations are classified into four blood types: O, A, B, and AB. For example, in the U.S., 45% of people have type O blood, 40% have type A, 11% have type B, and 4% have type AB (according to the American Red Cross, 2004). While there are other ways people's blood can differ, this problem will only take into account these four blood types.

   a.   Make a generic area model representing the blood types in this problem. List your friend's possible blood types along the top of the model and your possible blood types along the side.

   b.   What is the probability that you and your best friend have the same blood type?

   c.   Luckily, two people do not have to have the same blood type for the receiver of blood to survive a transfusion. Other combinations will also work, as shown in the diagram at right. Assuming that their blood is compatible in other ways, a donor with type O blood can donate to receivers with type O, A, B, or AB, while a donor with type A blood can donate to a receiver with A or AB. A donor with type B blood can donate to a receiver with B or AB, and a donor with type AB blood can donate only to AB receivers.

   Assuming that your best friend's blood is compatible with yours in other ways, determine the probability that he or she has a type of blood that can save your life!

4-72.   **Examine** the graph at right with slope triangles A, B, and C.

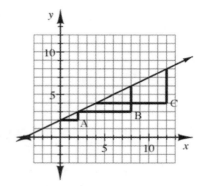

a.   Find the slope of the line using slope triangle A, slope triangle B, and then slope triangle C.

b.   Hernisha's slope triangle has a slope of $\frac{1}{2}$. What do you know about her line?

4-73.   Francis and John are racing. Francis is 2 meters in front of the starting line at time $t = 0$ and he runs at a constant rate of 1 meters per second. John is 5 meters in front of the starting line and he runs at a constant rate of 0.75 meters per second. After how long will Francis catch up to John?

4-74.   Can a triangle be made with sides of length 7, 10 and 20 units? **Justify** your answer.

4-75.   Solve each equation below for the given variable. Show all work and check your answer.

a. $\sqrt{x} - 5 = 2$

b. $-4(-2 - x) = 5x + 6$

c. $\frac{5}{x-2} = \frac{3}{2}$

d. $x^2 + 4x - 5 = 0$

4-76.   Find the perimeter of the shape at right. Clearly show all your steps.

4.2.4 How can I represent it?

Choosing a Probability Model

In Lesson 4.2.3, you used area models to represent probability situations where some outcomes were more likely than others. Today you will consider how to represent these situations using tree diagrams. You will then return to a problem that was introduced in Lesson 4.2.1 to decide if a rat's behavior is random or not.

4-77. Your teacher challenges you to a spinner game. You spin the two spinners with the probabilities listed at right. The first letter should come from Spinner #1 and the second letter from Spinner #2. If the letters can form a two-letter English word, you win. Otherwise, your teacher wins.

Spinner #1

I, U, A

$P(I) = \frac{1}{2}$
$P(U) = \frac{1}{6}$
$P(A) = \frac{1}{3}$

Spinner #2

T, F

$P(T) = \frac{1}{4}$
$P(F) = \frac{3}{4}$

a. Make a generic area model and find the probability that you will win this game.

b. Is this game fair? If you played the game 100 times, who do you think would win more often, you or your teacher? Can you be sure this will happen?

4-78. Sinclair wonders how to model the spinner game in problem 4-77 using a tree diagram. He draws the tree diagram at right.

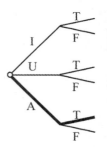

a. Sabrina says, "That can't be right. This diagram makes it look like all the words are equally likely." What is Sabrina talking about? Why is this tree diagram misleading?

b. To make the tree diagram reflect the true probabilities in this game, Sabrina writes numbers next to each letter showing the probability that the letter will occur. So she writes a "$\frac{1}{3}$" next to "A," a "$\frac{1}{4}$" next to each "T," etc. Following Sabrina's method, label the tree diagram with numbers next to each letter.

c. According to your area model from problem 4-77, what is the probability that you will spin the word "AT"? Now **examine** the bolded branch on the tree diagram shown above. How could the numbers you have written on the tree diagram be used to find the probability of spinning "AT"?

Problem continues on next page →

Geometry Connections

4-78.   *Problem continued from previous page.*

    d.   Does this method work for the other combinations of letters? Similarly calculate the probabilities for each of the paths of the tree diagram. At the end of each branch, write its probability. (For example, write "$\frac{1}{12}$" at the end of the "AT" branch.) Do your answers match those from problem 4-77?

    e.   Find all the branches with letter combinations that make words. Use the numbers written at the end of each branch to compute the total probability that you will spin a word. Does this probability match the probability you found with your area model?

4-79.   THE RAT RACE, Part Two

In problem 4-48, you read about Romeo, an amazing pet rat. As you previously learned, Sammy overheard Ryan at the county fair claiming that Romeo could learn to run a particular maze and find the cheese at the end.

"I don't think Romeo is that smart!" Sammy declares, "I think the rat just chooses a random path through the maze."

Ryan has built a maze with the floorplan shown at right. In addition, he has placed some cheese in an airtight container (so Romeo can't smell the cheese!) in room A.

    a.   Suppose that every time Romeo reaches a split in the maze, he is equally likely to choose any of the paths in front of him. Choose a method and find the probability that Romeo will end up in each room. In a sentence or two, explain why you chose the method you did.

    b.   If the rat moves through the maze randomly, how many out of 100 attempts would you expect Romeo to end up in room A? How many times would you expect him to end up in room B? Explain.

Problem continues on next page →

4-79.   *Problem continued from previous page.*

   c.   After 100 attempts, and Romeo finds the cheese 66 times. "See how smart Romeo is?" Ryan asks, "He clearly learned something and got better at the maze as he went along." Looking at your calculations, Sammy isn't so sure.

   Do you think Romeo learned and improved his ability to return to the same room over time? Or could he just have been moving randomly? Discuss this question with your team. Then, write an argument that would convince Ryan or Sammy.

4-80.   Always skeptical, Sammy says, "If Romeo really can learn, he ought to be able to figure out how to run this new maze I've designed." **Examine** Sammy's maze at right.

   a.   To give Romeo the best chance of finding the cheese, in which room should the cheese be placed? Choose a method, show all steps in your solution process, and **justify** your answer.

   b.   If the cheese is in room C and Romeo finds the cheese 6 times out of every 10 tries, does he seem to be learning? Explain your conclusion.

4-81.   Make an entry in your Learning Log describing the various ways of representing probabilities you have learned in this chapter. Which seems easiest to use so far? Which is most versatile? Are there any conditions under which certain ones cannot be used? Label this entry "Probability Methods" and include today's date.

METHODS AND MEANINGS

Probability Models

When all the possible outcomes of a probabilistic event have the same probability, probabilities can be calculated by listing the possible outcomes in a **systematic list**. However, when some outcomes are more probable than others, a more sophisticated model is required to calculate probabilities.

Spinner #1   **Spinner #2**

$P(I) = \frac{1}{2}$ $P(T) = \frac{1}{4}$

$P(U) = \frac{1}{6}$ $P(F) = \frac{3}{4}$

$P(A) = \frac{1}{3}$

One such model is an **area model**. In this type of model, the situation is represented by a square with area of 1 so that the areas of the parts are the probabilities of the different events that occur. For example, suppose you spin the two spinners shown above. The possible outcomes are represented in the area model at right. Notice that column "U" takes up $\frac{1}{6}$ of the width of the table since the "U" region is $\frac{1}{6}$ of Spinner #1. Similarly, the "T" row takes up $\frac{1}{4}$ of the height of the table, since the "T" region is $\frac{1}{4}$ of Spinner #2. Then the probability that the spinners come out "U" and "T" is equal to the area of the "UT" rectangle in the table: $\frac{1}{6} \cdot \frac{1}{4} = \frac{1}{24}$.

Spinner #1

	I $\left(\frac{1}{2}\right)$	**A** $\left(\frac{1}{3}\right)$	**U** $\left(\frac{1}{6}\right)$
T $\left(\frac{1}{4}\right)$	IT	AT	UT
F $\left(\frac{3}{4}\right)$	IF	AF	UF

Spinner #2

The situation can also be represented using a **tree diagram**. In this model, the branching points indicate probabilistic events, and the branches stemming from each event indicate the possible outcomes for the event. For example, in the tree diagram at right the first branching point represents spinning the first spinner. The first spinner can come out "I" "A" or "U", so each of those options has a branch. The numbers next to each letter represent the probability that that letter occurs.

The numbers at the far right of the table represent the probabilities of various outcomes. For example, the probability of spinning "U" and "T" can be found at the end of the bold branch of the tree. This probability, $\frac{1}{24}$, can be found by multiplying the fractions that appear on the bold branches.

4-82.   Choose a method to represent the following problem and use it to answer the questions below.

Kiyomi has 4 pairs of pants (black, green, blue jeans, and plaid) and she has 5 shirts (white, red, teal, black, and brown).

a.   If any shirt can be worn with any pair of pants, how many outfits does she own? That is, how many different combinations of pants and shirts can she wear?

b.   What is the probability that she is wearing black?

4-83.   Are the triangles at right similar? If so, write a flowchart that **justifies** your conclusion. If not, explain how you know.

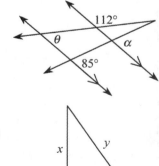

4-84.   You roll a die and it comes up a "6" three times in a row. What is the probability of rolling a "6" on the next toss?

4-85.   Find the values of θ and α in the diagram at right. State the relationships you used.

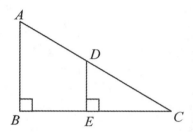

4-86.   Find x and y in the diagram at right. Show all of the steps leading to your answer.

4.2.5 Which model should I use?

Optional: Applications of Probability Methods

Beginning with Lesson 4.2.1, you have been learning about various methods to help you determine probabilities of different outcomes. Today you will apply what you know to two probability problems. As you work in your teams today, keep the following questions in mind to guide your discussion:

> Which probability do we need to find?
>
> How can we find the probability?
>
> Which probability model should we use?

4-87.   SHIFTY SHAUNA

Shauna has a bad relationship with the truth—she doesn't usually tell it! In fact, whenever Shauna is asked a question, she rolls a die. If it comes up 6, she tells the truth. Otherwise, she lies.

a.   If Shauna flips a fair coin and you ask her how it came out, what is the probability that she says "heads" and is telling the truth? Choose a method to solve this problem and carefully record your work. Be ready to share your solution method with the class.

b.   Suppose Shauna flips a fair coin and you ask her whether it came up heads or tails. What is the probability that she says "heads"? (Hint: The answer is not $\frac{1}{12}$!)

4-88.   MIDNIGHT MYSTERY

Each year, the students at Haardvarks School randomly select a student to play a prank. Late last night, Groundskeeper Millie saw a student steal the school's National Curling Championship trophy from the trophy case. All Millie can tell the headmaster about the crime is that the student who stole the trophy looked like he or she had red hair.

Problem continues on next page →

4-88.   *Problem continued from previous page.*

Unfortunately, of the 100 students at Haardvarks, the only ones with red hair are your friend Don Measley and his siblings. Groundskeeper Millie insists that one of the 5 Measley children committed the crime and should be punished. Don is incensed: "We Measleys would never play such a stupid prank! Groundskeeper Millie claims to have seen someone with red hair, but it was so dark at the time and Millie's eyes are so bad, there is no way she could have identified the color of someone's hair!"

The headmaster isn't convinced, so he walks around with Millie at night and points to students one by one, asking Millie whether each one has red hair. Millie is right about the hair color 4 out of every 5 times.

This looks like bad news for Don, but Professor McMonacle agrees to take up his defense. "I still think," McMonacle says, "that the thief probably wasn't one of the Measleys."

Your task: Model this situation with a tree diagram or a generic area model. The two chance events in your model should be "The thief is/is not a redhead" and "Millie is/is not correct about the thief's hair color."

4-89.   Look back at your model from problem 4-88 and circle every outcome in which Millie would report that the thief had red hair. (There should be two!) Then use your model to answer the following questions:

a.   Suppose that to help make Don's case, you perform the following experiment repeatedly: you pick a Haardvarks student at random, show the student to Millie late at night, and see what Millie says about the student's hair color. If you performed this experiment with 100 students, how many times would you expect Millie to say the student had red hair?

b.   If you performed this experiment with 100 students, how many times would you expect Millie to say the student had red hair and be correct about it?

c.   If you performed this experiment with 100 students, what percentage of the students Millie *said* had red hair would *actually* have red hair?

d.   Can you use these calculations to defend the Measleys? Is it likely that a Measley was the thief?

4-90.   Have you *proven* that none of the Measleys stole the Curling Trophy?

4-91.   Based on the measurements provided for each triangle below, decide if the angle θ must be more than, less than, or equal to 45°. Assume the diagram is not drawn to scale. Show how you know.

a.

b.

c.

4-92.   Find the area and perimeter of the triangle at right.

4-93.   After doing well on a test, Althea's teacher placed a gold star on her paper. When Althea **examined** the star closely, she realized that it was really a regular pentagon surrounded by 5 isosceles triangles, as shown in the diagram at right. If the star has the angle measurements shown in the diagram, find the sum of the angles inside the shaded pentagon. Show all work.

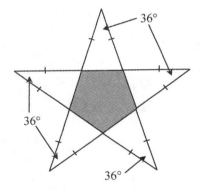

4-94.   Find the slope of the line through the points (–5, 86) and (95, 16). Then find at least one more point on the line.

4-95.   On graph paper, plot $\triangle ABC$ if $A(-1, -1)$, $B(3, -1)$, and $C(-1, -2)$.

a.   Enlarge (dilate) $\triangle ABC$ from the origin so that the ratio of the side lengths is 3. Name this new triangle $\triangle A'B'C'$. List the coordinates of $\triangle A'B'C'$.

b.   Rotate $\triangle A'B'C'$ 90° clockwise (↻) about the origin to find $\triangle A''B''C''$. List the coordinates of $\triangle A''B''C''$.

c.   If $\triangle ABC$ is translated so that the image of A is located at $(5, 3)$, where would the image of B lie?

Chapter 4 Closure   What have I learned?

Reflection and Synthesis

The activities below offer you a chance to reflect on what you have learned in this chapter. As you work, look for concepts that you feel very comfortable with, ideas that you would like to learn more about, and topics you need more help with. Look for connections between ideas as well as connections with material you learned previously.

①   TEAM BRAINSTORM

With your team, brainstorm a list for each of the following two subjects. Be as detailed as you can. How long can you make your list? Challenge yourselves. Be prepared to share your team's ideas with the class.

Topics: What have you studied in this chapter? What ideas and words were important in what you learned? Remember to be as detailed as you can.

Connections: How are the topics, ideas, and words that you learned in previous courses connected to the new ideas in this chapter? Again, make your list as long as you can.

The following is a list of the vocabulary used in this chapter. The words that appear in bold are new to this chapter. Make sure that you are familiar with all of these words and know what they mean. Refer to the glossary or index for any words that you do not yet understand.

α (alpha)	angle	**area model**
clinometer	conjecture	**dependent events**
hypotenuse	**independent events**	leg
orientation	probability	random
ratio	**slope angle**	slope ratio
slope triangle	**systematic list**	**tangent**
θ (theta)	**tree diagram**	**trigonometry**
Δx	**Δy**	

Make a concept map showing all of the connections you can find among the key words and ideas listed above. To show a connection between two words, draw a line between them and explain the connection, as shown in the example below. A word can be connected to any other word as long as there is a justified connection. For each key word or idea, provide a sketch of an example.

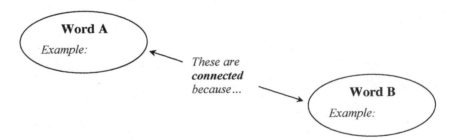

Your teacher may provide you with vocabulary cards to help you get started. If you use the cards to plan your concept map, be sure either to re-draw your concept map on your paper or to glue the vocabulary cards to a poster with all of the connections explained for others to see and understand.

While you are making your map, your team may think of related words or ideas that are not listed above. Be sure to include these ideas on your concept map.

③　　　SUMMARIZING MY UNDERSTANDING

This section gives you an opportunity to show what you know about certain math topics or ideas. Your teacher will direct you how to do this. Your teacher may give you a "GO" page to work on. "GO" stands for "Graphic Organizer," a tool you can use to organize your thoughts and communicate your ideas clearly.

④　　　WHAT HAVE I LEARNED?

This section will help you evaluate which types of problems you feel comfortable with and which types you need more help with. This section appears at the end of every chapter to help you check your understanding. Even if your teacher does not assign this section, it is a good idea to try these problems and find out for yourself what you know and what you need to work on.

Solve each problem as completely as you can. The table at the end of this closure section has answers to these problems. It also tells you where you can find additional help and practice on problems like these.

CL 4-96.　Solve for the missing side length or angle below.

a.

b.

c.

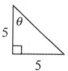

CL 4-97.　Use a flowchart to show how you know the triangles are similar. Then find the value of each variable.

a.

b.

CL 4-98.　Salvador has a hot dog stand 58 meters from the base of the Space Needle in Seattle. He prefers to work in the shade and knows that he can calculate when his hotdog stand will be in the shade if he knows the height of the Space Needle. To measure its height, Salvador stands at the hotdog stand, gets out his clinometer, and measures the angle of sight to be 80°. Salvador's eyes are 1.5 meters above the ground. Assuming that the ground is level between the hotdog stand and the Space Needle, how tall is the Space Needle?

CL 4-99. Use the diagram at right to answer the questions below.

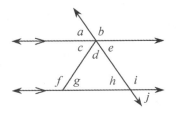

a. State the name of the geometric relationship between the angles below. Also describe the relationship between the angle measures, if one exists.

    i. $\angle a$ and $\angle h$
                           ii. $\angle b$ and $\angle e$

    iii. $\angle c$ and $\angle g$
                           iv. $\angle g$, $\angle d$, and $\angle h$

b. For each problem below, **justify** your answer. If $m\angle c = 32°$ and $m\angle e = 55°$, then find the measure of each angle below.

    i. $m\angle j$ ii. $m\angle d$ iii. $m\angle a$ iv. $m\angle g$

CL 4-100. Draw a pair of axes in the center of a half sheet of graph paper. Then draw the figure to the right and perform the indicated transformations. For each transformation, label the resulting image $A'B'C'D'E'$.

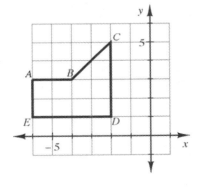

a. Rotate $ABCDE$ 180° ↻ around the origin.

b. Rotate $ABCDE$ 90° ↺ around the origin.

c. Reflect $ABCDE$ across the y-axis.

d. Translate $ABCDE$ up 5, left 7.

CL 4-101. In a certain town, 45% of the population has dimples and 70% has a widow's peak (a condition where the hairline above the forehead makes a "V" shape). Assuming that these physical traits are independently distributed, what is the probability that a randomly selected person has both dimples and a widow's peak? What is the probability that he or she will have neither? Use a generic area model or a tree diagram to represent this situation.

CL 4-102. Trace each figure onto your paper and label the sides with the given measurements.

3" base   10" base   11" base   12" base

a. On your paper, draw a height that corresponds to the labeled base for each figure.

b. Assume that the height for each figure above is 7 inches. Add this information to your diagrams and find the area of each figure.

CL 4-103. Find the perimeter of each shape below. Assume the diagram in part (b) is a parallelogram.

a.
7 mm
45°

b.
18 m
9 m
30 m

c.
7"
6"
60°
11"

CL 4-104. For each equation below, solve for x:

a. $\frac{x}{23} = \frac{15}{7}$

b. $(x + 2)(x - 5) = 6x + x^2 - 5$

c. $x^2 + 2x - 15 = 0$

d. $2x^2 - 11x = -3$

CL 4-105. Check your answers using the table at the end of this section. Which problems do you feel confident about? Which problems were hard? Have you worked on problems like these in math classes you have taken before? Use the table to make a list of topics you need help on and a list of topics you need to practice more.

HOW AM I THINKING?

This course focuses on five different **Ways of Thinking**: investigating, examining, reasoning and justifying, visualizing, and choosing a strategy/tool. These are some of the ways in which you think while trying to make sense of a concept or attempting to solve a problem (even outside of math class). During this chapter, you have probably used each Way of Thinking multiple times without even realizing it!

This closure activity will focus on one of these Ways of Thinking: **visualizing**. Read the description of this Way of Thinking at right.

Think about the problems you have worked on in this chapter. When did you need to think about what something looked like to make sense of it? What helps you to create mental pictures? Were there times when a problem didn't seem to make sense without seeing it? How have you used visualizing in a previous math class? You may want to flip through the chapter to refresh your memory about the problems that you have worked on. Discuss any of the methods you have developed to help you **visualize**.

> ### Visualizing
>
> To visualize means to make a picture in your mind that represents a situation or description. As you develop this Way of Thinking, you will learn how to turn a variety of situations into mental pictures. You think this way when you ask or answer questions like, "What does it look like when . . . ?" or "How can I draw . . . ?" When you catch yourself wondering what something might look like, you are visualizing.
>
>

Once your discussion is complete, think about the way you think as you answer the questions below.

a. **Visualization** is required when you imagine a situation and want to draw a diagram to represent it. Read the descriptions below and **visualize** what each situation looks like. Then draw a diagram for each. Label your diagrams appropriately with any given measurements.

(1) *Karen is flying a kite on a windy day. Her kite is 80 feet above ground and her string is 100 feet long. Karen is holding the kite 3 feet above ground.*

(2) *The bow of a rowboat (which is 1 foot above water level) is tied to a point on a dock that is 6 feet above the water level. The length of the rope between the dock and the boat is 8 feet.*

Problem continues on next page →

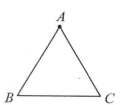

b.   Sometimes, **visualization** requires you to think
about how an object can move in relation to others.
For example, consider equilateral △*ABC* at right.

  (1)   **Visualize** changing △*ABC* by stretching
vertex *A* to point *D*, which is right above *A*.
What does the new triangle look like? Do
you have a name for it?

  (2)   What happened to $m\angle A$ as you stretched the triangle in part (1)? What
happened to $m\angle B$ and $m\angle C$?

  (3)   Now **visualize** the result after vertex *A* stretched to point *E*. What type of
triangle is the result? What happens to $m\angle B$ as the triangle is
stretched? What happens to $m\angle C$?

c.   An important use of **visualization** is to re-orient a right triangle to help you
identify which leg is Δx and which leg is Δy. For each triangle below,
visualize the triangle by rotating and/or reflecting it so that it is a slope
triangle. Draw the result and label the appropriate legs Δx or Δy.

(1)   (2)   (3)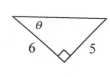

d.   Finally, **visualization** can help you view an object from
different perspectives. For example, consider the
square-based pyramid at right. **Visualize** what you
would see if you looked down at the pyramid from a
point directly above the top vertex. Draw this view on
your paper.

Answers and Support for
Closure Activity #4
What Have I Learned?

Problem	Solution	Need Help?	More Practice
CL 4-96.	a. $x \approx 9.23$ b. $x \approx 5.47$ c. $\theta = 45°$	Lessons 4.1.2 and 4.1.4 Math Notes boxes	Problems 4-11, 4-12, 4-16, 4-22, 4-25, 4-31, 4-34, 4-36, 4-46
CL 4-97.	a. $x \approx 3.6$ $\angle EDF = \angle BAC$ $\angle DEF = \angle ABC$ $\triangle EDF \sim \triangle BAC$ $AA \sim$ $\angle EDF = \angle BAC$ $\angle BCD = \angle ACE$ b. $x = 4.2$ $\triangle BCD \sim \triangle ACE$ $AA \sim$	Lessons 3.1.2, 3.1.3, 3.2.1, and 3.2.5 Math Notes boxes	Problems 3-23, 3-35, 3-36, 3-38, 3-46, 3-49, 3-53, 3-54, 3-55, 3-57, 3-64, 3-66, 3-80, 3-83, 3-84, 3-89, 4-7, 4-17, 4-18, 4-38, 4-39, 4-83
CL 4-98.	Total height ≈ 330.4 m 80° 58 m 1.5 m not to scale	Lesson 4.1.4 Math Notes box, Lesson 4.1.5	Problems 4-27, 4-30, 4-40, 4-41, 4-46, 4-57
CL 4-99.	a. *i.* corresponding angles, congruent *ii.* straight angle pair, supplementary *iii.* alternate interior angles, congruent *iv.* sum of the angles in a triangle, add up to 180° b. *i.* 55°: corresponding to *e* *ii.* 93°: straight angle with *e* and *c* *iii.* 55°: vertical to *e* *iv.* 32°: alternate interior to *c*	Lessons 2.1.1, 2.1.4, and 2.2.1 Math Notes boxes, Problem 2-3	Problems 2-13, 2-16, 2-17, 2-18, 2-23, 2-24, 2-25, 2-31, 2-32, 2-38, 2-49, 2-51, 2-62, 2-72, 2-111, 3-20, 3-31, 3-60, 3-70, 3-96, 4-6, 4-29, 4-44, 4-85, 4-93

Problem	Solution	Need Help?	More Practice
CL 4-100.	a. $A'(6, -3)$, $B'(4, -3)$, $C'(2, -5)$, $D'(2, -1)$, $E'(6, -1)$ b. $A'(-3, -6)$, $B'(-3, -4)$, $C'(-5, -2)$, $D'(-1, -2)$, $E'(-1, -6)$ c. $A'(6, 3)$, $B'(4, 3)$, $C'(2, 5)$, $D'(2, 1)$, $E'(6, 1)$ d. $A'(-13, 8)$, $B'(-11, 8)$, $C'(-9, 10)$, $D'(-9, 6)$, $E'(-13, 6)$	Lessons 1.2.2 and 1.2.3 Math Notes boxes	Problems 1-50, 1-51, 1-59, 1-60, 1-61, 1-64, 1-69, 1-73, 1-85, 1-96, 2-11, 2-19, 2-20, 2-33, 2-64, 2-113, 3-96
CL 4-101.	P(both) = 31.5% P(neither) = 16.5% 	Lesson 4.2.4 Math Notes box	Problems 4-52, 4-60, 4-62, 4-68, 4-69, 4-70, 4-71, 4-77, 4-78, 4-87
CL 4-102.	a. All heights should be 7". b. Areas in square inches: 10.5, 70, 77, 70	Lessons 1.1.3 and 2.2.4 Math Notes boxes	Problems 2-66, 2-68, 2-71, 2-75, 2-76, 2-78, 2-79, 2-82, 2-83, 2-90, 2-120, 3-51, 3-81, 3-97, 4-43, 4-67, 4-92
CL 4-103.	a. ≈ 23.899 mm b. $= 66$ m c. $\approx 32.93''$	Lessons 1.1.3, 4.1.2, and 4.1.4 Math Notes boxes	Problems 4-16, 4-20, 4-22, 4-36, 4-76, 4-92
CL 4-104.	a. $x = 49.286$ b. $x = \frac{-5}{9}$ c. $x = 3$ or $x = -5$ d. $x = \frac{11 \pm \sqrt{97}}{4} \approx 5.21$ or 0.29	Lessons 1.1.4 and 3.2.3 Math Notes box	Problems 1-17, 1-25, 1-32, 1-34, 1-45, 1-57, 1-74, 1-100, 1-124, 3-68, 3-90, 3-100, 4-8, 4-47, 4-75

COMPLETING THE TRIANGLE TOOLKIT

5

EAGLES BASKETBALL—PHILLY

CHAPTER 5 Completing the Triangle Toolkit

In Chapter 4, you **investigated** the powerful similarity and side ratio relationships in right triangles. In this chapter, you will learn about other side ratio relationships using the hypotenuse that will allow you to find missing side lengths and missing angle measures for any right triangles.

In addition, you will develop tools to complete your triangle toolkit so that you can find the missing angle measures and side lengths for any triangle, provided that enough information is given. You will then explore ways to **choose an appropriate tool** to solve new problems in unfamiliar contexts.

In this chapter, you will learn:

> how to recognize and use special right triangles.

> the trigonometric ratios of sine and cosine as well as the inverses of these functions.

> how to apply trigonometric ratios to find missing measurements in right triangles.

> new triangle tools called the Law of Sines and the Law of Cosines.

> how to recognize when the information provided is not enough to determine a unique triangle.

Guiding Questions

Think about these questions throughout this chapter:

Is there a shortcut?

How are the shapes related?

What information do I know?

Which tool(s) can I use?

Chapter Outline

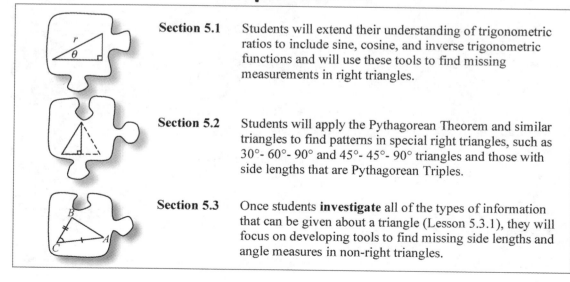

Section 5.1 Students will extend their understanding of trigonometric ratios to include sine, cosine, and inverse trigonometric functions and will use these tools to find missing measurements in right triangles.

Section 5.2 Students will apply the Pythagorean Theorem and similar triangles to find patterns in special right triangles, such as 30°- 60°- 90° and 45°- 45°- 90° triangles and those with side lengths that are Pythagorean Triples.

Section 5.3 Once students **investigate** all of the types of information that can be given about a triangle (Lesson 5.3.1), they will focus on developing tools to find missing side lengths and angle measures in non-right triangles.

5.1.1 What if I know the hypotenuse?

Sine and Cosine Ratios

In the previous chapter, you used the idea of similarity in right triangles to find a relationship between the acute angles and the lengths of the legs of a right triangle. However, we do not always work just with the legs of a right triangle—sometimes we only know the length of the hypotenuse. By the end of today's lesson, you will be able to use two new trigonometric ratios that involve the hypotenuse of right triangles.

5-1.   THE STREETS OF SAN FRANCISCO

While traveling around the beautiful city of San Francisco, Juanisha climbed several steep streets. One of the steepest, Filbert Street, has a slope angle of 31.5° according to her guidebook.

Once Juanisha finished walking 100 feet up the hill, she decided to figure out how high she had climbed. Juanisha drew the diagram below to represent this situation.

Can a tangent ratio be used to find Δy? Why or why not? Be prepared to share your thinking with the rest of the class.

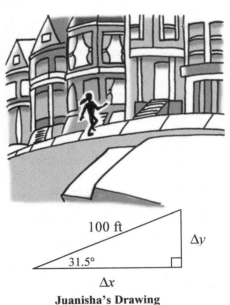

Juanisha's Drawing

5-2.   In order to find out how high Juanisha climbed in problem 5-1, you need to know more about the relationship between the ratios of the sides of a right triangle and the slope angle.

a.   Use **two different strategies** to find Δy for the slope triangles shown in the diagram at right.

b.   Find the ratio $\frac{\Delta x}{\text{hypotenuse}}$ for each triangle. Why must these ratios be equal?

c.   Find BC and AC in the triangle at right. Show all work.

5-3.   NEW TRIG RATIOS

In problem 5-2, you used a ratio that included the
hypotenuse of $\triangle ABC$. There are several ratios that
you might have used. One of those ratios is known
as the **sine ratio** (pronounced "sign"). This is the
ratio of the length of the side **opposite** the acute
angle to the length of the **hypotenuse**.

For the triangle shown at right, the sine of 60°
is $\frac{\sqrt{3}}{2} \approx 0.866$. This is written:

$$\sin 60° = \frac{\sqrt{3}}{2}$$

Another ratio comparing the length of the side **adjacent** to (which means "next to")
the angle to the length of the **hypotenuse**, is called the **cosine ratio** (pronounced
"co-sign"). For the triangle above, the cosine of 60° is $\frac{1}{2} = 0.5$. This is written:

$$\cos 60° = \frac{1}{2}$$

a.   Like the tangent, your calculator can give you both the sine and cosine ratios
       for any angle. Locate the "sin" and "cos" buttons on your calculator and use
       them to find the sine and cosine of 60°. Does your calculator give you the
       correct ratios?

b.   Use a trig ratio to write an equation and solve for a
       in the diagram at right. Does this require the sine
       ratio or the cosine ratio?

c.   Likewise, write an equation and solve for b for the
       triangle at right.

5-4.   Return to the diagram from Juanisha's
             climb in problem 5-1. Juanisha still
             wants to know how many feet she
             climbed vertically when she walked
             up Filbert Street. Use one of your
             new trig ratios to find how high she
             climbed.

Juanisha's Drawing

5-5.   For each triangle below, decide which side is
opposite and which is <u>adjacent</u> to the given
acute angle. Then determine which of the three
trig ratios will help you find *x*. Write and solve
an equation.

a.

b.

c.

d.

e.

f.

5-6.   TRIANGLE TOOLKIT

Obtain a Lesson 5.1.1 Resource Page ("Triangle Toolkit")
from your teacher. This will be a continuation of the
Geometry Toolkit you started in Chapter 1. Think about
the tools you have developed so far to solve for the
measure of sides and angles of a triangle. Then, in the
space provided, add a diagram and a description of each
tool you know. In later lessons, you will continue to add
new triangle tools to this toolkit, so be sure to keep this
resource page in a safe place. At this point, your toolkit
should include:

•   Pythagorean Theorem   •   Tangent

•   Sine   •   Cosine

5-7.   You now have multiple trig tools to find missing side
lengths of triangles. For the triangle at right, find the values
of *x* and *y*. Your Triangle Toolkit might help. Which tools
did you use?

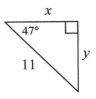

5-8.   Lori has written the conjectures below. For each one, decide if it is true or not. If you believe it is not true, find a **counterexample** (an example that proves that the statement is false).

   a.   If a shape as four equal sides, it cannot be a parallelogram.

   b.   If tan θ is more than 1, then θ must be more than 45°.

   c.   If two angles formed when two lines are cut by a transversal are corresponding, then the angles are congruent.

5-9.   Earl hates to take out the garbage and to wash the dishes, so he decided to make a deal with his parents: He will flip a coin once for each chore and will perform the chore if the coin lands on heads. What he doesn't know is that his parents are going to use a weighted coin that lands on heads 80% of the time!

   a.   What is the probability that Earl will have to do both chores?

   b.   What is the probability that Earl will have to take out the garbage, but will not need to wash the dishes?

5-10.   Copy the trapezoid at right on your paper. Then find its area and perimeter. Keep your work organized so that you can later explain how you solved it. (Note: The diagram is not drawn to scale.)

5-11.   Solve each of the equations below for the given variable. Be sure to check your answers.

   a. $4(2x + 5) - 11 = 4x - 3$ b. $\frac{2m-1}{19} = \frac{m}{10}$

   c. $3p^2 + 10p - 8 = 0$ d. $\sqrt{x+2} = 5$

5.1.2 Which tool should I use?

Selecting a Trig Tool

You now have several tools that will help you find the length of a side of a right triangle when given any acute angle and any side length. But how do you know which tool to use? And how can you identify the relationships between the sides and the given angle?

Today you will work with your team to develop **strategies** that will help you identify if cosine, sine, or tangent can be used to solve for a side of a right triangle. As you work, be sure to share any shortcuts you find that can help others identify which tool to use. As you work, keep the focus questions below in mind.

Is this triangle familiar? Is there something special about this triangle?

Which side is opposite the given angle? Which is adjacent?

Which tool should I use?

5-12. Obtain the Lesson 5.1.2 Resource Page from your teacher. On it, find the triangles shown below. Note: the diagrams are not drawn to scale.

$$\cos \theta = \frac{adj}{hyp}$$

$$\sin \theta = \frac{opp}{hyp}$$

$$\tan \theta = \frac{opp}{adj}$$

With your study team:

- Look through all the triangles first and see if any look familiar or are ones that you know how to answer right away without using a trig tool.

- Then, for all the other triangles, identify which tool you should use based on where the reference angle (the given acute angle) is located and which side lengths are involved.

- Write and solve an equation to find the missing side length.

a.

b.

c.

Problem continues on next page →

5-12.   *Problem continued from previous page.*

d.

e.

f.

g.

h.

i.

5-13.   Marta arrived for her geometry test only to find that she forgot her calculator. She decided to complete as much of each problem as possible.

a.   In the first problem on the test, Marta was asked to find the length *x* in the triangle shown at right. Using her algebra skills, she wrote and solved an equation. Her work is shown below. Explain what she did in each step.

$$\sin 25° = \frac{29}{x}$$
$$x(\sin 25°) = 29$$
$$x = \frac{29}{\sin 25°}$$

b.   Marta's answer in part (a) is called an **exact answer**. Now use your calculator to help Marta find the **approximate** length of *x*.

c.   In the next problem, Marta was asked to find *y* in the triangle shown at right. Find an exact answer for *y* without using a calculator. Then use a calculator to find an approximate value for *y*.

5-14.   In problem 5-12, you used trig tools to find a side length. But do you have a way to find an angle? **Examine** the triangles below. Do any of them look familiar? How can you use information about the side lengths to help you figure out the reference angle (θ)? Your Trig Table from Chapter 4 may be useful.

a.

b.

c.

5-15. Write a Learning Log entry explaining how you know which trig tool to use. Be sure to include examples with diagrams and anything else that would be useful to refer to later. Title this entry, "Choosing a Trig Tool" and include today's date.

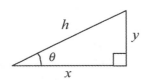

METHODS AND MEANINGS

Trigonometric Ratios

You now have three **trigonometric ratios** you can use to solve for the missing side lengths and angle measurements in any right triangle.
In the triangle below, when the sides are described relative to the angle θ, the opposite leg is y and the adjacent leg is x. The hypotenuse is h regardless of which acute angle is used.

$$\tan \theta = \frac{opposite\ leg}{adjacent\ leg} = \frac{y}{x}$$

$$\sin \theta = \frac{opposite\ leg}{hypotenuse} = \frac{y}{h}$$

$$\cos \theta = \frac{adjacent\ leg}{hypotenuse} = \frac{x}{h}$$

In some cases, you may want to rotate the triangle so that it looks like a slope triangle in order to easily identify the reference angle θ, the opposite leg y, the adjacent leg x, and the hypotenuse h. Instead of rotating the triangle, some people identify the opposite leg as the leg that is always opposite (not touching) the angle. For example, in the diagram at right, y is the leg opposite angle θ.

Review & Preview

5-16. For each triangle below, write an equation relating the **reference angle** (the given acute angle) with the two side lengths of the right triangle. Then solve your equation for x.

a.

b.

c.

5-17.   While shopping at his local home improvement store, Chen noticed that the directions for an extension ladder state, *"This ladder is most stable when used at a 75° angle with the ground."* He wants to buy a ladder to paint a two-story house that is 26 feet high. How long does his ladder need to be? Draw a diagram and set up an equation for this situation. Show all work.

5-18.   Kendra has programmed her cell phone to randomly show one of six photos when she turns it on. Two of the photos are of her parents, one is of her niece, and three are of her boyfriend, Bruce. Today, she will need to turn her phone on twice: once before school and again after school.

   a.   **Choose a model** (such as a tree diagram or generic area model) to represent this situation.

   b.   What is the probability that both photos will be of her boyfriend?

   c.   What is the probability that neither photo will be of her niece?

5-19.   Lori has written the conjectures below. For each one, decide if it is true or not. If you believe it is not true, find a **counterexample** (an example that proves that the statement is false).

   a.   If a triangle has a 60° angle, it must be an equilateral triangle.

   b.   To find the area of a shape, you always multiply the length of the base by the height.

   c.   All shapes have 360° rotation symmetry.

5-20.   **Examine** the triangles at right. Are the triangles similar? If so, show how you know with a flowchart. If not, explain how you know they cannot be similar.

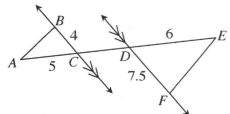

5.1.3 How can I find the angle?

Inverse Trigonometry

You now know how to find the missing side lengths in a right triangle given an acute angle and the length of any side. But what if you want to find the measure of an angle? If you are given the lengths of two sides of a right triangle, can you work backwards to find the measurements of the unknown angles? Today you will work on "undoing" the different trigonometric ratios to find the angles that correspond to those ratios.

5-21.   Mr. Gow needs to build a wheelchair access ramp for the school's auditorium. The ramp must rise a total of 3 feet to get from the ground to the entrance of the building. In order to follow the state building code, the angle formed by the ramp and the ground cannot exceed 4.76°.

Mr. Gow has plans from the planning department that call for the ramp to start 25 feet away from the building. Will this ramp meet the state building code?

a.   Draw an appropriate diagram. Add all the measurements you can. What does Mr. Gow need to find?

b.   To find an angle from a trig ratio you need to "undo" the trig ratio, just like you can undo addition with subtraction, multiplication with division, or squaring by finding the square root. These examples are all pairs of **inverse** operations.

When you use a calculator to do this, you use inverse trig functions which look like "$\sin^{-1}$", "$\cos^{-1}$", and "$\tan^{-1}$". These are pronounced, "inverse sine," "inverse cosine," and "inverse tangent." On many calculators, you must press the "inv" or "2nd" key first, then the "sin", "cos", or "tan" key.

Verify that your calculator can find an inverse trig value using the triangle at right from Lesson 5.1.2. When you find $\cos^{-1} \frac{8}{16}$, do you get 60°?

c.   Return to your diagram from part (a). According to the plan, what angle will the ramp make with the ground? Will the ramp be to code?

d.   At least how far from the building must the ramp start in order to meet the building code? If Mr. Gow builds the ramp exactly to code, how long will the ramp be? Show all work.

5-22. For the triangle at right, find the measures of $\angle A$ and $\angle B$. Once you have found the measure of the first acute angle (either $\angle A$ or $\angle B$), what knowledge about the angles in triangles could help you find the second acute angle?

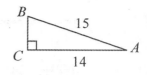

5-23. **Examine** the triangles below. Note: the diagrams are not drawn to scale.

$$\cos \theta = \frac{adj}{hyp} \qquad \sin \theta = \frac{opp}{hyp} \qquad \tan \theta = \frac{opp}{adj}$$

With your study team:

- Look through all the triangles first and see if any look familiar or are ones that you know how to answer right away without using a trig tool.

- Then, for all the other triangles, identify which tool to use based on where the reference angle (θ) is located and which side lengths are involved.

- Write and solve an equation to find the missing side length or angle.

a. 　　b. 　　c.

5-24. Peter cannot figure out what he did wrong. He wrote the equation below to find the missing angle of a triangle. However, his calculator gives him an error message each time he tries to calculate the angle.

Peter's work:　　$\cos \theta = \frac{8}{2.736}$

Jeri, his teammate, looked at his work and exclaimed, "Of course your calculator gives you an error! Your cosine ratio is impossible!" What is Jeri talking about? And how could she tell without seeing the triangle or checking on her calculator?

5-25. Write a Learning Log entry describing what you know about inverse trig functions. Be sure to include an example and a description of how to solve it. Title this entry, "Inverse Trig Functions" and include today's date.

5-26.   Solve the following equations for the given variable, if possible. Remember to check your answers.

    a. $6x^2 = 150$ b. $4m + 3 - m = 3(m+1)$

    c. $\sqrt{5x-1} = 3$ d. $(k - 4)^2 = -3$

5-27.   Mervin and Leela are in bumper cars. They are at opposite ends of a 100 meter track heading toward each other. If Mervin moves at a rate of 5.5 meters per second and Leela moves at a rate of 3.2 meters per second, how long does it take for them to collide?

5-28.   Donnell has a bar graph which shows the probability of a colored section coming up on a spinner, but part of the graph has been ripped off.

    a.   What is the probability of spinning red?

    b.   What is the probability of spinning yellow?

    c.   What is the probability of spinning blue?

    d.   If there is only one color missing from the graph, namely green, what is the probability of spinning green? Why?

5-29.   Find the area and the perimeter of the figure at right. Be sure to organize your work so you can explain your method later.

5-30.   While playing a board game, Mimi noticed that she could roll the dice 8 times in 30 seconds. How many minutes should it take her to roll the dice 150 times?

5.1.4 How can I use trig ratios?

Trigonometric Applications

Throughout this chapter, you have developed new tools to help you determine the length of any side or the measurement of any angle of a right triangle. Trig ratios, coupled with the Pythagorean Theorem, give you the powerful ability to solve problems involving right triangles. Today you will apply this knowledge to solve some real world problems.

As you are working with your team on the problems below, be sure to draw and label a diagram and determine which trig ratio to use before you start solving.

5-31.   CLIMBING IN YOSEMITE

David and Emily are climbing El Capitan, a big wall cliff in Yosemite National Park. David is on the ground holding the rope attached to Emily as she climbs. When Emily stops to rest, David wonders how high she has climbed. The rope is attached to his waist, about 3 feet off of the ground, and he has let out 40 feet of rope. This rope makes a 35° angle with the cliff wall.

a.   Assuming that the rope is taut (i.e., pulled tight), approximately how high up the wall has Emily climbed?

b.   How far away from the wall is David standing? Describe your method.

5-32.   The Bungling Brothers Circus is in town and you are part of the crew that is setting up its enormous tent. The center pole that holds up the tent is 70 feet tall. To keep it upright, a support cable needs to be attached to the top of the pole so that the cable forms a 60° angle with the ground.

a.   How long is the cable?

b.   How far from the pole should the cable be attached to the ground?

5-33.   Nathan is standing in a
meadow, exactly 185 feet from
the base of El Capitan. At
11:00 a.m., he observes Emily
climbing up the wall, and
determines that his angle of
sight up to Emily is about 10°.

a.   If Nathan's eyes are
about 6 feet above the
ground, about how high
is Emily at 11:00 a.m.?

b.   At 11:30 a.m., Emily has climbed some more, and Nathan's angle of sight to
her is now 25°. How far has Emily climbed in the past 30 minutes?

c.   If Emily climbs 32 feet higher in ten more minutes, at what angle will Nathan
have to look in order to see Emily?

5-34.   Forest needs to repaint the right side of his house because sunlight and rain have
caused the paint to peel. Each can of paint states that it will cover 150 sq. feet.
Help Forest decide how many cans of paint he should buy.

a.   Copy the shaded diagram below onto your paper. Work with your team to find
the area that will be painted green.

b.   Assuming that Forest can only buy whole cans of paint, how many cans of
paint should he buy? (Note: 1 square meter ≈ 10.764 square feet)

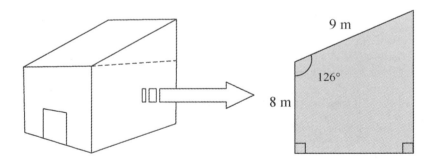

5-35.   TEAM CHALLENGE

It is 11:55 a.m., and Emily has climbed even higher. The rope now makes an angle
of 6° with the cliff wall. If David is 18 feet away from the base of El Capitan, at
what angle should Nathan (who is 185 feet from the base) look up to see Emily?

METHODS AND MEANINGS

Inverse Trigonometry

Just as subtraction "undoes" addition and multiplication "undoes" division, the inverse trigonometric functions "undo" the trig functions tangent, sine, and cosine. Specifically, **inverse trigonometric functions** are used to find the measure of an acute angle in a right triangle when a ratio of two sides is known. This is the **inverse**, or opposite, of finding the trig ratio from a known angle.

The inverse trigonometric functions that will be used in this course are $\sin^{-1}$, $\cos^{-1}$, and $\tan^{-1}$ (pronounced "inverse sine," "inverse cosine," and "inverse tangent"). Below is an example that shows how $\cos^{-1}$ may be used to find a missing angle, θ.

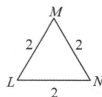

$$\cos\theta = \tfrac{10}{13}$$
$$\theta = \cos^{-1}\left(\tfrac{10}{13}\right)$$
$$\theta \approx 39.7°$$

To evaluate $\cos^{-1}\left(\tfrac{10}{13}\right)$ on a scientific calculator, most calculators require the "2nd" or "INV" button to be pressed before the "cos" button.

Review & Preview

5-36.   Which of the triangles below are similar to $\triangle LMN$ at right? How do you know? Explain.

a.   b.   c.   d.

5-37.   Find the equation of the line that has a 33.7° slope angle and a y-intercept at (0, 7). Assume the line has a positive slope.

Geometry Connections

5-38.   For each triangle below, write a trigonometric equation relating a, b, and θ.

a.

b.

c.

5-39.   Kendrick is frantic. He
remembers that several years ago
he buried his Amazing Electron
Ring in his little sister's sandbox,
but he cannot remember where.
A few minutes ago he heard that
someone is willing to pay $1000
for it. He has his shovel and is
ready to dig.

a.   The sandbox is rectangular, measuring 4 feet by 5
feet, as shown at right. If Kendrick only has time
to search in the 2 foot-square shaded region, what
is the probability that he will find the ring?

b.   What is the probability that he will not find the
ring? Explain how you found your answer.

c.   Kendrick decides instead to dig in the square
region shaded at right. Does this improve his
chances for finding the ring? Why or why not?

5-40.   Estelle is trying to find x in the triangle at right.
She lost her scientific calculator, but luckily her
teacher told her that $\sin 23° \approx 0.391$,
$\cos 23° \approx 0.921$, and $\tan 23° \approx 0.424$.

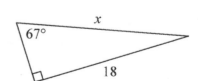

a.   Write an equation that Estelle could use to
solve for x.

b.   Without a calculator, how could Estelle find $\sin 67°$? Explain.

5.2.1 Is there a shortcut?

Special Right Triangles

You now know when triangles are similar and how to find missing side lengths in similar triangles. Today you will be using both of those ideas to **investigate** patterns within two types of special right triangles. These patterns will allow you to use a shortcut whenever you are finding side lengths in these particular types of right triangles.

5-41.   Darren wants to find the side lengths of the triangle at right. The only problem is that he left his calculator at home and he does not remember the value of cos 60°.

a.   "That's okay," says his teammate, Jan. "I think I see a short-cut." Using tracing paper, she created the diagram at right by reflecting the triangle across the side with length b. What is the resulting shape? How do you know?

b.   What if Jan had reflected across a different side? Would the result still be an equilateral triangle? Why or why not?

c.   Use Jan's diagram to find the value of a without using a trig ratio.

d.   Now find the length of b without a calculator. Leave your answer in **exact form**. In other words, do not approximate the height with a decimal.

5-42.   Darren's triangle is an example of a half-equilateral triangle, also known as a **30°- 60°- 90° triangle** because of its nice angle measures. Darren is starting to understand Jan's short-cut, but he still has some questions. Help Darren by answering his questions below.

a.   "Will this approach work on all triangles? In other words, can you always form an equilateral triangle by reflecting a right triangle?" Explain your **reasoning**.

b.   "What if the triangle looks different?" Use tracing paper to show how Darren can reflect the triangle at right to form an equilateral triangle. Then find the lengths of x and y without a calculator.

c.   "Is the longer leg of a 30°- 60°- 90° triangle always going to be the length of the shorter leg multiplied by $\sqrt{3}$? Why or why not?"

Problem continues on next page →

5-42.   *Problem continued from previous page.*

d.   "What if I only know the length of the shorter leg?"
     Consider the triangle at right. **Visualize** the
     equilateral triangle. Then find the values of n and m
     without a calculator.

e.   Darren drew the triangle at right and is
     wondering if it also is a 30°- 60°- 90° triangle.
     What do you think? How do you know?

5-43.   Darren wonders if he can find a similar pattern in another special
         triangle he knows, shown at right.

a.   Use what you know about this triangle to help Darren find
     the lengths of a and b without a trig tool or a calculator.
     Leave your answer in exact form.

b.   What should Darren name this triangle?

c.   Use the fact that all 45°- 45°- 90° triangles are similar to find the missing side
     lengths in the right triangles below. Leave your answers in exact, radical form.

(1)   (2)

5-44.   Use your new 30°- 60°- 90° and 45°- 45°- 90° triangle patterns to quickly find the
         lengths of the missing sides in each of the triangles below. Do not use a calculator.
         Leave answers in exact form. Note: The triangles are not necessarily drawn to
         scale.

a.   b.   c.

d.   e.   f.

5-45. In your Learning Log, explain what you know about 30°- 60°- 90° and 45°- 45°- 90° triangles. Include diagrams of each. Label this entry "Special Right Triangles" and include today's date.

LOOKING DEEPER

MATH NOTES

Rationalizing a Denominator

In Lesson 5.2.1, you developed some shortcuts to help find the lengths of the sides of a 30°- 60°- 90° and 45°- 45°- 90° triangle. This will enable you to solve similar problems in the future without a calculator or a Trig Table.

However, sometimes using the shortcuts leads to some strange looking answers. For example, when finding the length of a in the triangle at right, you will get the expression $\frac{6}{\sqrt{2}}$.

A number with a radical in the denominator is difficult to estimate. Therefore, it is sometimes beneficial to **rationalize the denominator** so that no radical remains in the denominator. Study the example below.

Example: Simplify $\frac{6}{\sqrt{2}}$.

First, multiply the numerator and denominator by the radical in the denominator. Since $\frac{\sqrt{2}}{\sqrt{2}} = 1$, this does not change the value of the expression.

Underlined _Example_

$$\frac{6}{\sqrt{2}} \cdot \frac{\sqrt{2}}{\sqrt{2}} = \frac{6\sqrt{2}}{2}$$
$$= 3\sqrt{2}$$

After multiplying, notice that the denominator no long has a radical, since $\sqrt{2} \cdot \sqrt{2} = 2$.

Often, the product can be further simplified. Since 2 divides evenly into 6, the expression $\frac{6\sqrt{2}}{2}$ can be rewritten as $3\sqrt{2}$.

5-46. For each triangle below, use your triangle shortcuts from this lesson to find the missing side lengths. Then find the area and perimeter of the triangle.

a.

b.

Geometry Connections

5-47.   Use the relationships found in each of the diagrams below to solve for *x* and *y*.
          Assume the diagrams are not drawn to scale. State which geometric relationships
          you used.

a.

b.

c.

d.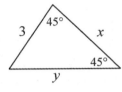

5-48.   On graph paper, graph $\overline{AB}$ if $A(1, 6)$ and $B(5, 2)$.

a.   Find AB (the length of $\overline{AB}$). Leave your answer in **exact form**. That is, do
      not approximate with a decimal. Explain your method.

b.   Reflect $\overline{AB}$ across the *y*-axis to create $\overline{A'B'}$. What type of shape is $ABB'A'$ if
      the points are connected in order? Then find the area of $ABB'A'$.

5-49.   Fill in the blank ovals below so that each flowchart is correct.

a.

b.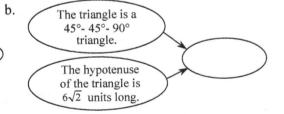

5-50. Decide if each pair of triangles below are similar. If they are similar, show a flowchart that organizes your **reasoning**. If they are not similar, explain how you know.

a.

b.

c.

d.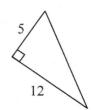

5.2.2 How can I use similar triangles?

Pythagorean Triples

In Lesson 5.2.1, you developed shortcuts that will help you quickly find the lengths of the sides of certain right triangles. What other shortcuts can be helpful? As you work today with your study team, look for patterns and connections between triangles.

5-51. Use the tools you have developed to find the lengths of the missing sides of the triangles below. If you know of a shortcut, share it with your team. Be ready to share your strategies with the class.

a.

b.

c.

d.

e.

f.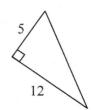

Problem continues on next page →

5-51. *Problem continued from previous page.*

g.

h.

i.

5-52. Karl noticed some patterns as he was finding the sides of the triangles in problem 5-46. He recognized that the triangles in parts (c), (d), (f), (g), (h), and (i) are integers. He also noticed that knowing the triangle in part (c) can help find the hypotenuse in parts (d) and (g).

   a. Groups of numbers like 3, 4, 5 and 5, 12, 13 are called **Pythagorean Triples**. Why do you think they are called Pythagorean Triples?

   b. What other sets of numbers are also Pythagorean Triples? How many different sets can you find?

5-53. With your team, find the missing side lengths for each triangle below. Try to use your new shortcuts when possible.

a.

b.

c.

d.

e.

f.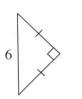

5-54. Diana looked at the next problems and thought she could not do them. Erik pointed out that they are the same as the previous triangles, but instead of numbers, each side length is given in terms of a variable. Use Erik's idea to help you find the missing side lengths of the triangles below:

a.

b.

c.

d.

e.

5-55. Use your shortcuts to find the area and perimeter of each shape below:

a.

b. $6\sqrt{2}$

c.

5-56. The sides of each of the triangles below can be found using one of the shortcuts from Section 5.2. Try to find the missing lengths using your patterns. Do not use a calculator.

a.

b.

c.

d.

5-57. Copy the diagram at right onto your paper.

a. Find the measures of all the angles in the diagram.

b. Make a flowchart showing that the triangles are similar.

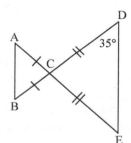

c. Cheri and Roberta noticed their similarity statements for part (b) were not the same. Cheri had stated $\triangle ABC \sim \triangle DEC$, while Roberta maintained that $\triangle ABC \sim \triangle EDC$. Who is correct? Or are they both correct? Explain your **reasoning**.

5-58. Using the triangle at right, write an expression representing cos 52°. Then write an expression for tan 52° and cos 38°.

5-59. Hadrosaurs, a family of duck-billed, plant-eating dinosaurs, were large creatures with thick, strong tails. It has recently been determined that hadrosaurs probably originated in North America.

Example of a hadrosaur footprint.

Scientists in Alaska recently found a hadrosaur footprint like the one at right that measured 14 inches across. It is believed that the footprint was created by a young dinosaur that was approximately 27 feet long. Adult hadrosaurs have been known to be 40 feet long. How wide would you expect a footprint of an adult hadrosaur to be? Show your **reasoning**.

5-60. Jeynysha has a Shape Bucket with a trapezoid, right triangle, scalene triangle, parallelogram, square, rhombus, pentagon, and kite. If she reaches in the bucket and randomly selects a shape, find:

    a.   P(at least one pair of parallel sides)   b.   P(hexagon)

    c.   P(not a triangle)   d.   P(has at least 3 sides)

5.3.1 What triangle tools do I still need?

Finding Missing Parts of Triangles

When do you have enough information to find all of the angle measures and side lengths of a triangle? For example, can you find all of the side lengths if you are only informed about the three angles? Does it matter if the triangle has a right angle or not? Today you will organize your triangle knowledge so that you know what tools you have and for which triangles you can accurately find all of the angle measures and side lengths.

5-61. How many ways can three pieces of information about a triangle be given? For example, the three given measurements could be one angle and two side lengths, as shown in the triangle at right. List as many other combinations of three pieces of information about a triangle as you can.

5-62.   HOW MUCH INFORMATION DO YOU NEED?

So far in this course you have developed several tools to find missing parts of triangles. But how complete is your Triangle Toolkit? Are there more tools that you need to develop?

Your Task: With your team, find the missing angles and sides of the triangles below. (Also printed on the Lesson 5.3.1 Resource Page). Notice that each triangle has three given pieces of information about its angles and sides. If there is not enough information or if you do not yet have the tools to find the missing information, explain why.

Discussion Points

- Are there any triangles that look familiar or that you already have a **strategy** for?

- What tools do you have to solve for parts of triangles? For what types of triangles do these tools work?

- Would it be helpful to subdivide any of the triangles into right triangles?

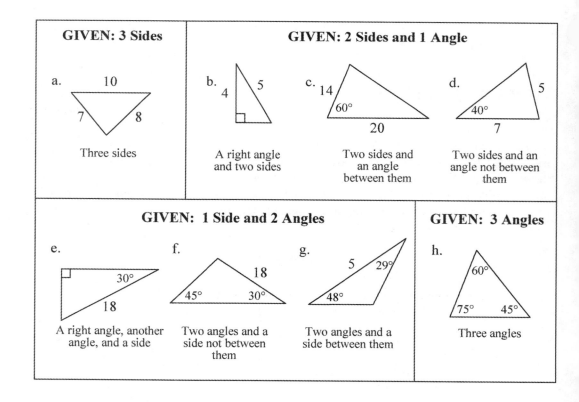

5-63.   While looking for different strategies to use, advice from a teammate can often help.

a.   Angelo thinks that the Pythagorean Theorem is a useful tool. For which types of triangles is the Pythagorean Theorem useful? Look for these types of triangles in problem 5-62 and use the theorem to solve for any missing sides.

b.   Tomas remembers using trigonometric ratios to find the missing sides and angles of a triangle. Which triangles from problem 5-62 can be analyzed using this **strategy**?

Three angles

c.   Ngoc thinks that more than one triangle exists with the angles at right. Is she correct? If so, how are these triangles related?

d.   Does it matter if the triangle is a right triangle? For example, both of these triangles (from parts (b) and (d)) give an angle and two sides. Can you use the same tool for both? Why or why not?

A right angle
and two sides

Two sides and an
angle not between
them

*Further Guidance
section ends here.*

5-64.   WHAT IF IT DOES NOT HAVE A RIGHT ANGLE?

If your team needs help on parts (c) and (f) of problem 5-62, Leila has an idea. She knows that she has some tools to use with right triangles but noticed that some of the triangles in problem 5-62 are <u>not</u> right triangles. Therefore, she thinks it is a good idea to split a triangle into two right triangles.

a.   Discuss with your team how to change the diagram at right so that the triangle is divided into two right triangles. Then use your right triangle tools to solve for the missing sides and angles.

b.   Leila wonders if her method would work for other triangles too. Test her method on the triangle from part (f) of problem 5-62 (also shown at right). Does her method work?

5-65. Ryan liked Leila's idea so much, he looked for a way to create a right triangle in the triangle from part (g) of problem 5-62. He decided to draw a height <u>outside</u> the triangle, forming a large right triangle. Use the right triangle to help you find the missing side lengths of the original triangle.

5-66. LEARNING LOG

Return to problem 5-62 and **examine** all of the ways three pieces of information can be given about a triangle. For which triangle(s) were you able to find missing side lengths and angles? For which triangle(s) do you not have enough given information? For which triangle(s) do you need a new **strategy**? Reflect on the strategies you have developed so far. Title this entry "Strategies to find Sides and Angles of a Triangle" and include today's date.

M
ETHODS AND MEANINGS

Special Right Triangles

MATH NOTES

So far in this chapter, you have learned about several special right triangles that will reappear throughout the rest of this course. Being able to recognize these triangles will enable you to quickly find the lengths of the sides and will save you time and effort in the future.

The half-equilateral triangle is also known as the **30°- 60°- 90° triangle**. The sides of this triangle are always in the ratio $1 : \sqrt{3} : 2$, as shown at right.

Another special triangle is the **45°- 45°- 90° triangle.** This triangle is also commonly known as an isosceles right triangle. The ratio of the sides of this triangle is always $1 : 1 : \sqrt{2}$.

You also discovered several **Pythagorean triples**. A Pythagorean triple is any set of 3 positive integers a, b, and c for which $a^2 + b^2 = c^2$. Two of the common Pythagorean triples that you will see throughout this course are shown at right.

5-67. To paint a house, Travis leans a ladder against the wall. If the ladder is 16 feet long and it makes contact with the house 14 feet above ground, what angle does the ladder make with the ground? Draw a diagram of this situation and show all work.

5-68. WACKY DIAGRAMS

After drawing some diagrams on his paper, Jason thinks there is something wrong. **Examine** each diagram below and decide whether or not the triangle could exist. If it cannot exist, explain why not.

a.

b.

5-69. William thinks that the hypotenuse must be the longest side of a right triangle, but Chad does not agree. Who is correct? Support your answer with an explanation and a counterexample, if possible.

5-70. Plot $\triangle ABC$ on graph paper with points $A(3, 3)$, $B(1, 1)$, and $C(6, 1)$.

a. Reflect $\triangle ABC$ across the x-axis. Then translate the result to the left 6 and down 3. Name the coordinates of the result.

b. Rotate $\triangle ABC$ 90° counterclockwise ($\circlearrowleft$) about the origin. Then reflect the result across the y-axis. Name the coordinates of the result.

5-71. Solve the equations below, if possible. If there is no solution, explain why.

a. $\frac{8-x}{x} = \frac{3}{2}$

b. $-2(5x-1)-3 = -10x$

c. $x^2 + 8x - 33 = 0$

d. $\frac{2}{3}x - 12 = 180$

5-72. **Multiple Choice:** Based on the relationships provided in the diagram, which of the equations below is correct? **Justify** your solution.

a. $4x + 2° + 9x - 3° = 90°$

b. $4x + 2° = 9x - 3°$

c. $4x + 2° + 9x - 3° = 180°$

d. $(4x + 2°)(9x - 3°) = 90°$

5.3.2 Is there a faster way?

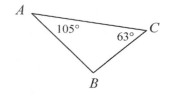

Law of Sines

In problem 6-64, you used a complicated **strategy** to find the lengths of sides and measures of angles for a non-right triangle. Is there a tool you can use to find angles and side lengths of non-right triangles directly, using fewer steps? Today you will explore the relationships that exist among the sides and angles of triangles and will develop a new tool called the Law of Sines.

5-73.   Is there a relationship between a triangle's side and the angle opposite to it? For example, assume that the diagram for $\triangle ABC$, shown at right, is not drawn to scale. Based on the angle measures provided in the diagram, which side must be longest? Which side must be shortest? How do you know?

5-74.   When Madelyn **examined** the triangle at right, she said, "I don't think this diagram is drawn to scale because I think the side labeled x has to be longer than 4."

    a.   Do you agree with Madelyn? Why or why not?

    b.   Leila thinks that x can be found by using right triangles. Review what you learned in Lesson 5.3.1 by finding the value of x.

    c.   Find the area of the triangle.

5-75.   Thui and Ivan came up with two different ways to find the height of the triangle at right.

- Using the right triangle on the left, Thui wrote: $\sin 58° = \frac{h}{12}$.

- Ivan also used the sine function, but his equation looked like this: $\sin 24° = \frac{h}{25}$.

    a.   Which triangle did Ivan use?

    b.   Calculate h using Thui's equation and again using Ivan's equation. How do their answers compare?

5-76. **LAW OF SINES**

Edwin wonders if Thui's and Ivan's methods can help find a way to relate the sides and angles of a non-right triangle. To find the height, Ivan and Thui each used the sine ratio with an acute angle and the hypotenuse of a right triangle.

a. Use the triangle above to find **two expressions** for h using the individual right triangles like you did in problem 5-75.

b. Use your expressions from part (a) to show that $\frac{\sin(m\angle B)}{b} = \frac{\sin(m\angle A)}{a}$.

c. Describe where $\angle B$ is located in relation to the side labeled b. How is $\angle A$ related to the side labeled a?

d. The relationship $\frac{\sin(m\angle B)}{b} = \frac{\sin(m\angle A)}{a}$ is called the **Law of Sines**. Read the Math Notes box for this lesson to learn more about this relationship. Then use this relationship to solve for x in the triangle at right.

5-77. **EXTENSION**

Does the Law of Sines work for a right triangle as well? Test this idea by solving for x in the triangle at right <u>twice</u>: once using the Law of Sines and again using right-triangle trigonometry (such as sine, cosine, or tangent). What happened? If it worked, do you think it will work for all right triangles?

5-78. **LEARNING LOG**

Reflect on what you have learned during this lesson about the sides and angles of a triangle. What is the Law of Sines and when can it be used? Include an example. Title this entry "Law of Sines" and include today's date.

METHODS AND MEANINGS

Law of Sines

For any $\triangle ABC$, the ratio of the sine of an angle to the length of the side opposite the angle is constant. This means that:

$$\frac{\sin(m\angle A)}{a} = \frac{\sin(m\angle B)}{b},$$

$$\frac{\sin(m\angle B)}{b} = \frac{\sin(m\angle C)}{c}, \text{ and}$$

$$\frac{\sin(m\angle A)}{a} = \frac{\sin(m\angle C)}{c}.$$

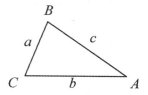

This property is called the **Law of Sines**. This is a powerful tool because it allows you to use the sine ratio to solve for measures of angles and lengths of sides of *any* triangle, not just right triangles. The law works for angle measures between 0° and 180°.

5-79. Lizzie noticed that two angles in $\triangle DEF$, shown at right, have the same measure. Based on this information, what statement can you make about the relationship between $\overline{ED}$ and $\overline{EF}$?

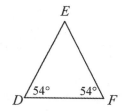

5-80. Find the length of $\overline{DF}$ in the diagram from problem 5-79 if $DE = 9$ units.

5-81. Find the area of the triangle at right. Show all work.

5-82. In the diagram at right, $\triangle ABC$ and $\triangle ADE$ are similar. If $AB = 5$, $BD = 4$, and $BC = 7$, then what is DE?

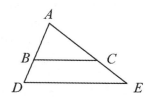

5-83.   A particular spinner only has two regions: green and purple. If the spinner is randomly spun twice, the probability of it landing on green twice is 16%. What is the probability of the spinner landing on purple twice?

5-84.   Solve the system of equations below. Write your solution as a point in (x, y) form. Check your solution.

$$y = -3x - 2$$
$$2x + 5y = 16$$

5.3.3   How can I complete my triangle toolkit?

Law of Cosines

So far, you have three tools that will help you solve for missing sides and lengths of a triangle. In fact, one of those tools, the Law of Sines, even helps when the triangle is not a right triangle. There are still two triangles from our exploration in Lesson 5.3.1 that you cannot solve directly with any of your existing tools. Today you will develop a tool to help find missing side lengths and angle measures for triangles such as those shown at right.

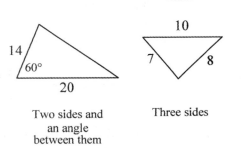

Two sides and an angle between them

Three sides

By the end of this lesson, you will have a complete set of tools to help solve for the side lengths and angle measures of *any* triangle, as long as enough information is given.

5-85.   LAW OF COSINES

Leila remembers that in problem 5-64, she solved for the side lengths and missing angles of the triangle at right by dividing the triangle into two right triangles. She thinks that using two right triangles may help find a tool that works for any triangle with two given sides and a given angle between them. Help Leila generalize this process by answering the questions below.

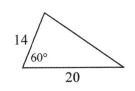

a.   **Examine** $\triangle ABC$ at right. Assume that you know the lengths of sides a and b and the measure of $\angle C$. Notice how the side opposite $\angle A$ is labeled a and the side opposite $\angle B$ is labeled b, and so on. Line segment $\overline{BD}$ is drawn so that $\triangle ABC$ is divided into two right triangles. If $CD = x$, then what is DA?

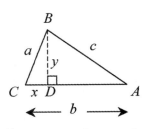

Problem continues on next page →

5-85.   *Problem continued from previous page.*

b.   Write an equation relating a, x, and y.
Likewise, write an equation relating the
side lengths of $\triangle BDA$.

c.   Leila noticed that both expressions
from part (b) have a y^2-term. "Can we
combine these equations so that we
have one equation that links sides a, b,
and c?" she asked. With your team, use
algebra to combine these two equations
so that y^2 is eliminated. Then simplify
the resulting equation as much as
possible.

d.   The equation from part (c) still has an x-term. Using only a and $m\angle C$, find an
expression for x using the left-hand triangle. Solve your equation for x, then
substitute this expression into your equation from part (c) for x.

e.   Solve your equation from part (d) for c^2. You have now found an equation
that links the lengths of two sides and the measure of the angle between them
to find the length of the side opposite the angle. This relationship is called the
Law of Cosines. Read the Math Notes box for this lesson to learn more about
the Law of Cosines.

f.   Use the Law of Cosines to solve for x in the
triangle at right.

5-86.   You now have many tools to solve for missing side lengths and angle measures.
Decide which tool to use for each of the triangles below and solve for x. Decide if
your answer is reasonable based on the diagram.

a.

b.

c.

5-87.   EXTENSION

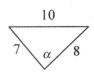

Not only can the Law of Cosines be used to solve for side lengths, but it can also be used to solve for angles. Consider the triangle from Lesson 5.3.1, shown at right.

a.   Write an equation that relates the three sides and the angle α. Then solve the equation for α.

b.   Now solve for the other two angles using any method. Be sure to name which tool(s) you used!

5-88.   You have now completed your Triangle Toolkit and can find the missing side lengths and angle measures for *any* triangle, provided that enough information is given. Add the Law of Sines and Law of Cosines to your Triangle Toolkit for reference later in this course.

METHODS AND MEANINGS

MATH NOTES

Law of Cosines

Just like the Law of Sines, the **Law of Cosines** represents a relationship between the sides and angles of a triangle.

Specifically, when given the lengths of any two sides, such as a and b, and the angle between them, $\measuredangle C$, the length of the third side, in this case c, can be found using this relationship:

$$c^2 = a^2 + b^2 - 2ab\cos C$$

Similar equations can be used to solve for a and b.

5-89.   Eugene wants to use the cosine ratio to find y on this triangle.

a.   Which angle should he use for his slope angle? Why?

b.   Set up an equation, and solve for y using cosine.

5-90.   Copy the graph at right onto graph paper.

a.   If the shape *ABCDE* were rotated about the origin 180°, where would point *A′* be?

b.   If the shape *ABCDE* were reflected across the *x*-axis, where would point *C′* be?

c.   If the shape *ABCDE* were translated so that each point (x, y) corresponds to $(x - 1, y + 3)$, where would point *B′* be?

5-91.   Jerry was trying to use a flowchart to describe how his friend Marcy feels about Whizzbangs candy. **Examine** his flowchart below.

a.   How do you know Jerry's flowchart is incorrect?

b.   Make a flowchart on your paper with the same three ovals, but with arrows drawn in so the flowchart makes sense. Explain why your flowchart makes more sense than the one at right.

5-92.   On graph paper, graph the line $y = \frac{3}{4}x + 6$. Then find the slope angle (the acute angle the line makes with the *x*-axis).

5-93.   The spinners at right are spun and the results are added.

a.   Find P(sum is 4).

b.   Find P(sum is 8).

Spinner #1   **Spinner #2**

5-94.   **Examine** the diagram at right. Which angle below is another name for $\angle ABC$? Note: More than one solution is possible.

a. $\angle ABE$ b. $\angle GBD$

c. $\angle FBG$ d. $\angle EBC$

e.   None of these

5.3.4 Is there more than one possible triangle?

Optional: Ambiguous Triangles

Now that you have completed your Triangle Toolkit, you can solve for the missing angles or sides of any triangle, provided that enough information is given. But how do you know if you have enough information? What if there is more than one possible triangle? Today you will explore situations where your tools may not be adequate to solve for the missing side lengths and angle measures of a triangle.

5-95.   **Examine** the triangle at right from problem 5-62. Notice that two side lengths and an angle measure not between the labeled sides are given. (This situation is sometimes referred to as **SSA**.)

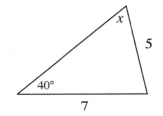

a.   Assuming that the triangle is not drawn to scale, what do you know about x? Is it more than 40° or less than 40°? **Justify** your conclusion.

b.   Solve for x. Was your conclusion from part (a) correct?

c.   "Hold on!" proclaims your teammate, Missy. "That's not what I got. I found out that $x \approx 115.9°$." She then drew the triangle at right. Do you agree with Missy? Use the Law of Sines to test her answer. That is, find out if the ratios of $\frac{\sin(angle)}{\text{opposite side}}$ are equal for each angle and its opposite side.

d.   What happened? How can there be two possible answers for x? **Examine** the diagram at right for clues.

e.   What is the relationship between the two solution angles? Do you think this relationship always exists? **Examine** the diagram above, which shows the two angle solutions, and use it to explain how the solutions are related.

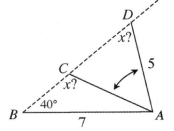

5-96.   In problem 5-95, you determined that it was possible to create two triangles because you were given only two side lengths and an angle not between them. When this happens, we call this **triangle ambiguity** since we cannot tell which triangle was the one we were supposed to find. Will there always be two possible triangles? Can there ever be more than two possible triangles? Think about this as you answer the questions below.

a.   Obtain the Lesson 5.3.4 Resource Page and some linguini (or other flat manipulative) from your teacher. Prepare pieces of linguini that are 1 inch, 1.5 inches, 2 inches, 2.5 inches, and 3 inches long.

b.   For each length of linguini, place one end at point A in the diagram on the resource page. Determine if you can form a triangle by connecting the linguini with the dashed side to close the triangle. If you can make a triangle, label the third vertex C and label $\overline{AC}$ with its length. Can you form more than one triangle with the same side length? Is a triangle always possible? Record any conjectures you make.

c.   If the technology is available, test your conjectures from part (b) with a dynamic geometry tool. Try to learn everything you can about SSA triangles. Use the questions below to guide your **investigation**.

   •   Can you find a way to create three possible triangles with one set of SSA information?

   •   Is it ever impossible to form a triangle?

   •   Is it possible to choose SSA information that will create only one triangle? How?

5-97.   Now that Alex knows that SSA (two sides and an angle not between them) can result in more than one possible triangle, he wants to know if other types of given information can also create ambiguous results. For example, when given three side lengths, is more than one triangle possible?

Examine each of the diagrams below (from problem 5-62) and determine if any other types of triangles are also ambiguous. You may want to imagine building the shapes with linguini. Remember that the given information cannot change – thus, if a side length is given, it cannot be lengthened or shortened.

a.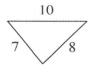
10
7   8

Three sides (SSS)

b.
14
60°
20

Two sides and an angle between them (SAS)

c.
18
45°   30°

Two angles and a side not between them (AAS)

d.
60°
75°   45°

Three angles (AAA)

5-98.   You now have many tools to use when solving for missing sides lengths and angle measures. Decide which tool to use for each of the triangles below and solve for x. If there is more than one solution, find both. Name the tool you use.

a.
16
42°
x 10

b.
9   56°
x

c.
25
120° 51°
x

5-99.   EXTENSION

While examining the triangle at right, Alex stated,
"Well, I know that there can be at most one solution."

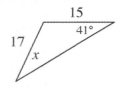

a.   **Examine** the information given in the triangle.
What do you know about x? Is it more than 41° or
less? How can you tell?

b.   Alex remembered that if there were two solutions, then they had to be
supplementary. Explain why this triangle cannot have two different values
for x.

5-100.   Farmer Jill has a problem. She lives on a
triangular plot of land that is surrounded
on all three sides by a fence. Yesterday,
one side of the fence was torn down in a
storm. She wants to determine the length
of the side that needs to be rebuilt so she
can purchase enough lumber. Since the
weather is still too poor for her to go
outside and measure the distance, she
decides to use the lengths of the two sides
that are still standing (116 feet and 224
feet) and the angle between them (58°).

a.   Draw a diagram of this situation. Label all of the sides and angles that Farmer
Jill has measurements for.

b.   Find the length of the fence that needs to be replaced. Show all work. Which
tool did you use?

5-101.   Mr. Miller has informed you that two shapes are similar.

a.   What does this tell you about the angles in the shapes?

b.   What does this tell you about the lengths of the sides of the shapes?

5-102.   Find the equation of the line that has a slope angle of 25° and a y-intercept of (0, 4).
Sketch a graph of this line. Assume the slope of the line is positive.

5-103.   Two sides of a triangle have lengths 9 and 14 units. Describe what you know about the length of the third side.

5-104.   Tehachapi High School has 839 students and is increasing by 34 students per year. Meanwhile, Fresno High School has 1644 students and is decreasing by 81 students per year. In how many years will the two high schools have the same number of students? Be sure to show all work.

5-105.   **Multiple Choice:** In the triangle at right, x must be:

a.   42°   b.   69°   c.   21°

d.   138°   e.   none of these

$5 \cdot 3 \cdot 5$ Which tool should I use?

Choosing a Tool

During this section, you have developed new tools such as the Law of Sines and the Law of Cosines to find the lengths of sides and the measures of angles of a triangle. These strategies are very useful because they work with all triangles, not just right triangles. But when is each **strategy** the best one to use? Today you will focus on which **strategy** is most effective to use in different situations. You will also apply your **strategies** to triangles in different contexts.

As you work on these problems, keep in mind that good communication and a joint brainstorming of ideas will greatly enhance your team's ability to **choose a strategy** and to solve these problems.

5-106.   LAKE TOFTEE, Part One

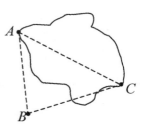

A bridge is being designed to connect two towns along the shores of Lake Toftee in Minnesota (one at point A and the other at point C). Lavanne has been given the responsibility of determining the length of the bridge.

Since he could not accurately measure across the lake (AC), he measured the only distance he could by foot (AB). He drove a stake into the ground at point B and found that $AB = 684$ feet. He also used a protractor to determine that $m\angle B = 79°$ and $m\angle C = 53°$. How long will the bridge need to be?

5-107.   LAKE TOFTEE, Part Two

Lavanne was not convinced that his measurements from
problem 5-106 were correct. He decided to measure the
distance between towns A and C again using a different
method to verify his results.

This time, he decided to drive a stake in the ground at point
D, which is 800 feet from town A and 694 feet from town C.
He also determined that $m\angle D = 68°$. Using these
measurements, how wide is the lake between points A and C? Does this confirm the
results from problem 5-106?

5-108.   The lid of a grand piano is propped open by a
supporting arm, as shown in the diagram at
right. Carson knows that the supporting arm
is 2 feet long and makes a 60° angle with the
piano. He also knows that the piano lid
makes a 23° angle with the piano. How wide
is the piano?

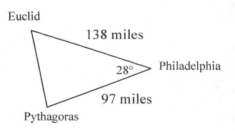

5-109.   PENNANT RACE

Your basketball team has made it to the semi-
finals and now needs to win only two more
games to go to the finals. Your plan is to
leave Philadelphia, travel 138 miles to the
town of Euclid, and then play the team there.
Then you will leave Euclid, travel to
Pythagoras, and play that team. Finally, you
will travel 97 miles to return home.

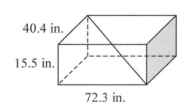

Euclid

138 miles

28° Philadelphia

97 miles

Pythagoras

Your team bus can travel only 300 miles on one tank of gas. Assuming that all of
the roads connecting the three towns are straight and that the two roads that connect
in Philadelphia form a 28° angle, will one tank of gas be enough for the trip? **Justify**
your solution.

5-110.   Shonte is buying pipes to install sprinklers for her
front lawn. She needs to fit the pipes into the bed of
her pickup truck to get them home from the store.
She knows that the longest dimension in her truckbed
is from the top of one corner to the bottom of the bed
at the opposite corner. After measuring the truckbed,
she drew the diagram at right. What is the longest
pipe she can buy?

40.4 in.

15.5 in.

72.3 in.

5-111. In problem 5-105 from homework, you used your intuition to state that if a triangle has two angles that are equal, then the triangle has two sides that are the same length. Now use your triangle tools to show that your intuition was correct. For example, for $\triangle PQR$, show that if $m\angle Q = m\angle R$, then $PQ = PR$.

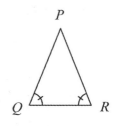

5-112. As Freda gazes at the edge of the Grand Canyon, she decides to try to determine the height of the wall opposite her. Using her trusty clinometer, she determines that the top of the wall is at a 38° angle above her, while the bottom is at a 46° angle below her, as shown in the diagram at right. If the base of the wall is 253 feet from the point on the ground directly below Freda, determine the height of the wall opposite her.

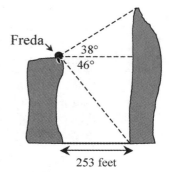

5-113. While facing north, Lisa and Aaron decide to hike to their campsite. Lisa plans to hike 5 miles due north to Lake Toftee before she goes to the campsite. Aaron plans to turn 38° east and hike 7.4 miles directly to the campsite. How far will Lisa have to hike from the lake to meet Aaron at the campsite? Start by drawing a diagram of the situation, then calculate the distance.

Review & Preview

5-114. Solve for the missing side lengths and angles in the triangle at right.

5-115. **Examine** the triangle shown at right. Solve for x twice, using two different methods. Show your work for each method clearly.

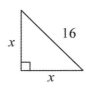

5-116. In Chapter 1 you learned that all rectangles are parallelograms because they all have two pairs of opposite parallel sides. Does that mean that all parallelograms are rectangles? Why or why not? Support your statements with **reasons**.

5-117.   Find the area and perimeter of each shape below. Show all work.

a.

b.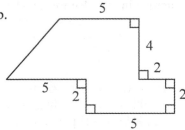

5-118.   △*ABC* was reflected across the *x*-axis, and then that result was rotated 90° clockwise about the origin to result in △*A′B′C′* , shown at right. Find the coordinates of points *A*, *B*, and *C* of the original triangle.

5-119.   Find the equation of a line parallel to the line $y = \frac{3}{4}x - 5$ that passes through the point (–4, 1). Show how you found your answer.

5-120.   **Examine** trapezoid *ABCD* at right.

a.   Find the measures of all the angles in the diagram.

b.   What is the sum of the angles that make up the trapezoid *ABCD*? That is, what is $m\angle A + m\angle ABC + m\angle BCD + m\angle D$?

5-121.   Use your triangle tools to solve the problems below.

a.   Find *PR* in the diagram at right.

b.   Find the perimeter of quadrilateral *PQRS*.

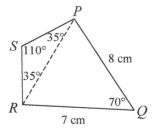

5-122. Find the area and perimeter of $\triangle ABC$ at right. Give approximate (decimal) answers, not exact answers.

5-123. Earl still hates to wash the dishes and take out the garbage. (See problem 5-9.) He found his own weighted coin, one that would randomly land on heads 30% of the time. He will flip a coin once for each chore and will perform the chore if the coin lands on heads.

   a. What is the probability that Earl will get out of doing both chores?

   b. What is the probability that Earl will have to take out the garbage, but will not need to wash the dishes?

5-124. On graph paper, draw $\triangle ABC$ if $A(3, 2)$, $B(-1, 4)$, and $C(0, -2)$.

   a. Find the perimeter of $\triangle ABC$.

   b. Dilate $\triangle ABC$ from the origin by a factor of 2 to create $\triangle A'B'C'$. What is the perimeter of $\triangle A'B'C'$?

   c. If $\triangle ABC$ is rotated 90° clockwise (↻) about the origin to form $\triangle A''B''C''$, name the coordinates of C''.

5-125. Solve each equation below for x. Check your solution if possible.

   a. $\frac{4}{5}x - 2 = 7$

   b. $3x^2 = 300$

   c. $\frac{4x-1}{2} = \frac{x+5}{3}$

   d. $x^2 - 4x + 6 = 0$

Chapter 5 Closure   What have I learned?

Reflection and Synthesis

The activities below offer you a chance to reflect on what you have learned in this chapter. As you work, look for concepts that you feel very comfortable with, ideas that you would like to learn more about, and topics you need more help with. Look for connections between ideas as well as connections with material you learned previously.

① TEAM BRAINSTORM

With your team, brainstorm a list for each of the following two subjects. Be as detailed as you can. How long can you make your list? Challenge yourselves. Be prepared to share your team's ideas with the class.

Topics: What have you studied in this chapter? What ideas and words were important in what you learned? Remember to be as detailed as you can.

Connections: How are the topics, ideas, and words that you learned in previous courses connected to the new ideas in this chapter? Again, make your list as long as you can.

②   MAKING CONNECTIONS

The following is a list of the vocabulary used in this chapter. The words that appear in bold are new to this chapter. Make sure that you are familiar with all of these words and know what they mean. Refer to the glossary or index for any words that you do not yet understand.

adjacent	**ambiguous**	angle
approximate	**cosine**	equilateral
exact answer	hypotenuse	**inverse sin, cos, tan**
law of cosines	**law of sines**	leg
opposite	**Pythagorean triple**	ratio
right triangle	**sine**	slope
tangent	theta (θ)	

Make a concept map showing all of the connections you can find among the key words and ideas listed above. To show a connection between two words, draw a line between them and explain the connection, as shown in the example below. A word can be connected to any other word as long as there is a justified connection. For each key word or idea, provide a sketch of an example.

Your teacher may provide you with vocabulary cards to help you get started. If you use the cards to plan your concept map, be sure either to re-draw your concept map on your paper or to glue the vocabulary cards to a poster with all of the connections explained for others to see and understand.

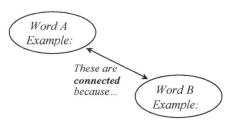

While you are making your map, your team may think of related words or ideas that are not listed above. Be sure to include these ideas on your concept map.

③   SUMMARIZING MY UNDERSTANDING

This section gives you an opportunity to show what you know about certain math topics or ideas. Your teacher will direct you how to do this. Your teacher may give you a "GO" page to work on. "GO" stands for "Graphic Organizer," a tool you can use to organize your thoughts and communicate your ideas clearly.

④   WHAT HAVE I LEARNED?

This section will help you recognize those types of problems you feel comfortable with and those you need more help with. This section will appear at the end of every chapter to help you check your understanding. Even if your teacher does not assign this section, it is a good idea to try these problems and find out for yourself what you know and what you need to work on.

Solve each problem as completely as you can. The table at the end of this closure section has answers to these problems. It also tells you where you can find additional help and practice on problems like these.

CL 5-126. For each diagram, write an equation and solve to find the value for each variable.

a.   b.   c.   d.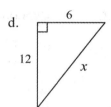

CL 5-127. Copy the diagram at right onto your paper.

a.   Are the triangles similar? If so, show your **reasoning** with a flowchart.

b.   If $m\angle B = 80°$, $m\angle ACB = 29°$, $AB = 14$, and $DE = 12$, find CE.

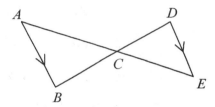

CL 5-128. Cynthia is planning a party. For entertainment, she has designed a game that involves spinning two spinners. If the sum of the numbers on the spinners is 10 or greater, the guests can choose a prize from a basket of candy bars. If the sum is less than 10, then the guest will be thrown in the pool. She has two possible pairs of spinners, shown below. For each pair of spinners, determine the probability of getting tossed in the pool. Assume that Spinners B, C, and D are equally subdivided.

a.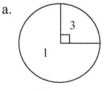

Spinner A   Spinner B

b.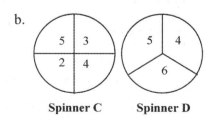

Spinner C   Spinner D

CL 5-129. While working on homework, Zachary was finding the value of each variable in the diagrams below. His first step for each problem is shown under the diagram. If his first step is correct, continue solving the problem to find the solution. If his first step is incorrect, explain his mistake and solve the problem correctly.

a.

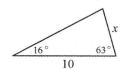

$$\sin 16° = \frac{x}{10}$$

b.

$$x^2 = 10^2 + 70^2 - 2(10)(70)\cos 50°$$

CL 5-130. **Examine** the diagram at right.

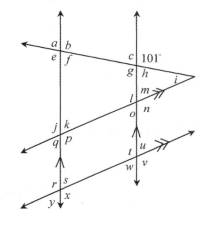

a.   Find the measures of each of the angles below, if possible. If it is not possible, explain why it is not possible. If it is possible, state your **reasoning**.

(1) $m∡b$ (2) $m∡f$

(3) $m∡m$ (4) $m∡g$

(5) $m∡h$ (6) $m∡i$

b.   If $m∡p = 130°$, can you now find the measures of any of the angles from part (a) that you couldn't before? Find the measures for all that you can. Be sure to justify your **reasoning**.

CL 5-131. Trace each figure at right onto your paper. The side labeled $\overline{AB}$ is the base in each figure. Then:

Trapezoid

Parallelogram

Triangle

a.   Draw a height for each figure to side $\overline{AB}$.

b.   Find the area of each figure assuming that the height of each shape is 4" long.

CL 5-132. Bob is hanging a swing from a pole high off the ground so that it can swing a total angle of 120°. Since there is a bush 5 feet in front of the swing and a shed 5 feet behind the swing, Bob wants to ensure that no one will get hurt when they are swinging. What is the maximum length of chain that Bob can use for the swing?

    a.   Draw a diagram of this situation.

    b.   What is the maximum length of chain that Bob can use? State what tools you used to solve this problem.

CL 5-133. **Examine** the triangle at right. Solve for *x* <u>twice</u> using two different methods.

CL 5-134. Graph the points (3, −4) and (7, 2) on graph paper and draw the line segment and a slope triangle that connects the points. Find:

    a.   The length of the segment   b.   The slope of the line segment

    c.   The area of the slope triangle   d.   The measure of the slope angle

CL 5-135. Trace the figure at right onto your paper and then perform all of the transformations listed below on the same diagram. Then find the perimeter of the final shape.

   •   Reflect △*ABC* across $\overline{AB}$.

   •   Rotate △*ABC* 180° around the midpoint of $\overline{BC}$.

   •   Reflect △*ABC* across $\overline{AC}$.

CL 5-136. Check your answers using the table at the end of this section. Which problems do you feel confident about? Which problems were hard? Have you worked on problems like these in math classes you have taken before? Use the table to make a list of topics you need help on and a list of topics you need to practice more.

HOW AM I THINKING?

This course focuses on five different **Ways of Thinking**: investigating, examining, reasoning and justifying, visualizing, and choosing a strategy/tool. These are some of the ways in which you think while trying to make sense of a concept or to solve a problem (even outside of math class). During this chapter, you have probably used each Way of Thinking multiple times without even realizing it!

This closure activity will focus on one of these Ways of Thinking: **choosing a strategy/tool**. Read the description of this Way of Thinking at right.

Think about the problems you have worked on in this chapter. When did you need to think about what method you would use to solve a problem? What helped you decide how to approach a problem? Were there times when more than one **strategy** seemed most useful? You may want to flip through the chapter to refresh your memory about the problems that you have worked on. Discuss these ideas with the class.

Once your discussion is complete, think about the way you think as you answer the questions below.

a.   List all the triangle tools that you have learned so far in this course. For each tool, find or create a problem that can be solved with this **strategy**.

b.   Sometimes, the key to being able to **choose a strategy or tool** is to recognize that different tools can be used on the same problem, but that sometimes some tools are more efficient than others.

> **Choosing a Strategy/Tool**
>
> To choose a strategy means to think about what you know about a problem and match that information with methods and processes for solving problems. As you develop this way of thinking you will learn how to choose ways of solving problems based in given information. You think this way when you ask/answer questions like "What strategy might work for…?" or, "How can I use this information to answer…?" When you catch yourself looking for a method to answer a problem, you are choosing a strategy/tool.
>
>

Solve for x in each diagram below <u>twice</u>. Each time, use a different **strategy** or tool. Then decide which method was easiest for that problem or state that both methods were of equal value.

(1)   (2)   (3)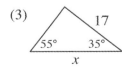

Problem continues on next page →

⑤   *Problem continued from previous page.*

c.   While you have focused most of this chapter on developing strategies for measuring triangles, you have developed strategies for several other topics so far in this course. Consider your **strategy** options as you answer the questions below.

(1)   **Examine** the diagram at right. Assume you know the measure of ∡*b* . How could you find *m*∡*h*? Describe two different **strategies**.

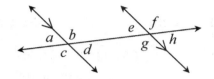

(2)   Now consider the trapezoid below. Find the area of the shape twice, using two different **strategies**.

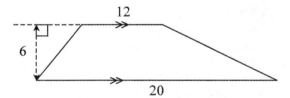

(3)   While shopping at the Two Tired Bike Shop, Barry notices that he may choose from many bicycles. Of the bikes at the store, $\frac{1}{4}$ were mountain bikes, while the rest were racing bikes. Also, $\frac{1}{2}$ of the bikes were blue, $\frac{1}{3}$ of the bikes were red, and $\frac{1}{6}$ of the bikes were purple. Barry decides that he will randomly choose a bicycle from the store.

Choose a probability model to represent this situation. Then find the probability that he chooses a purple racing bike. **[Students can use a scaled area model, generic area model, or a tree diagram; $\frac{1}{6} \cdot \frac{3}{4} = \frac{1}{8}$]**

d.   What about multiple strategies that you have learned in an earlier class? For example, you have multiple ways to approach a problem involving a system of equations. Consider the system below. Solve the system <u>twice</u>: once by graphing and again algebraically. Which **strategy** seemed most efficient? Why? **[(10, −2)]**

$$y = -x + 8$$
$$y = \tfrac{1}{2}x - 7$$

Answers and Support for
Closure Activity #4
What Have I Learned?

Problem	Solutions	Need Help?	More Practice
CL 5-126.	a. $\sin 15° = \frac{x}{20}$; $x \approx 5.176$ m b. $\tan 15° = \frac{5}{x}$; $x \approx 18.66$ in c. $\cos \theta = \frac{10}{11}$; $\theta \approx 24.62°$ d. $6^2 + 12^2 = x^2$; $x \approx 13.416$ un	Lessons 2.2.3, 4.1.4, 5.1.2, and 5.1.4 Math Notes boxes	Problems 4-11, 4-12, 4-16, 4-22, 4-25, 4-31, 4-34, 4-36, 4-46, 5-5, 5-7, 5-12, 5-16, 5-23, 5-89
CL 5-127.	a. b. $x \approx 24.38$	Lessons 3.1.2, 3.1.3, 3.2.1, 3.2.5, and 5.3.2 Math Notes boxes	Problems 3-64, 3-65, 3-83, 3-84, 3-89, 4-7, 4-17, 4-38, 4-39, 4-83, 5-20, 5-49, 5-50, 5-57, 5-76, 5-86, 5-91
CL 5-128.	a. $\frac{7}{12}$ b. $\frac{9}{12} = \frac{3}{4}$	Lesson 4.2.4 Math Notes box	Problems 4-52, 4-60, 4-62, 4-68, 4-69, 4-70, 4-71, 4-77, 4-78, 4-87, 5-9, 5-18, 5-28, 5-39, 5-83, 5-123
CL 5-129.	a. Cannot use sine in this manner in a non-right triangle. Use Law of Sines instead: $\frac{x}{\sin(16°)} = \frac{10}{\sin(101°)}$; $x \approx 2.807$ b. $x \approx 64.03$ un.	Lessons 5.3.2 and 5.3.3 Math Notes boxes	Problems 5-76, 5-77, 5-80, 5-81, 5-86, 5-98, 5-106, 5-107, 5-109, 5-114, 5-121
CL 5-130.	a. (1) $b = 101°$, corres. angles are equal (2) $f = 79°$, supplementary angles (3) not enough information (4) $g = 101°$, vertical angles are equal (5) $h = 79°$, supplementary angles (6) not enough information b. $m = 50°$; $v = 130°$; $i = 51°$	Lessons 2.1.1, 2.1.4, and 2.2.1 Math Notes boxes, Problem 2-3	Problems 2-13, 2-16, 2-17, 2-23, 2-24, 2-25, 2-31, 2-32, 2-38, 2-49, 2-51, 2-62, 2-72, 2-111, 3-20, 3-31, 3-60, 3-70, 3-96, 4-6, 4-29, 4-44, 4-85, 4-93, 5-47

Problem	Solutions	Need Help?	More Practice
CL 5-131.	Trapezoid Area: 22 square in. Parallelogram Area: 20 square in. Triangle Area: 14 square in.	Lessons 1.1.3 and 2.2.4 Math Notes boxes	Problems 2-66, 2-68, 2-71, 2-75, 2-76, 2-78, 2-79, 2-82, 2-83, 2-90, 2-120, 3-51, 3-81, 3-97, 4-43, 4-67, 4-92, 5-10, 5-29, 5-34, 5-55, 5-81, 5-117, 5-122
CL 5-132.	a. b. $x = \frac{10\sqrt{3}}{3} \approx 5.77$ ft.	Lessons 5.1.2, 5.3.2, and 5.3.3 Math Notes boxes	Problems 5-17, 5-76, 5-77, 5-80, 5-81, 5-86, 5-98, 5-106, 5-107, 5-109, 5-112, 5-114, 5-121
CL 5-133.	Both the Law of Sines and the Law of Cosines will work, as does dividing the triangle into two right triangles; $x \approx 17.06$ un.	Lessons 5.1.2, 5.3.2, and 5.3.3 Math Notes boxes	Problems 5-16, 5-17, 5-23, 5-76, 5-77, 5-80, 5-81, 5-86, 5-98, 5-106, 5-107, 5-109, 5-112, 5-114, 5-121
CL 5-134.	a. $\sqrt{52} \approx 7.21$ un. b. $\frac{3}{2}$ c. 12 sq. un. d. $56.31°$	Lessons 1.2.5, 2.3.3, 4.1.1, 4.1.4, 5.1.4 Math Notes boxes	Problems 2-116, 5-2, 5-37, 5-92, 5-102
CL 5-135.	The final shape is shown below: Perimeter: 24 feet 	Lessons 1.1.3, 1.2.2 and 1.2.3 Math Notes boxes	Problems 1-50, 1-51, 1-64, 1-69, 1-73, 1-85, 1-96, 2-11, 2-19, 2-20, 2-33, 2-64, 2-113, 3-96, 5-41, 5-70, 5-90, 5-118, 5-124

CHAPTER 6

In Chapter 5, you completed your work with the measurement of triangles, so you can now find the missing side lengths and angles of a triangle when sufficient information is given. Earlier, you developed ways to determine if two triangles are similar, and can use the ratios of similarity to learn more about the sides and angles of similar figures. But what if two triangles are congruent? What information can congruent triangles provide? In this chapter, you will find ways to determine whether two triangles are congruent.

In addition, Section 6.2 offers several projects and activities that will help you synthesize your understanding and make connections between different concepts you have learned so far. You will consolidate what you know, apply it in new ways, and identify what you still need to learn.

Guiding Questions

Think about these questions throughout this chapter:

How are the triangles related?

What is the connection?

What information do I need?

What do I still need to learn?

In this chapter, you will learn:

> what information is needed in order to conclude that two triangles are congruent.

> what a converse of a conditional statement is and how to recognize whether or not the converse is true.

> how to organize a flowchart that helps conclude that two triangles are congruent.

Chapter Outline

Section 6.1   This section turns the focus to congruent triangles. You will develop strategies to directly conclude that two triangles are congruent without first concluding that they are similar.

Section 6.2   This section includes several big problems and activities to help you learn how different threads of geometry are connected and to help you assess what you know and what you still need to learn.

6.1.1 Are the triangles congruent?

Congruent Triangles

In Chapter 3, you learned how to identify similar triangles and used them to solve problems. But what can be learned when triangles are congruent? In today's lesson, you will practice identifying congruent triangles using what you know about similarity. As you search for congruent triangles in today's problems, focus on these questions:

What do I know about these triangles?

How can I show similarity?

What is the common ratio?

6-1.   **Examine** the triangles at right.

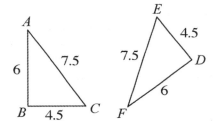

a.   Make a flowchart showing that these triangles are similar.

b.   Are these triangles also congruent? Explain how you know.

c.   While the symbol for similar figures is "~", the symbol for congruent figures is "≅". How is the congruence symbol related to the similarity symbol? Why do you think mathematicians chose this symbol for congruence?

d.   Luis wanted to write a statement to convey that these two triangles are congruent. He started with " $\triangle CAB$ ...", but then got stuck because he did not know the symbol for congruence. Now that you know the symbol for congruence, complete Luis's statement for him.

6-2.   The diagrams below are not drawn to scale. For each pair of triangles:

- Determine if the two triangles are congruent.

- If you find congruent triangles, write a congruence statement (such as $\triangle PQR \cong \triangle XYZ$).

- If the triangles are not congruent or if there is not enough information to determine congruence, write "cannot be determined."

a. $\overline{AC}$ is a straight segment:

b.

c.

d.

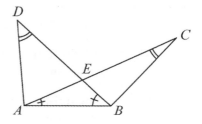

6-3.   Consider square *MNPQ* with diagonals intersecting at *R*, as shown at right.

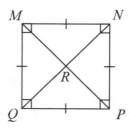

a.   How many triangles are there in this diagram? (Hint: There are more than 4!)

b.   How many lines of symmetry does *MNPQ* have? On your paper, trace *MNPQ* and indicate the location of each line of symmetry with a dashed line.

c.   Write as many triangle congruence statements as you can that involve triangles in this diagram. Be prepared to **justify** each congruence statement you write.

d.   Write a similarity statement for two triangles in the diagram that are not congruent. **Justify** your similarity statement with a flowchart.

MATH NOTES

METHODS AND MEANINGS

Congruent Shapes

The information below is from Chapter 3 and is reprinted here for your convenience.

If two figures have the same shape and are the same size, they are **congruent**. Since the figures must have the same shape, they must be similar.

Two figures are congruent if they meet both the following conditions:

- the two figures are similar, and
- their side lengths have a common ratio of 1.

6-4.   Use the diagram at right to answer the following questions.

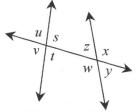

a.   What type of angle pair is ∡z and ∡t? That is, what is their geometric relationship?

b.   What type of angle pair do ∡s and ∡v form?

c.   Name all pairs of corresponding angles in the diagram. Hint: There are four different pairs.

6-5.   **Examine** the triangles at right.

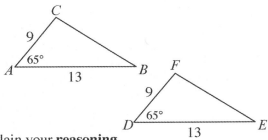

a.   Are these triangles similar? If so, use a flowchart to show how you know. If they are not similar, explain how you know.

b.   Are the triangles congruent? Explain your **reasoning**.

6-6.   Using the diagram at right, write an equation and find x. Check your answer.

6-7.   For each of the triangles below, find x.

a.

b.

c.

6-8.   Joey is in charge of selling cupcakes at the basketball games. The game is today at 5:00 p.m. At 3:00 p.m., Joey put some cupcakes into the oven and started working on his homework. He fell asleep and did not wake up until 3:55 p.m. What do you think happened?

Joey knows that the following four statements are facts:

   i.   If the cupcakes are burned, then the fans that attend the varsity basketball games will not buy them.

   ii.   If cupcakes are in the oven for more than 50 minutes, they will burn.

   iii.   If the fans do not buy the cupcakes, then the team will not have enough money for new uniforms next year.

   iv.   The cupcakes are in the oven from 3:00 p.m. to 3:55 p.m.

Copy the flowchart at right and decide how to organize the facts into the ovals. You will need to fill in one of the ovals with your own logical conclusion. Be sure that your ovals are in the correct order and that the arrows really show connections between the ovals. What conclusion should your flowchart make?

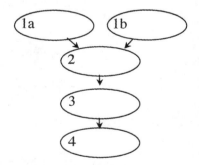

6-9.   **Multiple Choice:** $\triangle ABC$ is defined by points A(3, 2), B(4, 9), and C(6, 7). Which triangle below is the image of $\triangle ABC$ when it is rotated 90° counter-clockwise (↺) about the origin?

a. $A'(-2, 3)$, $B'(-9, 4)$, $C'(-7, 6)$ b. $A'(-3, 2)$, $B'(-4, 9)$, $C'(-6, 7)$

c. $A'(-2, 3)$, $B'(-7, 6)$, $C'(-9, 4)$ d. $A'(2, -3)$, $B'(9, -4)$, $C'(7, -6)$

e.   None of these

6.1.2 What information do I need?

Conditions for Triangle Congruence

In Lesson 6.1.1, you identified congruent triangles by looking for similarity and a common side length ratio of 1. Must you go through this two-step process every time you want to argue that triangles are congruent? Are there shortcuts for establishing triangle congruence? Today you will develop Triangle Congruence Shortcuts in order to quickly determine if two triangles are congruent.

6-10. Review your work from problem 6-5, which required you to determine if two triangles are congruent. Then work with your team to answer the questions below.

a. Derek wants to find general shortcuts that can help determine if triangles are congruent. To help, he draws the diagram at right to show the relationships between the triangles in problem 6-5.

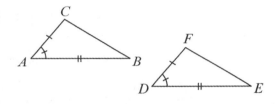

If two triangles have the relationship shown in the diagram, do they have to be congruent? How do you know?

b. Write a conjecture in the form of a conditional statement or arrow diagram based on this relationship. If you write a conditional statement, it should look like, "If two triangles …, then the triangles are congruent." What would be a good name (abbreviation) for this shortcut?

6-11.   TRIANGLE CONGRUENCE SHORTCUTS

Derek wonders, "What other types of information can determine that
two triangles are congruent?"

Your Task: Examine the pairs of triangles below to decide what other types of
information force triangles to be congruent. Notice that since no measurements are
given in the diagrams, you are considering the general case of each type of pairing.
For each pair of triangles below that you can prove are congruent, enter the
appropriate Triangle Congruence Conjecture on your Lesson 6.1.2 Resource Page
with an explanation defending your decision. An entry for SAS ≅ (the conjecture
you developed in problem 6-10) is already created on the resource page as an
example. Be prepared to share your results with the class.

Discussion Points

- In what ways can you show that triangles are similar?

- What must be true in order for triangles to be congruent?

- Which of the conditions below DO NOT assure congruence?

a.

Side-Side-Side: SSS

b.

Hypotenuse-Leg: HL

c.

Angle-Angle-Angle: AA

d.

Angle-Angle-Side: AAS

e.

Side-Side-Angle: SSA

f.

Angle-Side-Angle: ASA

6-12.   Use your triangle congruence conjectures to determine if the following pairs of triangles must be congruent. Note: the diagrams are not necessarily drawn to scale.

a.

b.

c.

d.

e.

f.

g.

h.

6-13.   **Examine** the relationships that exist in the diagram at right. Find the measures of angles *a*, *b*, *c*, and *d*. Remember that you can find the angles in any order, depending on the angle relationships you use.

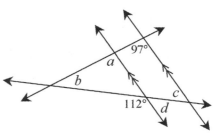

6-14.   **Examine** the triangles below. For each one, solve for x and name which **tool** you used. Show all work.

a.

b.

c.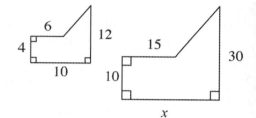

6-15.   The two shapes at right are similar.

a.   Find the value of x. Show all work.

b.   Find the area of each shape.

6-16.   On graph paper, graph $\triangle ABC$ if A(–2, 7), B(–5, 8), and C(–3, 1).

a.   Reflect $\triangle ABC$ across the x-axis to form $\triangle A'B'C'$. Name the coordinates of each new vertex.

b.   Now rotate $\triangle A'B'C'$ from part (a) 180° about the origin (0, 0) to form $\triangle A''B''C''$. Name the coordinates of each new vertex.

c.   Describe a single transformation that would change $\triangle ABC$ to $\triangle A''B''C''$.

6-17.   Solve the problem below using any method. Show all work.

Angle A of $\triangle ABC$ measures 5° more than 3 times the measure of angle B. Angle C measures 20° less than angle B. Find the measure of angles A, B, and C.

6-18.   **Multiple Choice:** Which list of side lengths below could form a triangle?

a.   2, 6, 7   b.   3, 8, 13   c.   9, 4, 2   d.   10, 20, 30

6.1.3 How can I organize my reasoning?

Flowcharts for Congruence

Now that you have shortcuts for establishing triangle congruence, how can you organize information in a flowchart to show that triangles are congruent? Consider this as you work today with your team.

6-19. In problem 6-1, you determined that the triangles at right are congruent.

a. Which triangle congruence conjecture shows that these triangles are congruent?

b. Make a flowchart showing your argument that these triangles are congruent.

c. How is a flowchart showing congruence different from a flowchart showing similarity? List every difference you can find.

6-20. In Don's congruence flowchart for problem 6-19, one of the ovals said "$\frac{AB}{FD} = 1$". In Phil's flowchart, one of the ovals said, "$AB = FD$". Discuss with your team whether these ovals say the same thing. Can equality statements like Phil's always be used in congruence flowcharts?

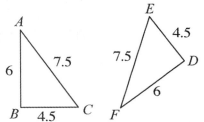

6-21. Make a flowchart showing that the triangles below are congruent.

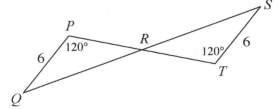

6-22.   In each diagram below, determine whether the triangles are congruent, similar but
         not congruent, or not similar. If you claim triangles are similar or congruent, make a
         flowchart **justifying** your answer.

a.

b.

c.

d.

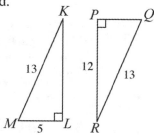

6-23.   Suppose you are working on a problem involving the two triangles $\triangle UVW$ and
         $\triangle XYZ$, and you know that $\triangle UVW \cong \triangle XYZ$. What can you conclude about the
         sides and angles of $\triangle UVW$ and $\triangle XYZ$? Write down every equation involving side
         lengths or angle measures that must be true.

MⒺTHODS AND MⒺANINGS

Triangle Congruence Shortcuts

To show that triangles are congruent, you can show that the triangles are similar and that the common ratio between side lengths is 1. However, you can also use certain combinations of congruent, corresponding parts as shortcuts to determine if triangles are congruent. These combinations, called **triangle congruence conjectures**, are:

SSS ≅ (Pronounced "side–side–side")
If all three pairs of corresponding sides have equal lengths, then the triangles are congruent.

SAS ≅ (Pronounced "side–angle–side")
If two pairs of corresponding sides have equal lengths *and* the angles between them (the included angle) are equal, then the triangles are congruent.

ASA ≅ (Pronounced "angle–side–angle")
If two angles and the side between them in a triangle are congruent to the corresponding angles and side in another triangle, then the triangles are congruent.

AAS ≅ (Pronounced "angle–angle–side")
If two pairs of corresponding angles *and* a pair of corresponding sides that are not between them have equal measures, then the triangles are congruent.

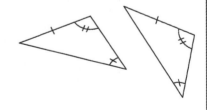

HL ≅ (Pronounced "hypotenuse–leg")
If the hypotenuse and a leg of one right triangle have the same lengths as the hypotenuse and a leg of another right triangle, the triangles are congruent.

6-24.   Use your conjectures about parallel lines and the angles formed with a third line to find the measures of the labeled angles below. Show each step you use and be sure to **justify** each with an angle conjecture from your Angle Relationships Toolkit. Be sure to write down your **reasoning** in the order that you find the angles.

a.   b.   c.

6-25.   In a basketball game, a player who gets fouled is awarded a free-throw called a "one-and-one." When this happens, the player gets a "free shot" from the free-throw line. If the player makes the free-throw, then he or she gets one point and gets to attempt another one-point shot. If the player misses the first free-throw, then no additional attempt is provided.

a.   If Vicki makes a free-throw 60% of the time, what is the probability that she will score no points? How did you get your answer?

b.   Is there a greater probability that she will make only one free-throw or two? Create a diagram or chart to show your **reasoning**.

6-26.   Solve the systems of equations below using any method, if possible. Show all work and check your solution. If there is no solution, explain why not.

a. $y = 2x + 8$

        $3x + 2y = -12$

b. $2x - 5y = 4$

        $5y - 2x = 10$

6-27.   **Examine** the triangles at right. Solve for x.

6-28.   **Examine** the triangle and line of reflection at right.

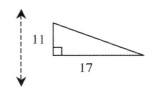

a.   On your paper, trace the triangle and the line of reflection. Then draw the image of the triangle after it is reflected across the line. Verify your reflection is correct by folding your paper along the line of reflection.

b.   Find the perimeter of the image. How does it compare with the perimeter of the original figure?

c.   Find the measure of both acute angles in the original triangle.

6-29.   **Multiple Choice:** Given the diagram at right, which of the statements below is not necessarily true?

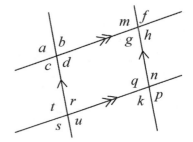

a. $a = d$ b. $d + r = 180°$

c. $u = n$ d. $t = m$

e.   These all must be true.

6.1.4 What's the relationship?

Converses

So far in this chapter, you have completed several problems in which you were given certain information and had to determine whether triangles were congruent. But what if you already know triangles are congruent? What information can you conclude then? Thinking this way requires you to take your Triangle Congruence Conjectures and reverse them. Today you will look more generally at what happens when you reverse a conjecture.

6-30.   Jorge is working with the diagram at right, and concludes
         that $\overrightarrow{AB} \parallel \overrightarrow{CD}$. He writes the following conditional
         statement to justify his reasoning:

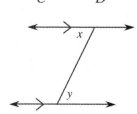

         If alternate interior angles are equal, then lines are parallel.

   a.   Margaret is working with a different diagram, shown
         at right. She concludes that $x = y$. Write a
         conditional statement or arrow diagram that justifies
         her reasoning.

   b.   How are Jorge's and Margaret's statements related?
         How are they different?

   c.   Conditional statements that have this relationship are
         called **converses**. Write the converse of the
         conditional statement below.

         If lines are parallel, then corresponding angles are equal.

6-31.   In problem 6-30, you learned that each conditional statement has a converse.
         Are all converses true? Consider the arrow diagram of a familiar conjecture below.

         Triangles congruent → *corresponding sides are congruent.*

   a.   Is this arrow diagram true?

   b.   Write the converse of this arrow diagram as an arrow diagram or as a
         conditional statement. Is this converse true? **Justify** your answer.

   c.   Now consider another true congruence conjecture below. Write its converse
         and decide if it is true.

         Triangles congruent → *corresponding angles are congruent.*

   d.   Write the converse of the arrow diagram below. Is this converse true? **Justify**
         your answer.

         A shape is a rectangle → *the area of the shape is $b \cdot h$.*

6-32.   CRAZY CONVERSES

For each of these problems below, make up a conditional statement or arrow diagram that meets the stated conditions. You must use a different example each time, and none of your examples can be about math!

a.   A true statement whose converse is true.

b.   A true statement whose converse is false.

c.   A false statement whose converse is true.

d.   A false statement whose converse is false.

6-33.   INFORMATION OVERLOAD

Raj is solving a problem about three triangles. He is trying to find the measure of $\angle H$ and the length of $\overline{HI}$. Raj summarizes the relationships he has found so far in the diagrams below:

  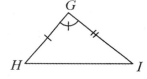

a.   Help Raj out! Assuming everything marked in the diagram is true, find $m\angle H$ and the length of $\overline{HI}$. Make sure to **justify** all your claims—don't make assumptions based on how the diagram looks

b.   Raj is still confused. Write a careful explanation of the **reasoning** you used to find the values in part (a). Whenever possible, use arrow diagrams or conditional statements in explaining your **reasoning**.

6-34.   Write an entry in your Learning Log about the converse relationship. Explain what a converse is, and give an example of a conditional statement and its converse. Also discuss the relationship between the truth of a statement and its converse. Title this entry "Converses" and include today's date.

METHODS AND MEANINGS

Converses

When conditional statements (also called "If …, then …" statements) are written backwards so that the condition (the "if" part) is switched with the conclusion (the "then" part), the new statement is called a **converse**. For example, examine the conjecture and its converse below:

Conjecture: If two parallel lines are cut by a transversal, then pairs of corresponding angles are equal.

Reversal: If two corresponding angles are equal, then the lines cut by the transversal are parallel.

The second statement (reversal) is called the **converse** of the first statement. Note that just because a conjecture is true does not mean that its converse must be true. For example, if the conditional statement, "If the dog has a meaty bone, then the dog is happy," is true, but its converse, "If the dog is happy, then the dog has a meaty bone," is not necessarily true. The dog could be happy for other reasons, such as going for a walk.

6-35.   Copy the diagram at right onto your paper. If $a = 53°$ and $g = 125°$, find the measures of each labeled angle. Explain how you find each angle, citing definitions and conjectures from your toolkit that support your steps. Remember that you can find the angles in any order, depending on the angle relationships you use.

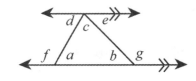

6-36.   On graph paper, graph the line $y = \frac{-3}{2}x + 6$. Name the x- and y-intercepts.

6-37.   As Samone looked at the triangles at right, she said, "I think these triangles are congruent." Her teammate, Darla, said, "But they don't look the same. How can you tell?" Samone smiled and said, "Never trust the picture! Look at the angles and the sides. The measures are all the same."

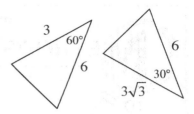

a.   Solve for the missing side of each triangle. How do they compare?

b.   Are you convinced that Samone is correct? Explain.

6-38.   Write a converse for each conditional statement below. Then, assuming the original statement is true, decide if the converse must be true or not.

a. If it rains, then the ground is wet.

b. If a polygon is a square, then it is a rectangle.

c. If a polygon is a rectangle, then it has four 90° angles.

d. If the shape has three angles, it is a triangle.

e. If two lines intersect, then vertical angles are congruent.

6-39.   In the diagram at right, $\triangle ABC \sim \triangle ADE$.

a.   Draw each triangle separately on your paper. Be sure to include all measurements in your diagrams.

b.   Find the length of $\overline{DE}$.

6-40.

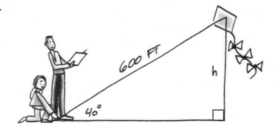

One measurement used in judging kite-flying competitions is the size of the angle formed by the kite string and the ground. This angle can be used to find the height of the kite. Suppose the length of the string is 600 feet and the angle at which the kite is flying measures 40°. Calculate the height, h, of the kite.

6.2.1 How can I use it? What's the connection?

Angles on a Pool Table

The activities in this section review several big topics you have studied so far. Work with your team to decide which combination of **tools** you will need for each problem. As you work together, think about which skills and tools you are comfortable using and which ones you need more practice with.

As you work on this activity, keep in mind the following questions:

What mathematical concepts did you use to solve this problem?

What do you still want to know more about?

What connections did you find?

6-41. TAKE IT TO THE BANK

Ricky just watched his favorite pool player, "Montana Mike," make a double bank shot in a trick-shot competition. Montana bounced a ball off two rails (sides) of the table and sank it in the corner pocket. "That doesn't look too hard," Ricky says, "I just need to know where to put the ball and which direction to hit it in."

A diagram of Montana's shot is shown at right. The playing area of a tournament pool table is 50 inches by 100 inches. Along its rails, a pool table is marked with a diamond every 12.5 inches. Montana started the shot with the ball against the top rail and the ball hit the bottom rail three diamonds from the right rail.

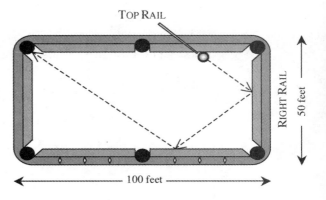

TOP RAIL

RIGHT RAIL

50 feet

100 feet

Your task: Figure out where on the top rail Ricky needs to place his ball and where he needs to aim to repeat Montana Mike's bank shot. Write instructions that tell Ricky how to use the diamonds on the table to place his ball correctly, and at what angle from the rail to hit the ball.

6-42.   EXTENSIONS

The algebraic and geometric **tools** you have developed so far will enable you to answer many questions about the path of a ball on a pool table. Work with your team to analyze the situations below.

a.   Ricky decided he wants to alter Montana's shot so that it hits the right rail exactly in at its midpoint. Where would Ricky need to place the ball along the top rail so that his shot reflects off the right rail, then the bottom rail, and enters the upper left pocket? At what angle with the top rail would he need to hit the ball?

b.   During another shot, Ricky noticed that Montana hit the ball as shown in the diagram at right. He estimated that the ball traveled 18 inches before it entered the pocket. Before the shot, the announcers noted that the distance of the ball to the top rail was 2 inches more than the distance along the top rail, as shown in the diagram. Where was the ball located before Montana hit it?

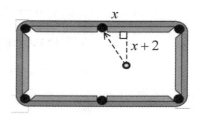

c.   Ricky wants to predict how Montana's next shot will end. The ball is placed at the second diamond from the left along the bottom rail, as shown at right. Montana is aiming to hit the ball toward the second diamond from the right along the top rail. Assuming he hits the ball very hard so that the ball continues traveling indefinitely, will the ball ever reach a pocket? If so, show the path of the ball. If not, explain how you know.

d.   After analyzing the path in part (c), Montana decided to start his ball from the third diamond from the left along the bottom rail, as shown at right. He is planning to aim at the same diamond as he did in part (c). If he hits the ball sufficiently hard, will the ball eventually reach a pocket? If so, show the path of the ball. If not, explain how you know.

6-43. Use your triangle **tools** to solve for x in the triangles below.

a.

b.

c.

d.

6-44. Penelope measured several sides and heights of $\triangle ABC$, as shown in the diagram at right. Find the area of $\triangle ABC$ **twice**, using two different methods.

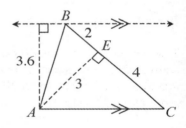

6-45. The shaded figures at right are similar.

a. Solve for m and n.

b. Find the area and perimeter of each figure.

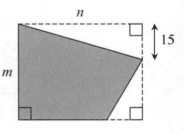

6-46. Decide if each triangle below is congruent to $\triangle ABC$ at right, similar but not congruent to $\triangle ABC$, or neither. **Justify** each answer.

a.

b.

c.

6-47.   On graph paper, graph the line $y = 3x + 1$.

a.   What is this line's slope angle? That is, what is the acute angle the line makes with the *x*-axis?

b.   Find the equation of a new line that has a slope angle of 45° and passes through the point (0, 3). Assume that the slope is positive.

c.   Find the intersection of these two lines using any method. Write your solution as a point in the form (*x*, *y*).

6-48.   **Multiple Choice:** Listed below are the measures of several different angles. Which angle is obtuse?

a.   0°   b.   52°   c.   210°   d.   91°

6.2.2 How can I use it? What's the connection?

Investigating a Triangle

The activities in this section review several big topics you have studied so far. Work with your team to decide which combination of **tools** you will need for each problem. As you work together, think about which skills and tools you are comfortable using and which ones you need more practice with.

As you work on this activity, keep in mind the following questions:

What mathematical concepts did you use to solve this problem?

What do you still want to know more about?

What connections did you find?

6-49.   GETTING TO KNOW YOUR TRIANGLE

a.   If you were asked to give every possible measurement of a triangle, what measurements could you include?

b.   Consider a triangle on a coordinate grid with the following vertices:

$A(2, 3)$, $B(32, 15)$, $C(12, 27)$

Your Task: On graph paper, graph $\triangle ABC$ and find all of its measurements. Be sure to find every measurement you listed in part (a) of this problem and show all of your calculations. With your team, be prepared to present your method for finding the area.

6-50.   **Examine** the diagram at right. Based on the information below, what statement can you make about the relationships between the lines? Be sure to **justify** each conclusion. Remember: each part below is a separate problem.

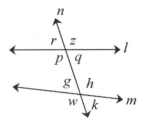

a. $p = h$ b. $w = k$

c. $r = q$ d. $z + k = 160°$

6-51.   Determine if each pair of triangles below are congruent, similar but not congruent, or if they are neither. If they are congruent, organize your **reasoning** into a flowchart.

a.   b.   c.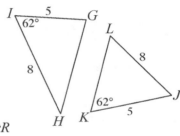

6-52.   On graph paper, plot and connect the points to form quadrilateral $WXYZ$ if $W(3, 7)$, $X(3, 4)$, $Y(9, 1)$, and $Z(5, 6)$.

a.   What is the shape of quadrilateral $WXYZ$? **Justify** your conclusion.

b.   Find the perimeter of quadrilateral $WXYZ$.

c.   If quadrilateral $WXYZ$ is reflected across the y-axis to form quadrilateral $W'X'Y'Z'$, then where is Y'?

d.   Rotate quadrilateral $WXYZ$ about the origin 90° clockwise (↻) to form quadrilateral $W''X''Y''Z''$. What is the slope of $\overline{W''Z''}$?

6-53.   As Ms. Dorman looked from the window of her third-story classroom, she noticed Pam in the courtyard. Ms. Dorman's eyes were 52 feet above ground and Pam was 38 feet from the building. Draw a diagram of this situation. What is the angle at which Ms. Dorman had to look down? That is, what is the angle of depression? (Assume that Ms. Dorman was looking at the spot on the ground below Pam.)

6-54.   **Examine** the diagram at right. Find two equivalent
          expressions that represent the area of the <u>inner</u> square.

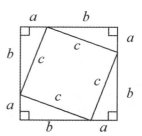

6-55.   **Multiple Choice:** To decide if his class would take a
          quiz today, he will flip a coin three times. If all three
          results are heads or all three results are tails, he will
          give the quiz. Otherwise, his students will not be
          tested. What is the probability that his class will take the quiz?

     a. $\frac{1}{8}$ b. $\frac{1}{4}$ c. $\frac{1}{2}$ d.   1

$6.2.3$ How can I use it? What's the connection?

Creating a Mathematical Model

The activities in this section review several big topics you have studied so far. Work with your
team to decide which combination of **tools** you will need for each problem. As you work
together, think about which skills and tools you are comfortable using and which ones you need
more practice with.

As you work on this activity, keep in mind the following questions:

              What mathematical concepts did you use to solve this problem?

                   What do you still want to know more about?

                      What connections did you find?

6-56.   AT YOUR SERVICE

Carina, a tennis player, wants to make her serve a truly powerful part of her game. She wants to hit the ball so hard that it appears to travel in a straight path. Unfortunately, the ball always lands beyond the service box. After a few practice serves, she realizes that the height at which you hit the ball determines where the ball lands. Before she gets tired from serving, she sits down to figure out how high the ball must be when she hits it so that her serve is legal.

In the game of tennis, every point begins with one player serving the ball. For a serve to be legal, the player must stand outside the court and hit the ball so that it crosses over the net and lands within the service box (shown shaded below). It can be difficult to make the ball land in the service box because the ball is often hit too low and touches the net or is hit too high and lands beyond the service box.

A tennis court is 78 feet long with the net located at the center. The distance from the net to the back of the service box is 21 feet, and the net is 3 feet tall.

Your task: Assuming Carina can hit the ball so hard that its path is linear, from what height must she hit the ball to have the serve just clear the net and land in the service box? Decide whether or not it is reasonable for Carina to reach this height if she is 5'7" tall. Also, at what angle does the ball hit the ground?

Your solution should include:

- a labeled diagram that shows a birds' eye view of the path of the ball.

- a labeled diagram that shows the side view of Carina, the ideal height of the tennis racket, the ideal path of the tennis ball, and the measurements that are needed from the birds' eye view diagram.

Discussion Points

What would you see if you were a bird looking down
on the court as Carina served?

Which distances do you know and which do you need to find?

6-57. To help solve this problem, copy the diagram at right, which shows the tennis court from above (called a "birds-eye" view). On your diagram, locate the position of Carina and the spot where the ball should land. Be sure to include the path of the ball.

a. Label all distances you already know. Do you see any triangles?

b. What distance(s) can you find? What geometric **tool(s)** can you use?

6-58. Next **visualize** the situation from the side and draw the path of the ball.

a. As you draw this diagram, be sure to include Carina, the net, and the spot where the ball should land.

b. Are there any similar triangles? Be careful to include any measurements that might help you determine the height of the serve.

c. What triangle **tool** can you use to find the angle of depression of the path of the ball? Find the acute angle the path of the ball makes with the ground.

6-59. How high must the ball be hit so that it just clears the net and lands in the service box? If Carina is 5'7" tall, is it possible for her to accomplish this serve? Assume that a tennis racquet is 2 feet long.

Further Guidance
section ends here.

6-60. You've been hired as a consultant for the National Tennis Association. They are considering raising the net to make the serve even more challenging. They want players to have to jump to make a successful serve (assuming that the powerful serves will be hit so hard that the ball will travel in a straight line). Determine how high the net should be so that the players must strike the ball from at least 10 feet.

Review & Preview

6-61. **Examine** the triangles in the diagram at right.

a. Are the triangles similar? **Justify** your conclusion.

b. Solve for *x*. Show all work.

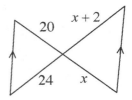

6-62.   For each diagram below, use geometric relationships
          to solve for the given variable(s). Check your answer.

a.

b.

c.

d.

6-63.   Find the area and perimeter of the trapezoid at right.

6-64.   A map of an island is shown at right. Each unit of length
          on the grid represents 32 feet.

a.   Find the actual dimensions of the island (the overall
          width and length).

b.   Find the area of the shape at right and the actual area
          of the island.

6-65.   **Examine** the two triangles at right.

a.   Are the triangles congruent? **Justify** your
          conclusion. If they are congruent, complete
          the congruence statement $\triangle DEF \cong$ _____.

b.   What transformation(s) are needed to change
          $\triangle DEF$ to $\triangle JKL$?

c.   If $DE = 4$ units, find KL .

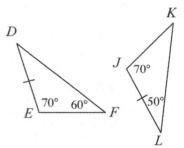

6-66.   **Multiple Choice:** The length of a rectangle is three units shorter than twice its
          width. Which expression below could represent the area of the rectangle?

a. $2x^2 - 3$ b. $2x^2 - 6x$ c. $2x^2 - 3x$ d. $(2x - 3)^2$

6.2.4 How can I use it? What's the connection?

Analyzing a Game

The activities in this section review several big topics you have studied so far. Work with your team to decide which combination of **tools** you will need for each problem. As you work together, think about which skills and tools you are comfortable using and which ones you need more practice with.

As you work on this activity, keep in mind the following questions:

What mathematical concepts did you use to solve this problem?

What do you still want to know more about?

What connections did you find?

6-67. THE MONTY HALL PROBLEM

Wow! Your best friend, Lee, has been selected as a contestant in the popular "Pick-A-Door" game show. The game show host, Monty, has shown Lee three doors and, because he knows what is behind each door, has assured her that behind one of the doors lies a new car! However, behind each of the other two doors is a goat.

"Which door do you pick?" Monty asks.

Lee's original choice

"I pick Door #1," Lee replies confidently.

"Okay. Now, before I show you what is behind Door #1, let me show you what is behind Door #3. It is a goat! Now, would you like to change your mind and choose Door #2 instead?" Monty asks.

What should Lee do? Should she stay with Door #1 or should she switch to Door #2? Does she have a better chance of winning if she switches, or does it not matter? Discuss this situation with the class and make sure you provide **reasons** for your statements.

6-68.   Now test your prediction from problem 6-67 by simulating this game with a partner using either a computer or a programmable calculator. If no technology is available, collect data by playing the game with a partner as described below.

Choose one person to be the contestant and one person to be the game show host. As you play, carefully record information about whether the contestant switches doors and whether the contestant wins. Play as many times as you can in the time allotted, but be sure to record at least 10 results from switching and 10 results from not switching. Be ready to report your findings with the class.

If playing this game without technology, the host should:

- Secretly choose the winning door. Make sure that the contestant has no way of knowing which door has been selected.

- Ask the contestant to choose a door.

- "Open" one of the remaining two doors that does not have the winning prize.

- Ask the contestant if he or she wants to change his or her door.

- Show if the contestant has won the car and record the results.

6-69.   **Examine** the data the class collected in problem 6-68.

a.   What does this data tell you? What should Lee do in problem 6-67 to maximize her chance of winning?

b.   Your teammate, Kaye, is confused. "Why does it matter? At the end, there are only two doors left. Isn't there a 50-50 chance that I will select the winning door?" Explain to Kaye why switching is better.

c.   Gerald asks, "What if there are 4 doors? If Monty now reveals two doors with a goat, is it still better to switch?" What do you think? Analyze this problem and answer Gerald's question.

6-70.   One of the topics you studied during Chapters 1 through 6 was probability. You investigated what made a game fair and how to predict if you would win or lose. Reflect on today's activity and write a Learning Log entry about the mathematics you used today to analyze the "Monty Hall" game. Title this entry "Game Analysis" and include today's date.

6-71.   Determine whether or not the triangles in each pair below are congruent. **Justify** your conclusion.

a.

b.

c.

d.

6-72.   **Examine** the geometric relationships in each of the diagrams below. For each one, write and solve an equation to find the value of the variable. Name all geometric relationships or conjectures that you use.

a.

b.

c.

d.

6-73.   In the diagram at right, $\overrightarrow{BD}$ **bisects** $\angle ABC$. This means that $\overrightarrow{BD}$ divides the angle into two equal parts. If $m\angle ABD = 3x + 24°$ and if $m\angle CBD = 5x + 2°$, solve for x. Then find $m\angle ABC$.

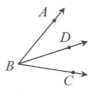

6-74.   Assume that 25% of the student body at your school is male and that 40% of the students walk to school. If a student from this school is selected at random, find the following probabilities.

   a.   P(student is female)

   b.   P(student is male and does not walk to school)

   c.   P(student walks to school or does not walk to school)

6-75.   If $b + 2a = c$ and $2a + b = 10$, then what is c? Explain how you know.

6-76.   **Multiple Choice:** The measure of $\angle ABD$ at right is:

   a.   27°   b.   161°

   c.   118°   d.   153°

   e.   None of these

$6.2.5$ How can I use it? What's the connection?

Using Transformations and Symmetry to Create a Snowflake

The activities in this section review several big topics you have studied so far. Work with your team to decide which combination of **tools** you will need for each problem. As you work together, think about which skills and tools you are comfortable using and which ones you need more practice with.

As you work on this activity, keep in mind the following questions:

What mathematical concepts did you use to solve this problem?

What do you still want to know more about?

What connections did you find?

6-77.   THE PAPER SNOWFLAKE

You have volunteered to help the decorating committee
make paper snowflakes for the upcoming winter school
dance. A paper snowflake is made by folding and
cutting a square of paper in such a way that when the
paper is unfolded, the result is a beautiful design with
symmetric patterns similar to those of a real snowflake.

Looking through your drawer of craft projects, you find the directions for how to
fold the paper snowflake (see below). However you cannot find any directions for
how to cut the folded paper to make specific designs in the final snowflake.

DESIGNING A PAPER SNOWFLAKE: Cut out a 20 unit by 20 unit square
from a piece of graph paper. Making sure that the gridlines are visible on the
outside of the shape, fold the square three times as shown in the diagram
below. Your final shape should be a 45°- 45°- 90° triangle that has folds
along the hypotenuse.

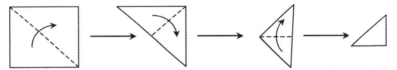

Once you have folded your paper, correctly label the
sides of your folded triangle "hypotenuse," "folded
leg," and "open leg" (the leg comprised of your
original square's edges) after orienting your triangle as
shown in the diagram at right.

Your Task: You want to be fully prepared to help the decorating committee for the
school dance. Explore and be ready to explain the relationships between the shapes
that are cut out and the design that appears after unfolding the paper. For each
possible location of a cutout, use what you know about symmetry and
transformations to describe the shapes that result when you unfold the paper.

Discussion Points

What are your goals for this task?

What **tools** would be useful to complete this task?

Visualize the result when a shape is cut along the hypotenuse.
What qualities will the result have?

6-78.   Since there are so many cuts that are possible, it is helpful to begin by considering a simple cutout along one side of the triangle.

a.   Sketch triangles onto your folded paper according to these directions, making sure that none of the shapes share a side or overlap:

- A 45°-45°-90° triangle with its hypotenuse along the paper triangle's hypotenuse. Each leg should be 3 units long.

- A 45°-45°-90° triangle with a 3-unit leg along the paper triangle's folded leg.

- A 45°-45°-90° triangle with a 3-unit leg along the paper triangle's open leg.

b.   Cut out the shapes you sketched from part (a). Then unfold the paper to view your snowflake. Identify the three different kinds of shapes that resulted from the triangles you cut. Describe them with as much specific vocabulary as you can.

c.   Find each pair of shapes shown below on your own snowflake. For each pair, describe <u>two different ways</u> to transform one shape into the other.

i.

ii.

iii.

iv.

Further Guidance section ends here.

6-79.   Some possible folded triangles with cutouts are shown below. What would each of these snowflakes look like when unfolded? Draw the resulting designs on the squares provided on the Activity 6.2.5 Resource Page (or draw the result on your paper.)

a.

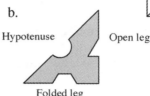

Hypotenuse   Open leg

Folded leg

b.

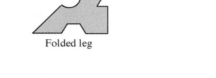

Hypotenuse   Open leg

Folded leg

6-80.   What shape must you cut out along your folded triangle hypotenuse to get the following shapes on your snowflake when your paper is unfolded? Sketch and label diagrams to show that you can accomplish each result.

a.   Rectangle with a length that is twice its width

b.   Kite

c.   Rhombus

d.   Pentagon

6-81.   EXTENSION

Get a final piece of grid paper from your teacher. Make one more snowflake that includes at least four of the following shapes. Make sure you sketch all of your planned cuts before cutting the paper with scissors. After you cut out your shapes and unfold your snowflake, answer questions (a) through (d) below.

- Draw a shape at the vertex where the hypotenuse and folded leg intersect that results in a shape with 8 lines of symmetry. Note that you will actually have to cut the vertex off to do this.

- Many letters, such as E, H, and I have reflection symmetry. Pick a letter (maybe one of your initials) and draw a shape along the folded triangle's hypotenuse or folded leg that results in a box letter when cut out and the snowflake is unfolded.

- Draw a shape along the folded triangle's hypotenuse or folded leg that results in a regular hexagon when cut out and the snowflake is unfolded.

- Draw a shape along the folded triangle's hypotenuse or folded leg that results in a star when cut out and the snowflake is unfolded.

- Draw curved shapes along the open leg so that there is at least one line of symmetry that is perpendicular to the open leg.

Problem continues on next page →

6-81.   *Problem continued from previous page.*

a.   What has to be true about the shape you cut out in order for your unfolded shape to have 8 lines of symmetry?

b.   There are two different shapes you could have drawn that would result in a regular hexagon. Sketch both shapes. Why do both shapes work?

c.   Some shapes are impossible to create by cutting along the hypotenuse of the folded paper triangle. Sketch several different examples of these shapes. What is the common characteristic of these impossible shapes?

d.   How is cutting along the open leg different from cutting along the folded leg or hypotenuse? Try to describe the difference in terms of symmetry. Use a diagram to help make your description clear.

6-82.   **Examine** the angles formed by parallel lines at right.

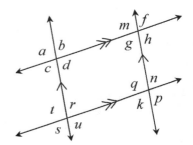

a.   If $r = 5x + 3°$ and $k = 4x + 9°$, solve for x. **Justify** your answer.

b.   If $c = 114°$, what is q? **Justify** your answer.

c.   If $g = 88°$, then what is q? **Justify** your answer.

6-83.   **Examine** the triangles below. For each, solve for x and name which **tool** you use. Show all work.

a.

b.

c.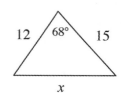

6-84.   For each part below, decide if the triangles are similar. If they are similar, use their similarity to solve for x. If they are not similar, explain why not.

a.

b.

c.

d.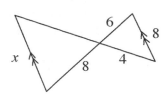

6-85.   For each shape below, use the geometric relationships to solve for the given variable(s). Show all work. Name the geometric relationships you used.

a.

b.

c.

d.

$$43$$

$$71°$$

$$43$$

$$x$$

6-86.   **Multiple Choice:** What is the distance between the points $(-2, -5)$ and $(6, 3)$?

a.   8   b. $8\sqrt{2}$ c.   16   d.   64

Chapter 6 Closure   What have I learned?

Reflection and Synthesis

The activities below offer you a chance to reflect on what you have learned in this chapter.
As you work, look for concepts that you feel very comfortable with, ideas that you would like to
learn more about, and topics you need more help with. Look for connections between ideas as
well as connections with material you learned previously.

① TEAM BRAINSTORM

With your team, brainstorm a list for each of the following two subjects. Be as
detailed as you can. How long can you make your list? Challenge yourselves. Be
prepared to share your team's ideas with the class.

Topics: What have you studied in this chapter? What ideas and words
were important in what you learned? Remember to be as detailed
as you can.

Connections: How are the topics, ideas, and words that you learned in previous
courses connected to the new ideas in this chapter? Again, make
your list as long as you can.

MAKING CONNECTIONS

The following is a list of the vocabulary used in this chapter. The words that appear in bold are new to this chapter. Make sure that you are familiar with all of these words and know what they mean. Refer to the glossary or index for any words that you do not yet understand.

AAS ≅	arrow diagrams	**ASA** ≅
conditional statement	congruent	conjecture
converse	corresponding	**diagonal**
flowchart	**HL** ≅	**SAS** ≅
similar	**SSS** ≅	

Make a concept map showing all of the connections you can find among the key words and ideas listed above. To show a connection between two words, draw a line between them and explain the connection, as shown in the example below. A word can be connected to any other word as long as there is a justified connection. For each key word or idea, provide a sketch of an example.

Your teacher may provide you with vocabulary cards to help you get started. If you use the cards to plan your concept map, be sure to either re-draw your concept map on your paper or glue the vocabulary cards to a poster with all of the connections explained for others to see and understand.

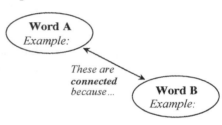

While you are making your map, your team may think of related words or ideas that are not listed above. Be sure to include these ideas on your concept map.

③   SUMMARIZING MY UNDERSTANDING

This section gives you an opportunity to show what you know about certain math topics or ideas. Your teacher will direct you how to do this.

④   WHAT HAVE I LEARNED?

This section will help you recognize those types of problems you feel comfortable with and those you need more help with. This section will appear at the end of every chapter to help you check your understanding. Even if your teacher does not assign this section, it is a good idea to try these problems and find out for yourself what you know and what you need to work on.

Solve each problem as completely as you can. The table at the end of this closure section has answers to these problems. It also tells you where you can find additional help and practice on similar problems.

CL 6-87. Write the converse of each statement and then determine whether or not the converse is true.

   a. If two lines are parallel, then corresponding angles are equal.

   b. In $\triangle ABC$, if the sum of $m\angle A$ and $m\angle B$ is 110°, then $m\angle C = 70°$.

   c. If alternate interior angles k and s are not equal, then the two lines cut by the transversal are not parallel.

   d. If Johan throws coins in the fountain, then he loses his money.

CL 6-88. Determine whether or not the two triangles in each pair are congruent. If they are congruent, show your **reasoning** in a flowchart. If the triangles are not congruent or you cannot determine that they are, **justify** your conclusion.

   a.

   b.

   c.

   d.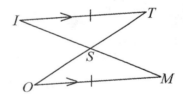

CL 6-89. For each part, determine which lines, if any, are parallel. Be sure to **justify** your decisions.

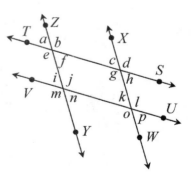

   a. $\angle e \cong \angle m$ b. $\angle c \cong \angle o$

   c. $\angle d \cong \angle o$ d. $\angle a \cong \angle m \cong \angle o$

   e. $\angle a \cong \angle k$ f. $\angle k \cong \angle c \cong \angle f$

CL 6-90. Determine whether or not the two triangles in each pair below are similar. If so, write a flowchart to show your **reasoning**. If not, explain why not.

a.

b.
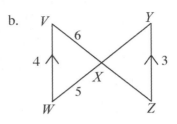

CL 6-91. For each diagram below, solve for the variable.

a.

b.

c.

CL 6-92. For each diagram, solve for the variable. Be sure to include the names of any relationships you used to get your solution.

a.

b.

c.
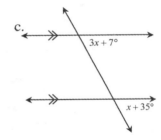

CL 6-93. Yee Ping thought about swimming across Redleaf Lake. She knows that she can swim about 1000 meters. She decided that she would feel more confident if she knew how far she would have to swim. To determine the length of the lake, she put posts at both ends of the lake (points *A* and *B*) and a third post on one side of the lake (point *C*). The distances between the posts are shown in the diagram at right. She measured the angle between the two posts and found that it was 150°. Use this information to determine the length of the lake. Do you think that Yee Ping will be able to swim between points *A* and *B*?

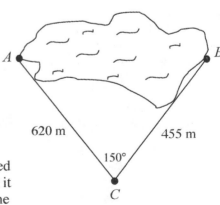

CL 6-94. Margarite has 9 pieces of copper pipe with which she plans to make 3 triangular frames. She has organized them into groups of three based on their coloring. The lengths of the pipes in each group are listed below.

     i.   23, 21, 4   *ii.*   2, 11, 10   *iii.*   31, 34, 3

a. Which groups, if any, will she actually be able to use to make a triangular frame if she is unable to cut any of the pipes? How do you know?

b. If possible, arrange the 9 pieces she has so that she can make 3 triangular frames. If so, how? If not, why not?

CL 6-95. At a story-telling class, Barbara took notes on the following story. However, all the parts of the story got mixed up. Help her make sense of the story by organizing the following details in a flowchart.

a. Maggie was happy she could play on the same team as Julie and Cheryl.

b. Julie was hoping to make the A team again this year as she grabbed her basketball and got on a bus in Bellingham.

c. Cheryl, having been named most valuable player in Port Townsend, started the drive to the statewide basketball camp.

d. Because of her skill in the first game, Maggie moved up to the A team.

e. At camp, Julie and Cheryl were placed on the A team.

f. Julie, Maggie and Cheryl met at a statewide basketball camp. Shortly after they met, they were placed on teams.

g. This year was Maggie's first year at camp, and was placed on the B team.

h. On the train to camp, Maggie thought about how surprising it was that her basketball coach chose her to attend camp.

CL 6-96. Check your answers using the table at the end of this section. Which problems do you feel confident about? Which problems were hard? Have you worked on problems like these in math classes you have taken before? Use the table to make a list of topics you need help on and a list of topics you need to practice more.

HOW AM I THINKING?

This course focuses on five different **Ways of Thinking**: investigating, examining, reasoning and justifying, visualizing, and choosing a strategy/tool. These are some of the ways in which you think while trying to make sense of a concept or attempting to solve a problem (even outside of math class). During this chapter, you have probably used each Way of Thinking multiple times without even realizing it!

Review each of the Ways of Thinking described in the closure sections of Chapters 1 through 5. Then choose three of these Ways of Thinking that you remember using while working in this chapter. Show and explain where and how you used each one. Describe why thinking in this way helped you solve a particular problem or understand something new. Be sure to include examples to demonstrate your thinking.

Answers and Support for Closure Activity #4
What Have I Learned?

Problem	Solutions	Need Help?	More Practice
CL 6-87.	a. True; If corresponding angles are equal, then the two lines are parallel	Lesson 6.1.4 Math Notes box	Problems 6-30, 6-31, 6-32, 6-38
	b. True; In triangle ABC, if angle C is 70°, then the sum of angles A and B is 110°.		
	c. True; If non-parallel lines form alternate interior angles, then those angles are not equal.		
	d. False; If Johan loses money, then he has thrown coins in the fountain.		

Problem	Solutions	Need Help?	More Practice

CL 6-88. b. Congruent

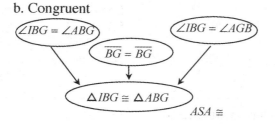

c. Not enough information.

d. Congruent:

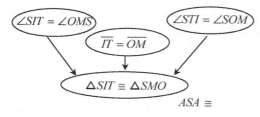

Need Help?
Lesson 6.1.3
Math Notes
box

More Practice
Problems 6-12,
6-21, 6-22, 6-37,
6-46, 6-51, 6-55,
6-65, 6-71

CL 6-89. a. $\overline{ST} \parallel \overline{UV}$; corres. angles are equal.

b. Not enough information.

c. $\overline{ST} \parallel \overline{UV}$; alt. interior angles are equal.

d. $\overline{ZY} \parallel \overline{XW}$; corres. angles are equal.

e. Not enough information.

f. $\overline{ZY} \parallel \overline{XW}$; $\overline{ST} \parallel \overline{UV}$; corres. angles and alternate interior angles are equal.

Need Help?
Lessons 2.1.1,
2.1.4, and
2.2.1 Math
Notes boxes,
Problem 2-3

More Practice
Problems 2-13,
2-16, 2-17, 2-23,
2-24, 2-25, 2-31,
2-32, 2-38, 2-49,
2-51, 2-62, 2-72,
2-111, 3-20, 3-31,
3-60, 3-70, 3-96,
4-6, 4-29, 4-44,
4-85, 4-93, 5-47,
6-30, 6-50

CL 6-90. a. Similar:

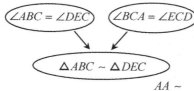

b. Similar; use of any 2 angles works.
Ex:

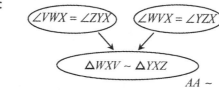

Need Help?
Lessons 2.1.4,
3.1.4, 3.2.1,
3.2.4, and
3.2.5 Math
Notes boxes

More Practice
Problems 3-64,
3-80, 3-83, 3-84,
3-86, 3-89, 4-7,
4-17, 4-38, 4-39,
4-83, 5-20, 5-49,
5-50, 5-57, 5-76,
5-86, 5-91, 6-5,
6-22, 6-46, 6-51,
6-61, 6-84

Problem	Solutions	Need Help?	More Practice
CL 6-91.	a. $x \approx 7.43$ b. $x \approx 8.28$ c. $\theta \approx 33.7°$	Lessons 4.1.4, 5.1.2, and 5.1.4 Math Notes boxes	Problems 4-12, 5-5, 5-7, 5-12, 5-16, 5-23, 5-89, 6-7, 6-14, 6-40, 6-43, 6-83
CL 6-92.	Reasons may vary. One possible set of reasons is listed for each: a. $x = 100°$ Triangle Angle Sum Theorem and supplementary angles b. $x = 30°$ Triangle Angle Sum Theorem, corresponding and supplementary angles c. $x = 14°$ corresponding angles	Lessons 2.1.1, 2.1.4, and 2.2.1 Math Notes boxes	Problems 2-17, 2-32, 2-38, 2-49, 2-51, 2-62, 2-72, 2-111, 3-20, 3-31, 3-60, 3-70, 3-96, 4-6, 4-29, 4-44, 4-85, 4-93, 5-47, 6-13, 6-24, 6-29, 6-35, 6-76, 6-82
CL 6-93.	The lake is about 1039 meters wide. This means Yee might have a problem.	Lesson 5.3.3 Math Notes box	Problems 5-100, 5-107, 5-109, 5-121, 6-14, 6-85

CL 6-94.	a. Sets *i* and *ii* work.
	
	b. It is possible
	    i. 4, 31, 34
	    ii. 3, 21, 23
	    iii. 2, 10, 11
		Lesson 2.3.2	Problems 2-107, 2-122, 3-60, 4-74, 6-18

CL 6-95.	One possible solution: 	Lesson 3.2.4 Math Notes box	Problems 3-62, 3-56, 3-67, 3-87, 4-39, 5-49, 5-91, 6-8

Appendix A What's the intersection?

Points, Lines, and Planes

In this course, you will study many shapes that are "built" with other shapes. For example, the rectangle at right is formed with four sides that are called **line segments**. Understanding the parts of shapes will help you not only *understand* the shapes better, but will also help you *describe* the shapes accurately.

A-1.   PLANES

A **plane** is a two-dimensional flat surface that extends without end. Even though a plane has no thickness, you can visualize it as the top surface of your desk or tabletop (if all sides of your desk extend infinitely). A graph with *x*- and *y*-axes that continue forever is a representation of a plane (see diagram at right).

a.   A plane is often represented by drawing a parallelogram, such as the one shown at right. Although the diagram seems to show edges, it is important to remember that a plane extends without end. The plane at right is named *Q*.

Use two pieces of cardboard to represent two planes. Remembering that planes extend infinitely and do not have borders (unlike your cardboard, which has edges), try to place your two planes so that they will never intersect (cross). Is it possible? If so, explain how the planes can be placed so that they do not intersect (or draw a diagram showing this situation). If not, explain why it is not possible.

b.   What happens when two planes intersect? What does their intersection look like? How could you describe the intersection?

c. .   What about three planes? Is it possible to have all three planes intersect each other? Is it possible to have two intersect, with a third plane somewhere else, never intersecting the other two? And is it possible for all three planes not to intersect anywhere? Consider these questions with your team members. For each case, explain how the planes are arranged and what their intersection(s) look(s) like. Be prepared to share your ideas with the class.

A-2.   LINES

In problem A-1, you discovered that when two planes intersect, their intersection is a line. While a plane is two-dimensional, a **line** is only one-dimensional. A line extends without end in two directions and has no thickness.

a.   Where have you used or seen a line before? In what contexts?

b.   If two lines intersect, how can you describe the intersection? Assume that the lines do not coincide (that is, assume that the lines do not lie directly on top of each other). Draw an example of two lines intersecting, and describe the intersection on your paper.

c.   When two lines intersect, their intersection is a **point**. A point has no dimension (and therefore, no thickness). Is it possible for two lines not to intersect? If so, is there more than one way for this to happen? To help you investigate this, use straight objects (such as two pencils) to represent lines. Be sure to keep in mind that lines extend infinitely in two directions. Explain what you find.

A-3.   Lines extend infinitely in two directions. However, what if a line extends infinitely in only one direction?

a.   On your paper, draw an example of a part of a line that extends infinitely in only one direction. This geometric figure is called a **ray**. A ray has one dimension, like a line. Where have you seen a ray before?

Ray

b.   A ray can be named using two points: the endpoint and one other point on the ray. For example, the ray above is called $\overrightarrow{AB}$. However, another way to represent a ray is on a number line, like the one shown below. This ray could be named $x \geq 2$.

On your paper, draw a number line. Then draw the ray $x \leq 3$. If this ray is named $\overrightarrow{EF}$, what is the coordinate of point E?

c.   Examine the ray at right. Name this ray at least three different ways.

A-4.   What about the points represented by the expression $-1 \le x \le 2$? What shape would these points form?

a.   On your paper, graph this shape on a number line. Then describe this shape.

b.   A portion of a line between two points is called a **line segment**. A line segment can be named using the two endpoints. For example, the line segment at right could be called $\overline{AB}$ or $\overline{BA}$.

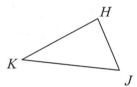

Using this notation, name the sides of the triangle at right.

c.   Examine the number line below. Name the line segment in as many ways as you can. Be ready to share your names with the class.

A-5.   In your Learning Log, write an entry describing what you learned today about points, lines, rays, line segments, and planes. Be sure to draw an example of each. Title this entry "Points, Lines, and Planes" and include today's date.

METHODS AND **M**EANINGS

MATH NOTES

Points, Lines, and Planes

A **point** is an undefined term in geometry. It has no dimension. It can be labeled with a capital letter (like point *A* at right) or with a coordinate (like 1).

A **line** has one dimension and extends without end in two directions. A number line is an example of a line. It is often named using two points on the line (like $\overleftrightarrow{BC}$ at right).

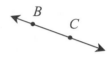

A **line segment** is a portion of a line between (and including) two points. It can be named using its endpoints (like $\overline{DE}$ at right) or with an interval on a number line (such as $-2 \leq x \leq 4$).

A **plane** is two-dimensional and extends without end. One way to think of a plane is as a flat surface, like the top of a table, that extends infinitely in all directions.

Review & Preview

A-6.   The ray at right can be named $\overrightarrow{AB}$ or $x \geq -3$. For each shape represented on the number lines below, write the name at least two different ways.

a.

b.

c.

d.

A-7.   In problem A-2, you showed that when two lines intersect and do not coincide (lie directly on top of each other), their intersection is a point.

   a.   Now consider three lines. If none of the lines coincide, how many arrangements are possible? Draw each case.

   b.   How can a line and a plane be arranged? For each case, describe the arrangement. If they intersect, describe the intersection.

A-8.   Draw a number line for $-4 \le x \le 4$ on your paper.

   a.   Label point A if its coordinate is 3.

   b.   Draw $\overline{EF}$ if it can be represented as $0 \le x \le 2$ and the coordinate of E is 0.

   c.   Explain where ray $\overrightarrow{FA}$ would exist. Then write another name for this ray.

A-9.   Part of this course is learning about geometry on a coordinate plane. What is the difference between how a point is represented on a number line and how it is represented on a coordinate plane?

   a.   To think about this question, first consider point A on the number line at right. What is the coordinate of A?

   b.   What happens when a y-axis is added to the diagram? Now how is point A represented with coordinates? Why is there a difference?

   c.   On graph paper, plot and label ray $\overrightarrow{AB}$ if A is (2, 3) and B is (4, 1).

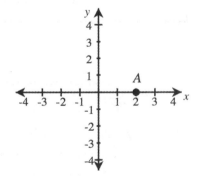

A-10.   On graph paper, find the intersection of line $\overleftrightarrow{AB}$ and ray $\overrightarrow{CD}$ if $A(4, 3)$, $B(-3, -4)$, $C(3, -4)$, and $D(1, -3)$.

Appendix B What can I assume?

Euclidean Geometry

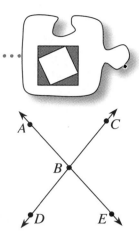

So far in this course, you have developed geometric ideas by assuming that certain geometric principals are true. For example, when you state that lines $\overline{AE}$ and $\overline{DC}$ intersect at point B, how can you be sure that they only intersect once? What are you assuming?

And when you became convinced that vertical angles are congruent (such as $\angle ABC$ and $\angle DBE$ at right), what assumptions did you make? What would be true if these assumptions were false?

To clarify issues like this, mathematicians have developed a geometric system of definitions, axioms, and theorems that includes assumptions as the basis for the mathematical ideas in the system. Perhaps the person most famous for this work is Euclid, a Greek mathematician who lived between 325 BC and 265 BC.

B-1. THE ELEMENTS

Euclid is often referred to as the "Father of Geometry," in large part because of a famous set of books he wrote, collectively called *Elements*. In this set of books, he provided critical definitions for many basic geometric figures and relationships, such as parallel lines and obtuse angles. In the left column of part (b) below are four of the geometric shapes defined by Euclid in *Elements*.

a. Complete this definition, which is a translation of Euclid's Definition 10: "*And when a straight-line stood upon another straight-line makes adjacent angles which are equal to one another, each of the equal angles is a right-angle, and the former straight line is called _____ to that upon which it stands.*" (Translation by Richard Fitzpatrick.)

b. Match each geometric term in the left column with its definition (translated into English from Greek) in the right column. One definition in the right column will be left over. Decide what shape Euclid was defining in the unmatched definition.

a. Line
b. Obtuse angle
c. Boundary
d. Point

1. Greater than a right angle.
2. A quadrilateral figure that is right-angled and equilateral.
3. That of which there is no part.
4. Length without breadth.
5. That which is the extremity of something.

B-2.   In addition to definitions, Euclid offered five **postulates** (also sometimes called **axioms**), which are statements that are assumed to be true. Euclid recognized that if these postulates were widely recognized as true, many other geometric properties and relationships could be proven true as well.

   a.   One of Euclid's postulates is translated, "*A straight line segment can be drawn by joining any two points.*" Draw two points on your paper and label them *A* and *B*. How many straight lines can connect points *A* and *B*? Draw as many as you can.

   b.   Another translated postulate states, "*All right angles are equal to one another.*" Do you agree with this assumption? If this postulate were not true, what would that mean?

   c.   Perhaps Euclid's most famous and studied postulate was his fifth postulate, which has been translated as, "*If a straight line falling across two other straight lines makes internal angles on the same side that are less than two right angles, then these two lines, when extended to infinity, will intersect on the same side as the angles and do not meet on the other side.*"

        Draw a diagram that could have accompanied this postulate. Is this assumption reasonable? What if this postulate were false?

B-3.   Another part of Book 1 of Euclid's *Elements* contains a series of Propositions (also called **theorems**), which are statements that are proven always to be true. By using definitions and postulates, Euclid set out to prove new geometric statements that, in turn, could be used to prove other new mathematical statements.

   Proposition 15 may look very familiar. Euclid proved that, "*If two straight lines cut one another, the angles that are vertically opposite are equal to one another.*" He then proved this by using a combination of several propositions and postulates.

   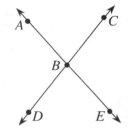

   a.   In his argument, Euclid states that if $\overline{DC}$ intersects $\overline{AE}$ at *B*, then ∡*ABC* and ∡*CBE* together form two right angles. What do you think he meant by that statement?

   b.   Euclid also used a common notion that "*things that are equal to the same thing are equal to each other.*" This is now referred to as the **Transitive Property**. Where have you used this property before?

LOOKING DEEPER

Euclid's *Elements*

In his set of books, collectively called *Elements*, Euclid defined many geometric terms to help fellow mathematicians and to create a common language about geometry. In addition, he also shared what he saw as five "common notions," listed below. Consider how you have used each of these notions in the past.

- If two things are equal to the same thing, then they are equal to each other.
- When equal things are added to equal things, then the sums are equal.
- When equal things are subtracted from equal things, then the differences are equal.
- When things coincide with one another, they are also equal to one another.
- The whole is greater than the part.

B-4. On graph paper, draw $\triangle ABC$ if $A(2, 4)$, $B(9, 5)$, and $C(4, 10)$.

a. Verify that $D(3, 7)$ is a midpoint of $\overline{AC}$.

b. Find the equation of the line through points D and B.

c. Is $\overline{BD}$ a height of $\triangle ABC$? Use slope to show that $\overline{BD}$ is perpendicular to $\overline{AC}$.

B-5. Draw a number line on your paper. If point A is at -1 and B is at 2, draw $\overrightarrow{AB}$. Describe the result.

B-6.   Consider points A and B on the number line at right. For the coordinates provided below, find the length of $\overline{AB}$. Assume that the coordinate of B is greater than or equal to the coordinate of A.

    a. A is 3 and B is 10   b. A is –2 and B is 8

    c. A is 6 and B is x d. A is x and B is y

B-7.   Examine $\triangle ABC$ on the graph at right.

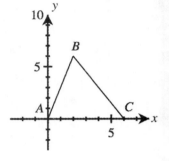

    a.   Find the midpoint of $\overline{AB}$ and call it D.

    b.   Find the midpoint of $\overline{BC}$ and call it E.

    c.   Find the equation of $\overleftrightarrow{DE}$.

    d.   Is $\overleftrightarrow{DE}$ parallel to $\overleftrightarrow{AC}$? Use slope to justify your conclusion.

B-8.   On a piece of graph paper, graph $y = -\frac{1}{2}x + 4$ and label its x-intercept A and its y-intercept B. Label the origin $(0, 0)$ point C.

    a.   Find the area of $\triangle ABC$.

    b.   Draw a height to $\overline{AB}$ through C. What is the slope of this height? Show how you found this slope.

    c.   If the height you drew in part (b) intersects side $\overline{AB}$ at point D, find the equation of the line through C and D.

Glossary

AA ~ (Triangle Similarity)   If two angles of one triangle are congruent to the two corresponding angles of another triangle, then the triangles are similar. For example, given $\triangle ABC$ and $\triangle A'B'C'$ with $\angle A \cong \angle A'$ and $\angle B \cong \angle B'$, then $\triangle ABC \sim \triangle A'B'C'$. You can also show that two triangles are similar by showing that *three* pairs of corresponding angles are congruent (which would be called AAA~), but two pairs are sufficient to demonstrate similarity. (pp. 151 and 171)

AAS ≅ (Triangle Congruence)   If two angles and a non-included side of one triangle are congruent to the corresponding two angles and non-included side of another triangle, the two triangles are congruent. Note that AAS ≅ is equivalent to ASA ≅. (p. 299)

absolute value   The absolute value of a number is the distance of the number from zero. Since the absolute value represents a distance, without regard to direction, it is always non-negative. Thus the absolute value of a negative number is its opposite, while the absolute value of a non-negative number is just the number itself. The absolute value of x is usually written $|x|$. For example, $|-5| = 5$ and $|22| = 22$. (pp. 453 and 575)

acute angle   An angle with measure greater than 0° and less than 90°. One example is shown at right. (p. 24)

adjacent angles   For two angles to be adjacent, they must satisfy these three conditions: (1) The two angles must have a common side; (2) They must have a common vertex; and (3) They can have no interior points in common. This means that the common side must be between the two angles; no overlap between the angles is permitted. In the example at right, $\angle ABC$ and $\angle CBD$ are adjacent angles.

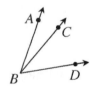

adjacent leg   In a right triangle, the leg adjacent to an acute angle is the side of the angle that is not the hypotenuse. For example, in $\triangle ABC$ shown at right, $\overline{AB}$ is the leg adjacent to $\angle A$. (p. 241)

alpha (α)   A Greek letter that is often used to represent the measure of an angle. Other Greek letters used to represent the measure of an angle include theta (θ) and beta (β). (p. 190)

alternate interior angles   Angles between a pair of lines that switch sides of a third intersecting line (called a transversal). For example, in the diagram at right the shaded angles are alternate interior angles. If the lines intersected by the transversal are parallel, the alternate interior angles are congruent. Conversely, if the alternate interior angles are congruent, then the two lines intersected by the transversal are parallel. (p. 91)

altitude   See *height*.

ambiguous   Information is ambiguous when it has more than one interpretation or conclusion. (pp. 270)

angle In general, an angle is formed by two rays joined at a common endpoint. Angles in geometric figures are usually formed by two segments, with a common endpoint (such as the angle shaded in the figure at right). (pp. 22 and 24)

angle measure *See* measurement.

angle of depression When an object (*B*) is below the horizontal line of sight of the observer (*A*), the angle of depression is the angle formed by the line of sight to the object and the horizontal line of sight.

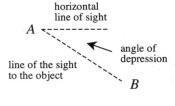

angle of elevation When an object (*B*) is above the horizontal line of sight of the observer (*A*), the angle of elevation is the angle formed by the line of sight to the object and the horizontal line of sight.

apex In a cone or pyramid, the apex is the point that is the farthest away from the flat surface (plane) that contains the base. In a pyramid, the apex is also the point at which the lateral faces meet. An apex is also sometimes called the "vertex" of a pyramid or cone. (p. 533)

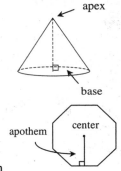

apothem A segment that connects the center of a regular polygon to a point on one of its sides, and is perpendicular to that side. (p. 410)

approximate Close, but not exact. An approximate answer to a problem is often a rounded decimal. For example, if the exact answer to a problem is $\sqrt{2}$, then 1.414 and 1.41 are approximate answers. (p. 123)

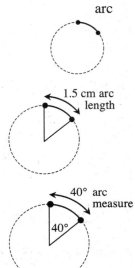

arc A connected part of a circle. Because a circle does not contain its interior, an arc is more like a portion of a bicycle tire than a slice of pizza. (pp. 426 and 485)

arc length The length of an arc (in inches, centimeters, feet, etc.) is the distance from one of the arc's endpoints to the arc's other endpoint, measured around the circle. Note that arc length is different from arc measure. Arcs of two different circles may have the same arc measure (like 90°), but have different arc lengths if one circle has a larger radius than the other one. For an example, see concentric circles. (p. 490)

arc measure The measure in degrees of an arc's central angle. Note that arc measure is measured in degrees and is different from arc length. (p. 490)

area On a flat surface (plane), the number of non-overlapping square units needed to cover the region. *Also see* surface area. (p. 490)

area model A tool that uses the area of rectangles to represent the probabilities of possible outcomes when considering two independent events. For example, suppose you are going to randomly select a student from a classroom. If the probability of selecting a female student from the room is $\frac{2}{3}$ and the probability of selecting a 9th grader from the room is $\frac{1}{4}$, the area of the shaded rectangle at right represents the probability that a randomly selected student is a female 9th grader ($\frac{2}{3} \cdot \frac{1}{4} = \frac{1}{6}$). A generic area model is a tool that enables you to find the probabilities of outcomes without drawing a diagram to scale. (p. 219)

	male $\frac{1}{3}$	female $\frac{2}{3}$
9th grader $\frac{1}{4}$	$\frac{1}{12}$	$\frac{1}{6}$
not 9th grader $\frac{3}{4}$	$\frac{1}{4}$	$\frac{1}{2}$

Area model

arrow diagram A pictorial representation of a conditional statement. The arrow points toward the conclusion of the conditional (the "then" part of the "If… then" statement). For example, the conditional statement *"If two lines cut by a transversal are parallel, then alternate interior angles are congruent"* can be represented by the arrow diagrams below. (p. 84)

Lines cut by a transversal are parallel → *alternate interior angles are congruent.*

arrowheads To indicate a line on a diagram, we draw a segment with arrowheads on its ends. The arrowheads show that our diagram indicates a line, which extends indefinitely. Marks on pairs of lines or segments such as ">>" and ">>>" indicate that the lines or segments are parallel. Both types of marks are used in the diagram above. (p. 54)

ASA $\cong$ (Triangle Congruence) If two angles and the included side of one triangle are congruent to the corresponding two angles and included side of another triangle, the triangles are congruent. Note that ASA $\cong$ is equivalent to AAS $\cong$. (p. 299)

auxiliary lines Segments and lines added to existing figures. Auxiliary lines are usually added to a figure to allow us to prove something about the figure.

axioms Statements accepted as true without proof. Also known as "postulates."

base (a) Triangle: Any side of a triangle to which a height is drawn. There are three possible bases in each triangle (p. 112); (b) Trapezoid: the two parallel sides (p. 107); (c) Parallelogram (and rectangle, rhombus, and square): Any side to which a height is drawn. There are four possible bases (p. 106); (d) Solid: *See* cone, cylinder, prism, and pyramid.

binomial An expression that is the sum or difference of exactly two terms, each of which is a monomial. For example, $-2x + 3y^2$ is a binomial. (p. 104)

bisect To bisect a geometric object is to divide it into two congruent parts. (p. 317)

center of a circle On a flat surface, the fixed point from which all points on the circle are equidistant. *See* circle. (p. 341)

central angle   An angle with its vertex at the center of a circle. (p. 490)

centroid   The point at which the three medians of a triangle intersect. The centroid is also the center of balance of a triangle. The other points of concurrency studied in this course are the circumcenter and the incenter. (pp. 471 and 501)

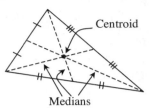

chord   A line segment with its endpoints on a circle. A chord that passes through the center of a circle is called a "diameter." *See* circle. (p. 485)

circle   The set of all points on a flat surface that are the same distance from a fixed point. If the fixed point (center) is O, the symbol $\odot O$ represents a circle with center O. If r is the length of a circle's radius and d is the length of its diameter, the circumference of the circle is $C = 2\pi r$ or $C = \pi d$. The area of the circle is $A = \pi r^2$. The equation of a circle with radius length r and center $(0, 0)$ is $x^2 + y^2 = r^2$. (pp. 341, 485, and 490)

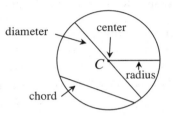

circular angle   An angle with a measure of 360°. (pp. 22 and 24)

circumcenter   The center of the circle that passes through the vertices of a triangle. It can be found by locating the point of intersection of the perpendicular bisectors of the sides of the triangle. The other points of concurrency studied in this course are the centroid and the incenter. (p. 501)

circumference   The perimeter of (distance around) a circle. (p. 426)

circumscribe   A circle circumscribes a polygon when it passes through all of the vertices of the polygon. (p. 500)

$\odot C$ circumscribes the pentagon.

clinometer   A device used to measure angles of elevation and depression. (p. 202)

clockwise   Clockwise identifies the direction of rotation shown in the diagram at right. The word literally means "in the direction of the rotating hands of a clock." The opposite of clockwise is counter-clockwise. (p. 34)

compass   (a) A tool used to draw circles; (b) A tool used to navigate the Earth. A compass uses the Earth's magnetic field to determination which direction is north.

complementary angles   Two angles whose measures add up to 90°. Angles T and V are complementary because $m\angle T + m\angle V = 90°$. Complementary angles may also be adjacent, like $\angle ABC$ and $\angle CBD$ in the diagram at far right. (p. 74)

concentric circles   Circles that have the same center. For example, the circles shown in the diagram at right are concentric. (p. 460)

concurrency (point of) The single point where two or more lines intersect on a plane. (p. 501)

conditional statement A statement written in "If …, then …" form. For example, "*If a rectangle has four congruent sides, then it is a square*" is a conditional statement. (p. 108)

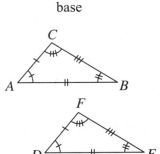

cone A three-dimensional figure that consists of a circular face, called the "base," a point called the "apex," that is not in the flat surface (plane) of the base, and the lateral surface that connects the apex to each point on the circular boundary of the base. (pp. 542 and 547)

congruent Two shapes are congruent if they have exactly the same shape and size. Congruent shapes are similar and have a scale factor of 1. The symbol for congruence is ≅. (pp. 159 and 291)

congruence statement A statement indicating that two figures are congruent. The order of the letters in the names of the shapes indicates which sides and angles are congruent to each other. For example, if $\triangle ABC \cong \triangle DEF$, then $\angle A \cong \angle D$, $\angle B \cong \angle E$, $\angle C \cong \angle F$, $\overline{AB} \cong \overline{DE}$, $\overline{BC} \cong \overline{EF}$, and $\overline{AC} \cong \overline{DF}$. (p. 346)

conic section A curve that is the intersection of a plane with a double cone. Conic sections include parabolas, circles, ellipses, and hyperbolas. Conic sections that degenerate (collapse) into a point or line are excluded. (p. 578)

conjecture An educated guess. Conjectures often result from noticing a pattern during an investigation. Conjectures are also often written in conditional ("If…, then…") form. Once a conjecture is proven, it becomes a theorem. (pp. 10 and 304)

construction The process of using a straightedge and compass to solve a problem and/or create a geometric diagram. (pp. 459 and 468)

converse The converse of a conditional statement can be found by switching the hypothesis (the "if" part) and the conclusion (the "then" part). For example, the converse of "*If P, then Q*" is "*If Q, then P.*" Knowing that a conditional statement is true does not tell you whether its converse is true. (p. 304)

convex polygon A polygon is convex if any pair of points inside the polygon can be connected by a segment without leaving the interior of the polygon. (p. 396)

coordinate geometry The study of geometry on a coordinate grid. (p. 395)

corresponding angles (a) When two lines are intersected by a third line (called a transversal), angles on the same side of the two lines and on the same side of the transversal are called corresponding angles. For example, the shaded angles in the diagram at right are corresponding angles. Note that if the two lines cut by the transversal are parallel, the corresponding angles are congruent. Conversely, if the corresponding angles are congruent, then the two lines intersected by the transversal are parallel. (p. 91); (b) Angles in two figures may also correspond, as shown at right. See corresponding parts for more information. (pp. 143 and 150)

Glossary

corresponding parts   Points, sides, edges, or angles in two or more figures that are images of each other with respect to a transformation. If two figures are congruent, their corresponding parts are congruent to each other. (p. 143, 150, 346)

cosine ratio   In a right triangle, the cosine ratio of an acute $\angle A$ is $\cos A = \frac{\text{length of adjacent side}}{\text{length of hypotenuse}}$.   In the triangle at right, $\cos A = \frac{AB}{AC} = \frac{4}{5}$. (p. 241)

counter-clockwise   Counter-clockwise identifies the direction of rotation shown in the diagram at right. The opposite of counter-clockwise is clockwise. (p. 34)

counterexample   An example showing that a generalization has at least one exception; that is, a situation in which the statement is false. For example, the number 4 is a counterexample to the statement "All even numbers are greater than 7." (p. 238)

cross-section   The intersection of a three-dimensional solid and a plane. The cross-sections of a cone (and double-cone) are called "conic sections." (pp. 538 and 578)

cube   A polyhedron all of whose faces are squares. (p. 527)

cylinder (circular)   A three-dimensional figure that consists of two parallel congruent circular regions (called *bases*) and a lateral surface containing segments connecting each point on the circular boundary of one base to the corresponding point on the circular boundary of the other. (pp. 30 and 451)

bases

decagon   A polygon with ten sides. (p. 393)

delta (Δ)   A Greek letter that is often used to represent a difference. Its uses include Δx and Δy, which represent the lengths of the horizontal and vertical legs of a slope triangle, respectively. (p. 47)

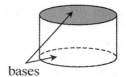

dependent events   Two events are dependent if the outcome of one event affects the probability of the other event. For example, assume you will randomly select two cards, one at a time, without replacement from a deck of cards. The probability that the first card is red is $\frac{26}{52} = \frac{1}{2}$ because 26 of the 52 cards are red. However, the probability of the second card now depends on the result of the first selection. If the first card was red, there are now 25 red cards remaining in a deck of 51 cards, and the probability that the second card is red is $\frac{25}{51}$. The second event (selecting the second card) is dependent on the first event (selecting the first card). (p. 207)

diagonal   In a polygon, it is a segment that connects two vertices of the polygon but is not a side of the polygon. (p. 400)

diagonal

diameter   A line segment drawn through the center of a circle with both endpoints on the circle. The length of a diameter is usually denoted d. Note that the length of a circle's diameter is twice the length of its radius. *See* circle. (pp. 341 and 485)

dilation   A transformation which produces a figure similar to the original by proportionally shrinking or stretching the figure. In a dilation, a shape is stretched (or compressed) proportionally from a point, called the point of dilation. (p. 138)

dimension   (a) Flat figures have two dimensions (which can be labeled "base" and "height"); (b) Solids have three dimensions (such as "width," "height," and "depth"). (pp. 98 and 452)

directrix   A line that, along with a point (called a focus), defines a conic section (such as a parabola). (p. 574)

dissection The process of dividing a flat shape or solid into parts that have no interior points in common.

dodecahedron   A polyhedron with twelve faces. (p. 529)

double cone   Two cones placed apex to apex so that their bases are parallel. Generally we think of the cones as extending to infinity beyond their bases. (p. 588)

Double cone

edge   In three dimensions, a line segment formed by the intersection of two faces of a polyhedron. (p. 527)

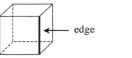

edge

ellipse   A type of conic section. An example is shown at right. The sum of the distances between each point on an ellipse and two fixed points (called the foci) is constant. (p. 585)

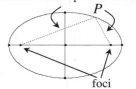

distances from point *P* to foci

foci

endpoints   See *line segment.*

enlarge   To enlarge something is to increase its size. For this course, an enlargement is a dilation of a figure whose result is similar to but larger than the original. (p. 140)

equator   If we represent the Earth as a sphere, the equator is the great circle equally distant between the North and South poles. The equator divides the Earth into two halves called the Northern and Southern hemispheres. The equator also marks a latitude of 0°. *See* latitude. (p. 549)

equilateral   A polygon is equilateral if all its sides have equal length. The word "equilateral" comes from "equi" (meaning "equal") and "lateral" (meaning "side"). Equilateral triangles not only have sides of equal length, but also angles of equal measure. However, a polygon with more than three sides can be equilateral without having congruent angles. For example, see the rhombus at right. (pp. 351 and 396)

exact answer An answer that is precisely accurate and not approximate. For example, if the length of a side of a triangle is exactly $\sqrt{10}$, the exact answer to the question "How long is that side of the triangle?" would be $\sqrt{10}$, while 3.162 would be approximate answer. (p. 123)

expected value For this course, the expected value of a game is the average amount expected to be won or lost on each play of the game if the game is played many times. The expected value need not be a value one could actually win on a single play of the game. For example, if you play a game where you roll a die and win one point for every dot on the face that comes up, the expected value of this game is $\frac{1+2+3+4+5+6}{6} = 3.5$ points for each play. (p. 516)

exterior angle When a side of a polygon is extended to form an angle with an adjacent side outside of the polygon, that angle is called an exterior angle. For example, the angles marked with letters in the diagram at right are exterior angles of the quadrilateral. Note that an exterior angle of a polygon is always adjacent and supplementary to an interior angle of that polygon. The sum of the exterior angles of a convex polygon is always 360°. (pp. 403 and 407)

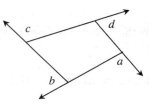

face of a polyhedron One of the flat surfaces of a polyhedron, including the base(s). (p. 527)

fair game For the purposes of this course, a fair game has an expected value of 0. Therefore, over many plays, a person would expect to neither win nor lose points or money by playing a fair game. (p. 510)

flowchart A diagram showing an argument for a conclusion from certain evidence. A flowchart uses ovals connected by arrows to show the logical structure of the argument. When each oval has a reason stated next to it showing how the evidence leads to that conclusion, the flowchart represents a proof. See the example at right. (p. 167)

focus (plural: foci) A point that, along with a line (called a directrix), can be used to define all or part of a conic section (such as a parabola). (pp. 574 and 581)

fraction buster "Fraction busting" is a method of simplifying equations involving fractions. Fraction busting uses the Multiplicative Property of Equality to alter the equation so that no fractions remain. To use this method, multiply both sides of an equation by the common denominator of all the fractions in the equation. The result will be an equivalent equation with no fractions. For example, when given the equation $\frac{x}{7} + 2 = \frac{x}{3}$, we can multiply both sides by the "fraction buster" 21. The resulting equation, $3x + 42 = 7x$, is equivalent to the original but contains no fractions. (p. 512)

function A relation in which for each input value there is one and only one output value. For example, the relation $f(x) = x + 4$ is a function; for each input value (x) there is exactly one output value. In terms of ordered pairs (x, y), no two ordered pairs of a function have the same first member (x). (p. 589)

graph   A graph represents numerical information spatially. The numbers may come from a table, situation (pattern), rule (equation or inequality), or figure. Most of the graphs in this course show points, lines, figures, and/or curves on a two-dimensional coordinate system like the one at right.

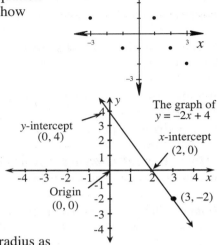

A complete graph includes all the necessary information about a line or a curve. To be complete, a graph must have the following components: (1) the *x*-axis and *y*-axis labeled, clearly showing the scale; (2) the equation of the graph written near the line or curve; (3) the line or curve extended as far as possible on the graph with arrows if the line or curve continues beyond the axes; (4) the coordinates of all special points, such as *x*- and *y*-intercepts, shown in (*x*, *y*) form. (p. 29)

great circle   A cross-section of a sphere that has the same radius as the sphere. If the Earth is represented with a sphere, the equator is an example of a great circle. (p. 549)

golden ratio   The number $\frac{1+\sqrt{5}}{2}$, which is often labeled with the Greek letter phi (ϕ), pronounced "fee." (p. 599)

height   (a) Triangle: the length of a segment that connects a vertex of the triangle to a line containing the opposite base (side) and is perpendicular to that line; (b) Trapezoid: the length of any segment that connects a point on one base of the trapezoid to the line containing the opposite base and is perpendicular to that line; (c) Parallelogram (includes rectangle, rhombus, and square): the length of any segment that connects a point on one base of the parallelogram to the line containing the opposite base and is perpendicular to that line; (d) Pyramid and cone: the length of the segment that connects the apex to a point in the plane containing the figure's base and is perpendicular to that plane; (e) Prism or cylinder: the length of a segment that connects one base of the figure to the plane containing the other base and is perpendicular to that plane. Some texts make a distinction between height and altitude, where the altitude is the segment described in the definition above and the height is its length. (pp. 106, 110, 448, 534, and 547)

hemisphere   A great circle of a sphere divides it into two congruent parts, each of which is called a hemisphere. If the Earth is represented as a sphere, the Northern hemisphere is the portion of the Earth north of (and including) the equator. Likewise, the Southern hemisphere is the portion of the Earth south of (and including) the equator. (p. 549)

heptagon   A polygon with seven sides. (p. 393)

heptahedron   A polyhedron with seven faces. (p. 529)

hexagon   A polygon with six sides. (pp. 43 and 393)

hexahedron   A polyhedron with six faces. A regular hexahedron is a cube. (p. 529)

HL ≅ (Triangle Shortcut) If the hypotenuse and one leg of one right triangle are congruent to the hypotenuse and corresponding leg of another right triangle, the two right triangles are congruent. Note that this congruence conjecture applies only to right triangles. (p. 299)

hypotenuse The longest side of a right triangle (the side opposite the right angle). (pp. 119 and 241)

hypothesis A conjecture (or educated guess) in science.

icosahedron A polyhedron with twenty faces. (p. 529)

"If …, then …" statement A statement written in the form "If …, then …." Also known as a conditional statement. (p. 108)

image The shape that results from a transformation, such as a translation, rotation, reflection, or dilation. (p. 34)

incenter The center of the circle inscribed in a triangle. It can be found by locating the point at which the angle bisectors of a triangle intersect. The other points of concurrency studied in this course are the centroid and the circumcenter. (p. 193)

independent events If the outcome of a probabilistic event does not affect the probability of another event, the events are independent. For example, assume you plan to roll a normal six-sided die twice and want to know the probability of rolling a 1 twice. The result of the first roll does not affect the probability of rolling a 1 on the second roll. Since the probability of rolling a 1 on the first roll is $\frac{1}{6}$ and the probability of rolling a 1 on the second roll is also $\frac{1}{6}$, then the probability of rolling two 1s in a row is $\frac{1}{6} \cdot \frac{1}{6} = \frac{1}{36}$. (p. 207)

indirect proof *See* proof by contradiction.

inequality symbols The symbols < (less than), > (greater than), ≤ (less than or equal to), and ≥ (greater than or equal to).

inscribed angle An angle with its vertex on the circle and sides intersecting the circle at two distinct points. (p. 490)

Inscribed Angle Theorem The measure of an inscribed angle is half the measure of its intercepted arc. Likewise, the measure of an intercepted arc is twice the measure of an inscribed angle whose sides pass through the endpoints of the arc. In the figure at right, if $m\overset{\frown}{AC} = 60°$, then $m\angle ABC = 30°$. (p. 494)

inscribed circle A circle is inscribed in a polygon if each side of the polygon intersects the circle at exactly one point.

$\odot B$ is inscribed in the pentagon.

inscribed polygon A polygon is inscribed in a circle if each vertex of the polygon lies on the circle. (p. 461)

$\odot C$ circumscribes the pentagon.

integers   The set of numbers { . . . −3, −2, −1, 0, 1, 2, 3, . . . }.

intercepted arc   The arc of a circle bounded by the points where the two sides of an inscribed angle meet the circle. In the circle at right, $\angle ABC$ intercepts $\overarc{AC}$. (p. 489)

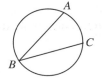

interior angle (of a polygon)   An angle formed by two consecutive sides of the polygon. The vertex of the angle is a vertex (corner) of the polygon. (p. 402)

Interior angle

Interior Angle Sum Conjecture   The sum of the interior angles of a polygon with n-sides is $180°(n − 2)$. (p. 407)

inverse trigonometric functions   When the ratio between the lengths of two sides of a right triangle is known, $\sin^{-1}$, $\cos^{-1}$, or $\tan^{-1}$ can be used to find the measure of one of the triangle's acute angles. (p. 248)

irrational numbers   The set of numbers that cannot be expressed in the form $\frac{a}{b}$, where a and b are integers and $b \neq 0$. For example, π and $\sqrt{2}$ are irrational numbers. (pp. 115 and 467)

isosceles trapezoid   A trapezoid with a pair of equal base angles (from the same base). Note that this will cause the non-parallel sides to be congruent. (pp. 77 and 371)

isosceles triangle   A triangle with two sides of equal length. (p. 48)

Isosceles Triangle Theorem   If a triangle is isosceles, then the base angles (which are opposite the congruent sides) are congruent. For example, if $\triangle ABC$ is isosceles with $\overline{BA} \cong \overline{BC}$, then the angles opposite these sides are congruent; that is, $\angle A \cong \angle C$.

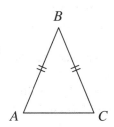

iteration   The act of repeating an action over and over. (p. 598)

justify   To give a logical reason supporting a statement or step in a proof. More generally, to use facts, definitions, rules, and/or previously proven conjectures in an organized sequence to convincingly demonstrate that your claim (or your answer) is valid (true). (p. 167)

kite   A quadrilateral with two distinct pairs of consecutive congruent sides. (p. 353)

lateral surface area   The sum of the areas of all of the faces of a prism or pyramid, with the exception of the base(s). (p. 534)

latitude   An angular measure (in degrees) that indicates how far north or south of the equator a position on the Earth is. All points on the equator have a latitude of 0°. The North Pole have a latitude of 90°, while the South Pole has a latitude of -90°. (p. 549)

Law of Cosines For any $\triangle ABC$ with sides a, b, and c opposite $\angle A$, $\angle B$, and $\angle C$ respectively, it is always true that $c^2 = a^2 + b^2 - 2ab \cdot \cos(C)$, $b^2 = a^2 + c^2 - 2ac \cdot \cos(B)$, and $a^2 = b^2 + c^2 - 2bc \cdot \cos(A)$. (p. 267)

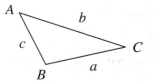

Law of Sines For any $\triangle ABC$ with sides a, b, and c opposite $\angle A$, $\angle B$, and $\angle C$ respectively, it is always true that $\frac{\sin A}{a} = \frac{\sin B}{b} = \frac{\sin C}{c}$. (p. 264)

legs The two sides of a right triangle that form the right angle. Note that legs of a right triangle are always shorter than its hypotenuse. (p. 119)

line A line is an undefined term in geometry. It is one-dimensional and extends without end in two directions. It is made up of points and has no thickness. A line can be named with a letter (such as l), but also can be labeled using two points on the line, such as $\overleftrightarrow{AB}$ below. (p. 81)

line of symmetry A line that divides a shape into two congruent parts that are mirror images of each other. If you fold a shape over its line of symmetry, the shapes on both sides of the line will match each other perfectly. Some shapes have more than one line of symmetry, such as the example at right. Other shapes may only have one line of symmetry or no lines of symmetry. (p. 5)

line segment The portion of a line between two points. A line segment is named using its endpoints. For example, the line segment at right can be named either $\overline{AB}$ or $\overline{BA}$. (p. 81)

linear scale factor (a) In the case of two similar two-dimensional figures, the linear scale factor is the ratio of the lengths of any pair of corresponding sides. This means that once it is determined that two figures are similar, all of their pairs of corresponding sides have the same ratio. The linear scale factor can also be called the *ratio of similarity*. When the ratio is comparing a figure and its image after a dilation, this ratio can also be called the *zoom factor*. (b) In the case of two similar polyhedra, the linear scale factor is the ratio of the lengths of any pair of corresponding edges. (pp. 140, 415, 457)

logical argument A logical sequence of statements and reasons that lead to a conclusion. A logical argument can be written in a paragraph, represented with a flowchart, or documented in a two-column proof. (pp. 10, 353, and 366)

longitude An angular measure (in degrees) that indicates how far west or east of the Prime Meridian a position on the Earth is. Lines of longitude (which are actually circles) are all great circles that pass through the North and South Poles. (pp. 549 and 551)

major arc An arc with measure greater than 180°. Each major arc has a corresponding minor arc that has a measure that is less than 180°. A major arc is named with three letters on the arc. For example, the highlighted arc at right is the major arc $\overset{\frown}{ABC}$. (p. 485)

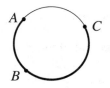

mat plan A top (or bottom) view of a multiple cube solid. The number in each square is the number of cubes in that stack. For example, the mat plan at right represents the solid at the far right. (p. 443)

measurement For the purposes of this course, a measurement is an indication of the size or magnitude of a geometric figure. For example, an appropriate measurement of a line segment would be its length. Appropriate measurements of a square would include not only the length of a side, but also its area and perimeter. The measure of an angle represents the number of degrees of rotation from one ray to the other about the vertex. (p. 15)

median A line segment that connects a vertex of a triangle with the midpoint of side opposite to the vertex. For example, since D is a midpoint of $\overline{BC}$, then $\overline{AD}$ is a median of $\triangle ABC$. The three medians of a triangle intersect at a point called the centroid. (p. 471)

midpoint A point that divides a segment into two segments of equal length. For example, D is the midpoint of $\overline{BC}$ in $\triangle ABC$ at right. (p. 381)

midsegment A segment joining the midpoints of two sides of a triangle. (p. 371)

minor arc An arc with measure less than $180°$. Minor arcs are named using the endpoints of the arc. For example, the highlighted arc at right is named $\overset{\frown}{AC}$. (p. 485)

Möbius strip A one-sided surface in a closed loop which can be formed by giving a rectangular strip of paper a half-twist and affixing its ends. (p. 8)

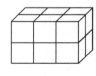

monomial An expression with only one term. It can be a number, a variable, or the product of a number and one or more variables. For example, 7, $3x$, $-4ab$, and $3x^2y$ are each monomials.

n-gon A polygon with n sides. A polygon is often referred to as an "n-gon" when we do not yet know the value of n. (p. 422)

net A diagram that, when folded, forms the surface of a three-dimensional solid. A net is essentially the faces of a solid laid flat. It is one of several ways to represent a three-dimensional diagram. The diagram at right is a representation of the solid at the far right. Note that the shaded region of the net indicates the (bottom) base of the solid. (p. 446)

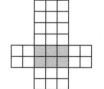

nonagon A polygon with nine sides. (p. 393)

nonahedron A polyhedron with nine faces. (p. 529)

non-convex polygon A polygon that is not convex. An example of a non-convex polygon is shown at right. *See* convex. (pp. 395 and 396)

oblique A prism (or cylinder) is oblique when its lateral surface(s) are not perpendicular to the base. A pyramid (or cone) is oblique when its apex is not directly above the center of the base. (pp. 451 and 538)

obtuse angle Any angle that measures between (but not including) 90° and 180°. (p. 24)

octagon A polygon with eight sides. (p. 393)

octahedron A polyhedron with eight faces. In a regular octahedron, all of the faces are equilateral triangles. (p. 529)

opposite In a figure, opposite means "across from." For example, in a triangle, an "opposite side" is the side that is across from a particular angle and is not a side of the angle. For example, the side $\overline{AB}$ in $\triangle ABC$ at right is opposite $\measuredangle C$, while $\overline{AC}$ is opposite the right angle. (p. 241)

orientation In this course, orientation refers to the placement and alignment of a figure in relation to others or an object of reference (such as coordinate axes). Unless it has rotation symmetry, the orientation of a figure changes when it is rotated (turned) less than 360°. Also, the orientation of a shape changes when it is reflected, except when reflected across a line of symmetry. (p. 241)

parabola The graph of a quadratic function (any equation that can be written in the form $y = ax^2 + bx + c$) is a parabola. There are several other ways to find a parabola, including the intersection of a right circular cone with a flat surface parallel to an edge of the cone. (p. 574)

parallel lines Two lines on a flat surface are parallel if they never intersect. Two line segments on a flat surface are parallel if the lines they lie on never intersect. There is a constant distance between two parallel lines (or line segments). Identical arrow markings are used to note parallel lines or line segments. (p. 47)

parallelogram A quadrilateral with two pairs of parallel sides. (p. 361)

pentagon A polygon with five sides. (p. 393)

pentahedron A polyhedron with five faces. (p. 529)

perimeter The distance around the exterior of a figure on a flat surface. For a polygon, the perimeter is the sum of the lengths of its sides. The perimeter of a circle is also called a circumference. (p. 15)

perpendicular Two rays, line segments, or lines that meet (intersect) to form a right angle (90°) are called perpendicular. A line and a flat surface can also be perpendicular if the line does not lie on the flat surface but intersects it and forms a right angle with every line on the flat surface passing through the point of intersection. A small square at the point of intersection of two lines or segments indicates that the lines are perpendicular. (p. 47)

phi (ϕ)   A Greek letter, pronounced "fee," that represents the golden ratio, $\frac{1+\sqrt{5}}{2}$. (p. 599)

pi (π)   The ratio of the circumference (C) of the circle to its diameter (d). For every circle, $\pi = \frac{\text{circumference}}{\text{diameter}} = \frac{C}{d}$. Numbers such as 3.14, 3.14159, or $\frac{22}{7}$ are approximations of π. (p. 426)

plane   A plane is an undefined term in geometry. It is a two-dimensional flat surface that extends without end. It is made up of points and has no thickness.

platonic solid   A convex regular polyhedron. All faces of a platonic solid are congruent, regular polygons. There are only five possible platonic solids: tetrahedron (with four faces of equilateral triangles), cube (with six faces of squares), octahedron (with eight faces of equilateral triangles), dodecahedron (with twelve faces of regular pentagons), and icosahedron (with twenty faces of equilateral triangles). (pg. 529)

polygon   A two-dimensional closed figure of three or more line segments (sides) connected end to end. Each segment is a side and only intersects the endpoints of its two adjacent sides. Each point of intersection is a vertex. At right are two examples of polygons. (p. 42, 393, and 396)

polyhedron (plural: polyhedra)   A three-dimensional object with no holes that is bounded by polygons. The polygons are joined at their sides, forming the edges of the polyhedron. Each polygon is a face of the polyhedron. (p. 448)

postulates   Statements accepted as true without proof. Also known as "axioms."

preimage   The original figure in a transformation.

prism   A three-dimensional figure that consists of two parallel congruent polygons (called *bases*) and a lateral surface containing segments connecting each point on each side of one base to the corresponding point on the other base. The lateral surface of a prism consists of parallelograms. (p. 448)

probability   A number that represents how likely an event is to happen. When a event has a finite number of equally-likely outcomes, the probability that one of those outcomes, called A, will occur is expressed as a ratio and written as:

$$P(A) = \frac{\text{number of successful outcomes}}{\text{total number of possible outcomes}}.$$

For example, when flipping a coin, the probability of getting tails, P(tails), is $\frac{1}{2}$ because there is only one tail (successful outcome) out of the two possible equally likely outcomes (a head and a tail). Probability can be written as a ratio, decimal, or percent. A probability of 0 (or 0%) indicates that it is impossible for the event to occur, while a probability of 1 (or 100%) indicates that the event must occur. Events that "might happen" will have values somewhere between 0 and 1 (or between 0% and 100%). (p. 60)

proof   A convincing logical argument that uses definitions and previously proven conjectures in an organized sequence to show that a conjecture is true. A proof can be written in a paragraph, represented with a flowchart, or documented in a formal two-column proof. (p. 10, 353, and 366)

proof by contradiction   A proof that begins by assuming that an assertion is true and then shows that this assumption leads to a contradiction of a known fact. This demonstrates that the assertion is false. Also known as an *indirect proof.* (p. 96)

proportional equation   An equation stating that two ratios (fractions) are equal. (p. 145)

protractor   A geometric tool used for physically measuring the number of degrees in an angle. (p. 22)

pyramid   A polyhedron with a polygonal base formed by connecting each point of the base to a single given point (the **apex**) that is above or below the flat surface containing the base. Each triangular lateral face of the pyramid is formed by the segments from the apex to the endpoints of a side of the base and the side itself. A tetrahedron is a special pyramid because any face can act as its base. (p. 533)

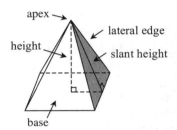

Pythagorean Theorem   The statement relating the lengths of the legs of a right triangle to the length of the hypotenuse: $(\text{leg \#1})^2 + (\text{leg \#2})^2 = \text{hypotenuse}^2$. The Pythagorean Theorem is powerful because if you know the lengths of any two sides of a right triangle, you can use this relationship to find the length of the third side. (p. 123)

Pythagorean triple   Any three positive integers a, b, and c that make the relationship $a^2 + b^2 = c^2$ true. Commonly used Pythagorean triples include 3, 4, 5 and 5, 12, 13. (p. 260)

quadratic equation   An equation that can be written in the form $ax^2 + bx + c = 0$, where a, b, and c are real numbers and a is nonzero. A quadratic equation written in this form is said to be in standard form. For example, $3x^2 - 4x + 7.5 = 0$ is a quadratic equation. (p. 163)

Quadratic Formula   The Quadratic Formula states that if $ax^2 + bx + c = 0$ and $a \neq 0$, then $x = \frac{-b \pm \sqrt{b^2 - 4ac}}{2a}$. For example, if $5x^2 + 9x + 3 = 0$, then $x = \frac{-9 \pm \sqrt{9^2 - 4(5)(3)}}{2(5)} = \frac{-9 \pm \sqrt{21}}{10}$. (p. 163)

quadrilateral   A polygon with four sides.

radius (plural: radii)   Of a circle: A line segment drawn from the center of a circle to a point on the circle. (p. 341); Of a regular polygon: A line segment that connects the center of a regular polygon with a vertex. The length of a radius is usually denoted r. (p. 410)

random   An event is random if its result cannot be known (and can only be guessed) until the event is completed. For example, the flip of a fair coin is random because the coin can either land on heads or tails and the outcome cannot be known for certain until after the coin is flipped.

ratio   A ratio compares two quantities by division. A ratio can be written using a colon, but is more often written as a fraction. For example, in the two similar triangles at right, a ratio can be used to compare the length of $\overline{BC}$ in $\triangle ABC$ with the length of $\overline{EF}$ in $\triangle DEF$. This ratio can be written as 5:11 or as the fraction $\frac{5}{11}$. (p. 60)

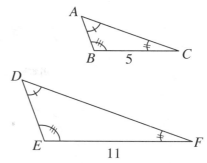

ratio of similarity   The ratio of any pair of corresponding sides of two similar figures. This means that once it is determined that two figures are similar, all of their pairs of corresponding sides have the same ratio. For example, for the similar triangles $\triangle ABC$ and $\triangle DEF$ above, the ratio of similarity is $\frac{5}{11}$. The ratio of similarity can also be called the *linear scale factor*. When the ratio is comparing a figure and its image after a dilation, this ratio can also be called the *zoom factor*. (pp. 140, 415, and 457)

rationalizing the denominator   Rewriting a fractional expression that has radicals in the denominator in order to eliminate them. (p. 252)

ray   A ray is part of a line that starts at one point and extends without end in one direction. In the example at right, ray $\overrightarrow{AB}$ is part of $\overleftrightarrow{AB}$ that starts at A and contains all of the points of $\overleftrightarrow{AB}$ that are on the same side of A as point B, including A. Point A is the endpoint of $\overrightarrow{AB}$.

rectangle   A quadrilateral with four right angles. (pp. 5 and 361)

reflection   A transformation across a line that produces a mirror image of the original (preimage) shape. The reflection is called the "image" of the original figure. The line is called a "line of reflection." See the example at right. Note that a reflection is also sometimes referred to as a "flip." (pp. 34 and 38)

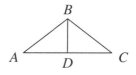

original   image

Line of reflection

Reflexive Property   The Reflexive Property states that any expression is always equal to itself. That is, $a = a$. This property is often useful when proving that two triangles that share a side or an angle are congruent. For example, in the diagram at right, since $\triangle ABD$ and $\triangle CBD$ share a side ($\overline{BD}$), the Reflexive Property justifies that $BD = BD$. (p. 354)

reflection symmetry   *See* symmetry.

regular   A polygon is regular if it is a convex polygon with congruent angles and congruent sides. For example, the shape at right is a regular hexagon. (pp. 42, 351, and 396)

REGULAR HEXAGON

relation An equation that relates two or more variables. For example, $y = 3x - 2$ and $x^2 + y^2 = 9$ are both relations. A relation can also be thought of as a set of ordered pairs. (p. 589)

relationship For this course, a relationship is a way that two objects (such as two line segments or two triangles) are connected. When you know that the relationship holds between two objects, learning about one object can give you information about the other. Relationships can be described in two ways: a geometric relationship (such as a pair of vertical angles or two line segments that are parallel) and a relationship between the measures (such as two angles that are complementary or two sides of a triangle that have the same length). Common geometric relationships between two figures include being similar (when two figures have the shape, but not necessarily the same size) and being congruent (when two figures have the same shape and the same size). (pp. 76, 91, 150, and 159)

reasoning *See* logical reasoning *and* proof.

remote interior angles If a triangle has an exterior angle, the remote interior angles are the two angles not adjacent to the exterior angle. Also called "opposite interior angles." (p. 397)

rhombus A quadrilateral with four congruent sides. (pp. 361 and 464)

right angle An angle that measures 90°. A small square is used to note a right angle, as shown in the example at right. (pp. 22 and 24)

right triangle A triangle that has one right angle. The side of a right triangle opposite the right angle is called the "hypotenuse," and the two sides adjacent to the right angle are called "legs." (p. 119)

rigid motions Movements of figures that preserve their shape and size. Also called "rigid transformations." Examples of rigid motions are reflections, rotations, and translations. Also called "isometries." (p. 34)

rotation A transformation that turns all of the points in the original (preimage) figure the same number of degrees around a fixed center point (such as the origin on a graph). The result is called the "image" of the original figure. The point that the shape is rotated about is called the "center of rotation." To define a rotation, you need to state the measure of turn (in degrees), the direction the shape is turned (such as clockwise or counter-clockwise), and the center of rotation. See the example at right. Note that a rotation is also sometimes referred to as a "turn." (p. 34)

rotation symmetry *See* symmetry.

$r : r^2 : r^3$ **Ratios of Similarity** When a two-dimensional figure is enlarged (or reduced) proportionally, its lengths and area change. If the linear scale factor is r, then all lengths (such as sides, perimeter, and heights) of the original (preimage) figure is multiplied by a factor of r while the area is multiplied by a factor of r^2.

When a polyhedron is enlarged (or reduced) proportionally, its lengths, surface area, and volume also change. If the linear scale factor is r, then the surface area is multiplied by a factor of r^2 and the volume is multiplied by a factor of r^3. Thus, if a polyhedron is enlarged proportionally by a linear scale factor of r, then the new edge lengths, surface area, and volume can be found using the relationships below. (p. 457)

New edge length = $r \cdot$ (corresponding edge length of original polyhedron)

New surface area = $r^2 \cdot$ (original surface area)

New volume = $r^3 \cdot$ (original volume)

This principle also applies to other solids such cylinders, cones, and spheres.

same-side interior angles Two angles between two lines and on the same side of a third line that intersects them (called a transversal). The shaded angles in the diagram at right are an example of a pair of same-side interior angles. Note that if the two lines that are cut by the transversal are parallel, then the two angles are supplementary (add up to 180°). (p. 91)

sample space The total number of outcomes that can happen in an event. The sample space for rolling a standard 6-sided die is the set {1, 2, 3, 4, 5, 6} because those are the only possible outcomes.

SAS ≅ (Triangle Congruence) Two triangles are congruent if two sides and their included angle of one triangle are congruent to the corresponding two sides and included angle of another triangle. Also referred to as "SAS Congruence" or "SAS ≅". (p. 299)

SAS ~ (Triangle Similarity) If two triangles have two pairs of corresponding sides that are proportional and have congruent included angles, then the triangles are similar. Also referred to as "SAS Similarity" or "SAS ~". (p. 171)

scale The ratio between a length of the representation (such as a map, model, or diagram) and the corresponding length of the actual object. For example, the map of a city may use one inch to represent one mile.

scalene triangle A triangle with no congruent sides. (p. 55)

secant A line that intersects a circle at two distinct points. (p. 557)

sector

sector A region formed by two radii of a central angle and the arc between their endpoints on the circle. You can think of it as a portion of a circle and its interior, resembling a piece of pizza. (p. 426)

semicircle In a circle, a semicircle is an arc with endpoints that are endpoints of any diameter of the circle. It is a half circle and has a measure of 180°. (p. 492)

side of an angle   One of the two rays that form an angle.

side of a polygon   *See* polygon.

similar figures   Two shapes are similar if they have exactly the same shape but are not necessarily the same size. The symbol for similar is ~. (pp. 136 and 155)

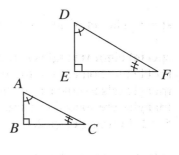

similarity statement   A statement that indicates that two figures are similar. The order of the letters in the names of the shapes determine which sides and angles correspond to each other. For example, if $\triangle ABC \sim \triangle DEF$, then $\angle A$ must correspond to $\angle D$ and $\overline{AB}$ must correspond to $\overline{DE}$. (p. 150)

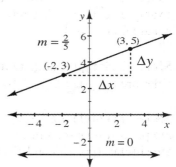

sine ratio   In a right triangle, the sine ratio of an acute $\angle A$ is $\sin A = \frac{\text{length of opposite side}}{\text{length of hypotenuse}}$. In the triangle at right, $\sin A = \frac{BC}{AC} = \frac{3}{5}$. (p. 241)

skew lines   Lines that do not lie in the same flat surface.

slant height   (a) Pyramid: The height of a lateral face drawn from the apex; (b) Cone: The distance from the apex of the cone to any point on the circular boundary of the base. (p. 534)

slide   See *translation*.

slope   A ratio that describes how steep (or flat) a line is. Slope can be positive, negative, or even zero, but a straight line has only one slope. Slope is the ratio $\frac{\text{vertical change}}{\text{horizontal change}}$ or $\frac{\text{change in } y \text{ value}}{\text{change in } x \text{ value}}$, sometimes written $\frac{\Delta y}{\Delta x}$. When the equation of a line is written in $y = mx + b$ form, m is the slope of the line. A line has positive slope if it slopes upward from left to right on a graph, negative slope if it slopes downward from left to right, zero slope if it is horizontal, and undefined slope if it is vertical. Parallel lines have equal slopes, and the slopes of perpendicular lines are opposite reciprocals of each other (e.g. , $\frac{3}{5}$ and $-\frac{5}{3}$). (pp. 47 and 190)

slope angle   *See* slope triangle.

slope-intercept form   A form of a linear equation: $y = mx + b$. In this form, m is the slope and the point $(0, b)$ is the y-intercept. (p. 123)

slope triangle   A right triangle with legs (parallel to the x- and y-axes) that meet the hypotenuse at two points on a given line or line segment. The lengths of the legs of the slope triangle can be used to find the slope of the line. The angle (θ) formed in a slope triangle by the hypotenuse and the horizontal leg is called the slope angle. (pp. 47 and 190)

solid   A closed three-dimensional shape and all of its interior points. Examples include regions bounded by pyramids, cylinders, and spheres. (p. 443)

solve   To find all the solutions to an equation or an inequality (or a system of equations or inequalities). For example, solving the equation $x^2 = 9$ gives the solutions $x = 3$ and $x = -3$. The solution(s) may be number(s), variable(s), or an expression. (pp. 19, 87, and 163)

space   The set of all points in three-dimensions.

special right triangles   A right triangle with particular notable features that can be used to solve problems. Sometimes, these triangles can be recognized by the angles, such as the $45°\text{-}45°\text{-}90°$ triangle (also known as an "isosceles right triangle") and a $30°\text{-}60°\text{-}90°$ triangle. Other right triangles are special because the length of each side is an integer, such as a 3, 4, 5 triangle or a 5, 12, 13 triangle. (p. 260)

sphere   The set of all points in space that are the same distance from a fixed point. The fixed point is the center of the sphere and the distance is its radius. (p. 555)

Sphere

square   A quadrilateral with four right angles and four congruent sides. (p. 361)

Square

square root   A number a is a square root of b if $a^2 = b$. For example, the number 9 has two square roots, 3 and −3. A negative number has no real square roots; a positive number has two; and zero has just one square root, namely, itself. In a geometric context, the principal square root of a number x (written $\sqrt{x}$) represents the length of a side of a square with area x. For example, $\sqrt{16} = 4$. Therefore if the side of a square has a length of 4 units, then its area is 16 square units. (p. 115)

SSS $\cong$ (Triangle Congruence)   Two triangles are congruent if all three pairs of corresponding sides are congruent. (p. 299)

SSS $\sim$ (Triangle Similarity)   If two triangles have all three pairs of corresponding sides that are proportional (this means that the ratios of corresponding sides are equal), then the triangles are similar. (pp. 155 and 171)

straight angle   An angle that measures 180°. This occurs when the rays of the angle point in opposite directions, forming a line. (p. 24)

180°

straightedge   A tool used as a guide to draw lines, rays, and segments. (p. 468)

statement   A recording of fact to present evidence in a logical argument (proof). (p. 459)

Substitution Method   A method for solving a system of equations by replacing one variable with an expression involving the remaining variable(s). For example, in the system of equations at right the first equation tells you that y is equal to $-3x + 5$. We can substitute $-3x + 5$ in for y in the second equation to get $2(-3x + 5) + 10x = 18$, then solve this equation to find that $x = 2$. Once we have x, we substitute that value back into either of the original equations to find that $y = -1$. (p. 87)

$$y = -3x + 5$$
$$2y + 10x = 18$$

Substitution Property The Substitution Property states that in an expression, one can replace a variable, number, or expression with something equal to it without altering the value of the whole. For example, if $x = 3$, then $5x - 7$ can be evaluated by replacing x with 3. This results in $5(3) - 7 = 8$. (p. 87)

supplementary angles Two angles a and b for which $a + b = 180°$. Each angle is called the supplement of the other. In the example at right, angles A and B are supplementary. Supplementary angles are often adjacent. For example, since $\angle LMN$ is a straight angle, then $\angle LMP$ and $\angle PMN$ are supplementary angles because $m\angle LMP + m\angle PMN = 180°$. (p. 74)

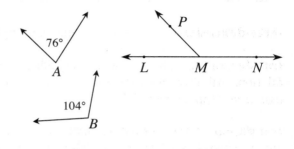

surface area The sum of all the area(s) of the surface(s) of a three-dimensional solid. For example, the surface area of a cylinder is the sum of the areas of its top base, its bottom base, and its lateral surface. (pp. 446 and 452)

symmetry (a) Rotation symmetry: A shape has rotation symmetry when it can be rotated for less than 360° and it appears not to change. For example the hexagon at right appears not to change if it is rotated 60° clockwise (or counter-clockwise); (b) Reflection symmetry: A shape has reflection symmetry when it appears not to change after being reflected across a line. The regular hexagon at right also has reflection symmetry across any line drawn through opposite vertices, such as those shown in the diagram. *See* reflection, rotation, *and* line *of* symmetry. (pp. 43, 44, 45)

system of equations A system of equations is a set of equations with the same variables. Solving a system of equations means finding one or more solutions that make each of the equations in the system true. A solution to a system of equations gives a point of intersection of the graphs of the equations in the system. There may be zero, one, or several solutions to a system of equations. For example, $(1.5, -3)$ is a solution to the system of linear equations at right; $x = 1.5$, $y = -3$ makes both of the equations true. Also, $(1.5, -3)$ is a point of intersection of the graphs of these two equations. (p. 87)

$$y = 2x - 6$$
$$y = -2x$$

systematic list A list created by following a system (an orderly process). (p. 219)

tangent A line on the same flat surface as a circle that intersects the circle in exactly one point. A tangent of a circle is perpendicular to a radius of the circle at their point of intersection (also called the "point of tangency." (p. 496)

tangent ratio In a right triangle, the tangent ratio of an acute $\angle A$ is $\tan A = \frac{\text{length of opposite side}}{\text{length of adjacent side}}$. In the triangle at right, $\tan A = \frac{BC}{AB} = \frac{3}{4}$. (p. 200)

tetrahedron A polyhedron with four faces. The faces of a tetrahedron are triangles. In a regular tetrahedron, all of the faces are congruent equilateral triangles. (p. 533)

theorem   A conjecture that has been proven to be true. Some examples of theorems are the Pythagorean Theorem and the Triangle Angle Sum Theorem. (p. 367)

theta (θ)   A Greek letter that is often used to represent the measure of an angle. Other Greek letters used to represent the measure of an angle include alpha (α) and beta (β). (p. 190)

three-dimensional   An the object that has length, width, and depth. (p. 340)

transformation   This course studies four transformations: reflection, rotation, translation, and dilation. All of them preserve shape, and the first three preserve size. *See each term for its own definition.* (pp. 34 and 138)

translation   A transformation that preserves the size, shape, and orientation of a figure while sliding (moving) it to a new location. The result is called the "image" of the original figure (preimage). Note that a translation is sometimes referred to as a "slide." (p. 34)

image
original

transversal   A line that intersects two or more other lines on a flat surface (plane). In this course, we often work with a transversal that intersects two parallel lines. (p. 79)

trapezoid   A quadrilateral with at least one pair of parallel sides. (pp. 107 and 361)

tree diagram   A structure used to organize the possible outcomes of two or more events. For example, the tree diagram at right represents the possible outcomes when a coin is flipped twice. (p. 219)

triangle   A polygon with three sides.

Triangle Angle Sum Theorem   The sum of the measures of the interior angles in any triangle is 180°. For example, in $\triangle ABC$ at right, $m\angle A + m\angle B + m\angle C = 180°$. (p. 99)

Triangle Congruence Conjectures   Conjectures that use the minimum number of congruent corresponding parts to prove that two triangles are congruent. They are: SSS $\cong$, SAS $\cong$, AAS $\cong$, ASA $\cong$, and HL $\cong$. (p. 299)

Triangle Inequality   In a triangle with side lengths a, b, and c, c must be less than the sum of a and b and greater than the difference of a and b. In the example at right, a is greater than b (that is, $a > b$), so the possible values for c are all numbers such that $c > a - b$ and $c < a + b$. (p. 119)

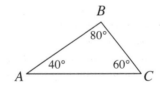

Triangle Midsegment Theorem   The segment that connects the midpoints of any two sides of a triangle measures half the length of the third side is and parallel to that side. (p. 371)

trigonometry   Literally, the "measure of triangles." In this course, this word is used to refer to the development of triangle tools such as trigonometric ratios (sine, cosine, and tangent) and the Laws of Sines and Cosines. (p. 192)

turn See *rotation*

two-column proof A form of proof in which statements are written in one column as a list and the reasons for the statements are written next to them in a second column. (p. 366)

two-dimensional A figure that that lies on a flat surface and that has length and width. *See* plane. (p. 340)

unit of measure A standard quantity (such as a centimeter, second, square foot, or gallon) that is used to measure and describe an object. A single object can be measured using different units of measure, which will usually yield different results. For example, a pencil may be 80 mm long, meaning that it is 80 times as long as a unit of 1 mm. However, the same pencil is 8 cm long, so that it is the same length as 8 cm laid end-to-end. (This is because 1 cm is the same length as 10 mm.) (p. 98)

Venn diagram A type of diagram used to classify objects. It is usually composed of two or more overlapping circles representing different conditions. An item is placed or represented in the Venn diagram in the appropriate position based on the conditions it meets. In the example of the Venn diagram at right, if an object meets one of two conditions, it is placed in region **A** or **C** but outside region **B**. If an object meets both conditions, it is placed in the intersection (**B**) of both circles. If an object does not meet either condition, it is placed outside of both circles (region **D**). (p. 51)

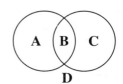

vertex (plural: vertices) (a) For a two-dimensional geometric shape, a vertex is a point where two or more line segments or rays meet to form a "corner," such as in a polygon or angle. (b) For a three-dimensional polyhedron, a vertex is a point where the edges of the solid meet. (c) On a graph, a vertex can be used to describe the highest or lowest point on the graph of a parabola or absolute value function (depending on the graph's orientation). (pp. 74 and 527)

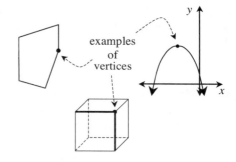

examples
of
vertices

vertical angles The two opposite (that is, non-adjacent) angles formed by two intersecting lines. "Vertical" is a relationship between pairs of angles, so one angle cannot be called vertical. Angles that form a vertical pair are always congruent. (pp. 75 and 91)

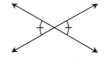

volume A measurement of the size of the three-dimensional region enclosed within an object. It is expressed as the number of 1x1x1 unit cubes (or parts of cubes) that fit inside a solid. (pp. 453 and 452)

weighted average In this course, weighted average is used to calculate expected value. The weighted average takes into account the relative probabilities of all possible outcomes and uses them to calculate the average win or loss of each game. *See* expected value *for an example*. (p. 508 and 516)

x-intercept A point where a graph crosses the *x*-axis. A graph may have several *x*-intercepts, no *x*-intercepts, or just one.

y-intercept A point where a graph crosses the *y*-axis. A function has at most one *y*-intercept; a relation may have several.

zoom factor The amount each side of a figure is multiplied by when the figure is proportionally enlarged or reduced in size. It is written as the ratio of a length in the new figure (image) to a length in the original figure (preimage). For the triangles at right, the zoom factor is $\frac{8}{6}$ or $\frac{4}{3}$. See also "ratio of similarity" and "linear scale factor." (pp. 140 and 142)

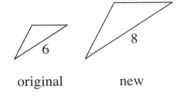

original   new

Index
Student Version

Many of the pages referenced here contain a definition or an example of the topic listed, often within the body of a Math Notes box. Others contain problems that develop or demonstrate the topic. It may be necessary to read the text on several pages to fully understand the topic. Also, some problems listed here are good examples of the topic and may not offer any explanation. The page numbers listed below reflect the pages in the Student Version. References to Math Notes boxes are bolded.

Greek Alphabet used in text

α (alpha), **190**
β (beta), **190**
Δ (delta), **47**, 599
θ (theta), **190**
φ (phi), 598, **599**

Number

30°-60°-90° triangle, **260**
30°-60°-90° triangles, 250
3-4-5 triangles, 255
45°-45°-90° triangle, **260**
45°-45°-90° triangles, 251

A

AA ~, **155**, **171**
AAS ≅, **299**
Absolute value, 453, 575
Acute angles, **24**
Adjacent leg, **241**
Adjacent side, 236
Alpha (α), **190**
Alternate interior angles, 84, **91**
Angle Notation, **190**
    alpha, **190**
    beta, **190**
    theta, **190**
Angles, 22, **24**
    acute, **24**
    alternate interior, 84, **91**
    central, 382, 394, 488, **490**
    circular, 22, **24**
    complementary, 74, **76**
    congruent, **76**
    consecutive, 370
    corresponding, **91**
    equal measure, **351**
    exterior, 358, 403
    inscribed, 489, **490**, **494**
    naming, **81**
    obtuse, **24**
    remote interior, 397
    right, 22, **24**
    same-side interior, 84, **91**
    slope, **190**
    straight, **24**
    supplementary, 74, **76**
    vertex, 74
    vertical, **91**
Index

Apothem, **410**
Approximate, **123**, 240
Arc, 425, **426**, 430, 483, **485**, 488
    chord, 484, **485**
    intercepted, 489
    length, 488, **490**
    major, 484, **485**
    measure, 488, **490**
    minor, 484, **485**
    quarter circle, 405
    semicircle, 492
Area, **15**, 99
    of a triangle, 103
    of circle, **426**
    of parallelogram, **112**
    of regular polygons, **422**
    of trapezoid, **112**
    of triangle, **112**
    sector, **430**
    similar figures, 12
    surface, 446, **555**
Area model, 213, **219**
Argument
    proof, 365, 370
Arrow diagram, 84
ASA ≅, **299**
At Your Service Problem, 312
Average, weighted, 508

B

Base, 107
Base angles of an isosceles triangle, 90
Bases, 447, **448**
    lateral surface, 530
Beta (β), **190**
Bisect, 317
Bisector
    perpendicular, 459
Blood types, 214
Building a Kaleidoscope Problem, 21

C

Carpetmart Problem, 12
Center, **341**, **410**
  circumcenter, 500
  concentric circles, 460
  of balance, **471**
  of balance, **471**
  of circle, **490**
  radius, 410
Center of rotation, **34**
Central angle, 382, 394, 488, **490**
Centroid, **471**, **501**
Chance, 57, **60**
Choosing a strategy/tool, 283
Chords, 484, **485**
  diameter, **485**
  intersecting, 498
Circle, **341**
  arc, 425, **426**, 483, **485**, 488
  arc length, **430**
  arc measure, **490**
  area, **426**
  area of sector, **430**
  center, **341**, **490**
  central angle, 488, **490**
  chord, **485**
  circumcenter, 500
  circumference, 424, **426**
  diameter, 335, **341**, **485**
  great, 549
  inscribed angle, **490**, **494**
  length of arc, **490**
  pi (π), **426**
  quarter, 405
  radius, **341**
  secant, 496
  sector, 425, **426**
  semicircle, 492
  tangent, 496
Circles, concentric, 460
Circular angles, 22, **24**
Circumcenter, 500, **501**
Circumference, 424, **426**
Clinometer, 202
Coincide, **87**
Common ratio, 143
Compass, 460, **468**
Complementary angles, 74
Concentric circles, 460
  focus-directrix paper, 576
Concept map, 63
Concurrency, **471**, **501**
Conditional statement, 80, **108**
  arrow diagram, 84
Cone
  conic sections, 573, **578**
  ellipse, **585**
  lateral surface, **547**
  volume, **547**
Congruent, 140, **159**, **291**
  angles, 75, **76**
  shapes, **159**, **291**

Congruent corresponding parts, 346
Conic sections, 573, **578**
  ellipse, **585**
  graphing, 576
  hyperbola, 584
  parabola, 574
Conjecture, **10**, 75, **304**
  proven, 354
  theorem, 367
Consecutive angles, 370
Constant diameter
  Reuleaux curves, 337
Construction, 459
  compass, 460
  ellipse, 583
  hyperbola, 583
  perpendicular bisector, 459, **468**
  straightedge, 460
Contradiction, proof by, **96**
Converse, **304**
Convex polygon, 395, **396**
Coordinate geometry
  dilation, 136
  finding a midpoint, **381**
Correspondence
  similarity statement, **150**
Corresponding angles, **91**
Corresponding parts
  congruent triangles, **346**
$\cos^{-1}$, 243, **248**
Cosine ratio (cos), 236, **241**
Counterexample, 238
Cross-sections
  conic sections, 573, **578**
  ellipse, **585**
  of three-dimensional solids, **538**
Cube, 527
Cubic units, **452**
Curves, Reuleaux, 337
Cylinder, 30, 451
  lateral surface, 530
  oblique, 451

D

Decagon, 393
Decimal, non-repeating, 467
Delta (Δ), **47**
Dependent events, 207
Designing a Quilt Problem, 3, 5
Diagonals, **400**
  of a rhombus, **364**
Diagram
  tree, 206, **219**
  Venn, 50, **51**
Diagram markings, 54
Diameter, 335, **341**, **485**
Dilation, 135, 136, **138**
  creating with rubber bands, 135
Dimensions, 98
  cubic units, **452**
Directrix, 574
Dual polyhedron, 530

E

Earth
    equator, 549
    great circle, 549
    hemisphere, 549
    latitude lines, 549
    longitude lines, 549, **551**
    prime meridian, 549
Edges, 527
    vertex, 527
Ellipse, 581, 583, **585**
    foci, **585**
Enlargement
    zoom factor, 140
Equality
    Reflexive Property, **354**
Equations
    graphing, **29**
    proportional, **145**
    Quadratic Formula, **163**
    solving linear, **19**
Equator, 549
    great circle, 549
Equiangular, **351**, 396
Equilateral, **351**
    polygon, **396**
Equilateral triangles, 11, 22
Equivalent, **512**
Euler, Leonhard, 595
Euler's Formula for Polyhedra, 595
Exact answer, **123**, 240
Examining, 129
Expected value, 507, **516**
    weighted average, 508
Experiment, 7
Exploration, **10**
Exterior angle, 358, 397, 403, **407**
    sum of, **407**

F

Faces, 527
    edge, 527
    lateral, 447, **448**, **534**
    total surface area, **452**
Facilitator, 4
Factoring, **163**
Family Fortune, The Problem, 18, 170
Flipping a shape (reflection), 27, **34**, **38**
Flowchart, 157, 167, 353
Focus (foci), 574, 581, **585**
    ellipse, 581
    hyperbola, 584
Focus-directrix paper, 576
Formula
    quadratic, **163**
Fraction busters, **512**
Function, **589**
    absolute value, 575

G

Geometry, 548
George Washington's Nose Problem, 147
Getting To Know Your Triangle Problem, 309
Golden ratio, 597, 598, **599**
    golden rectangles, 598
    golden triangles, 598
    spiral, 598, **599**
Golden rectangle, 598
Golden spiral, 598, 599
Golden triangles, 598
Graph
    focus-directrix, 576
Graphing an equation, 29
Great circle, 549

H

Half-equilateral triangle, 40, 250
Half-square, 40
Height
    of pyramid, **534**
    slant, **534**
Hemisphere, 549
Heptagon, 393
Hexagon, 43, 393
Hinged Mirror Team Challenge, The Problem, 349
HL $\cong$, **299**
Horizontal change, **47**, **190**
How Tall Is It? Problem, 202
Hyperbola, 584
Hypotenuse, **119**, **241**

I

Icon
    Learning Log, 28
    stoplight, 88
    toolkit, 54
Image, 34
Incenter, **501**
Independent events, 207
Inscribed angle, 489, **490**
Inscribed Angle Theorem, **494**
Inscribed polygon, 461
Intercepted arc, 489
Interior angles, 402
    sum of, **407**
Interior Design Problem, 343
Intersecting chords, 498
Intersecting tangents, **560**
Intersections
    secant, 557
    tangents, **560**
Inverse, **248**
Inverse operations, 243
    trigonometric ratios, 243
Inverse trigonometric functions
    inverse cosine, **248**
    inverse sine, **248**
    inverse tangent, **248**

Investigating, 7, 66
Investigative process, **10**
Irrational number, **115**, 467
Isosceles trapezoid, 77, 371
Isosceles triangle, 38, 48
    base angles, 90
Iteration, 598

J

Justifying, 16, **167**

K

Kaleidoscope, Building a Problem, 21
Kite, 353

L

Lateral
    face, **534**
    faces, 447, **448**
    slant height, **534**
    surface area, **534**
    surface of a cone, **547**
    surface of a cylinder, 530
Latitude lines, 549
    equator, 549
Law of Cosines, 266, **267**
Law of Sines, 263, **264**
Leaning Tower of Pisa Problem, 187, 198
Learning Log, 28
Leg, **119**
Length
    of arc, 488, **490**
Lessons From Abroad Problem, 174
Light, reflection of, 85
Likelihood
    probability, **505**
Line
    naming, **81**
    of reflection, **34**, 38
    of symmetry, **5**, 43
Line segment, 38
    midsegment, 369, **371**
    naming, **81**
Linear scale factor, 414, **415**
    Ratios of similarity, **457**
    zoom factor, 140
Lines
    latitude, 549
    longitude, 549
List, systematic, **219**
Log, Learning, 28
Longitude lines, 549, **551**
    meridian, **551**
    prime meridian, 549

M

m, **47**
Major arc, 484, **485**
Map, concept, 63
Mapping, **34**
Marking a diagram, 54
Mat plan, 443
Maximum limits, 119
Measure
    of arc, 488, **490**
Measurement
    area, **15**, 99
    dimensions, 98
    perimeter, **15**
    unit of measure, 98, 99
    unit square, 99
Medians, **471**
    centroid, **471**
Meridian, **551**
    a.m., **551**
    p.m., **551**
    prime, 549
Midnight Mystery Problem, 221
Midpoint, 40, 41, 342, **381**
    midsegment, 369, **371**
Midsegment, 369, **371**
Mighty Mascot Problem, 413
Minimum limits, 119
Minor arc, 484, **485**
Mirror, hinged, 21, 73
Möbius strip, 7, 8, 9
Models
    area, **219**
    probability, **219**

N

Nature
    golden ratio, 599
Net, 446
n-gon, 393, **422**
Nonagon, 393
Non-convex polygon, 395, **396**
Number
    irrational, 467

O

Oblique cylinder, 451
Oblique prism, 451
Oblique pyramid, 538
Obtuse angles, **24**
Octagon, 393
    regular, 402
Operations
    inverse, 243
Opposite leg, **241**
Opposite side, 236
Optimization, 343
Orientation, **241**

R

$r : r^2 : r^3$ ratios, **457**
Radius, **341**, 410
Rat Race, The Problem, 204, 217
Ratio, **60**
    cosine, 236
    golden, 597, 598, 599
    Law of Sines, **264**
    linear scale factor, 414, **415**
    of similar figures, **457**
    of similar solids, **457**
    of similarity, **142**
    proportion, **145**
    sine, 236
    slope, **47**, **190**
    zoom factor, **415**
Rationalizing the denominator, **252**
Ratios of similarity, **457**
Reasoning and justifying, 16, 180
Recorder/Reporter, 4
Rectangle, 5, **361**
    diagonals, **400**
Rectangular prism, 451
Reflection, 27, **34**, **38**
    line of, **34**, **38**
    of light, 85
Reflection symmetry, 3, **5**, 43, 44
Reflexive Property of Equality, **354**
Regular hexagon, 21, 43
Regular octagon, 402
Regular pentagon, 23
Regular polygons, 42, 349, **351**, **396**
    apothem, **410**
    area of, **422**
    center, **410**
    central angle, 382
    radius, **410**
Regular polyhedra, 528
    dual polyhedron, 530
    platonic solids, 529
Relation, **589**
Relationship
    angles, 74, **76**, 84
    Law of Cosines, **267**
    Law of Sines, **264**
    Pythagorean Theorem, 122, 123
    similarity, 136, 139, **150**
Relationships
    angles, 84
Remote interior angles, 397
Representation
    solids, 443, 444
Reuleaux curves, 337
Reversal, **304**
Rhombus, 356, **361**, **400**, **464**
    diagonals, **364**, **400**, **464**
Right angles, 22, **24**
Right pyramid, 538

Right triangle, **119**
    hypotenuse, **119**
    leg, **119**
    Pythagorean Theorem, 122
    special, **260**
Rotation, **34**
Rotation symmetry, 43, 45, 52
Rotation, center of, **34**
Rubber band, use of, 135

S

Same-side interior angles, 84, **91**
SAS $\cong$, **299**
SAS $\sim$, **171**
Secant, 496, 557
Sector, 425, **426**
Segment, 38
Semicircle, 492
Shape bucket, 50
Shape Factory, The Problem, 40, 118
Shapes
    congruent, 140, **159**, **291**
    ratio of areas, **457**
    ratio of perimeters, **457**
    similar, 136, 139
    three-dimensional, 340
    two-dimensional, 340
Side
    face, 527
Side view, 444
Sides
    congruent, **351**
Similar figures
    area of, 12, **457**
Similarity, 136, 139, **171**, **415**
    AA $\sim$, **155**
    congruent, 140, **159**, **291**
    proportional equation, **145**
    ratio, **142**
    SSS $\sim$, **155**
    SSS $\sim$, AA $\sim$, and SAS $\sim$, **171**
    statement, **150**
    zoom factor, 140, **142**
$\sin^{-1}$, 243, **248**
Sine ratio (sin), 236, **241**, **264**
Slant height, **534**
Sliding a shape (translation), **34**
Slope, 20, **47**
    negative, **47**
    of parallel lines, **47**
    of perpendicular lines, **47**
    positive, **47**
    triangle, **47**, **190**, **200**
    undefined, **47**
    zero, **47**
Slope angle, **190**, 202
    clinometer, 202
    common, **194**
Slope ratio, **200**, **241**
    common, **194**

T

Index of Symbols

$\geq$	"greater than or equal to"	$\angle A$	angle with vertex A
$\leq$	"less than or equal to"	$m\angle A$	measure of angle A
$>$	"greater than"	$36°$	"36 degrees"
$<$	"less than"	$\cong$	"congruent to"
$=$	"equal to"	$\tan \theta$	"tangent of theta"
$\sqrt{\ }$	square root or radical	$\sin \theta$	"sine of theta"
$\triangle ABC$	a triangle with vertices A, B, and C	$\cos \theta$	"cosine of theta"
		$\sim$	"similar to"
$X'Y'Z'$	"X prime, Y prime, Z prime"	$P:Q$	ratio of P to Q
$ABCD$	quadrilateral $ABCD$	$P(A)$	probability of event A
cm^2	square centimeter	π	"pi"
in^2	square inch	$\odot C$	circle C
$//$	"parallel to"	$\overarc{ABC}$	arc ABC
$\perp$	"perpendicular to"	$m\overarc{ABC}$	measure of arc ABC
AB	length of line segment $\overline{AB}$	α	alpha
$\overleftrightarrow{AB}$	line through points A and B	β	beta
$\overline{AB}$	line segment with endpoints at A and B	Δ	delta
$\overrightarrow{AB}$	ray starting at A and passing through B	θ	theta
		ϕ	phi

Equation Reference

$y = mx + b$	Slope-intercept form of a line	$x^2 + y^2 = r^2$	Equation of a circle with center at the origin $(0, 0)$, with radius r
$y = ax^2 + bx + c$	Standard form of a quadratic equation		

THIS BOOK IS THE PROPERTY OF:

Book No._____

ISSUED TO	Year Used	CONDITION	
		ISSUED	RETURNED

PUPILS to whom this texbook is issued must not write on any part of it in any way, unless otherwise instructed by the teacher.